RADICAL CURIOSITY

ONE MAN'S SEARCH
FOR COSMIC MAGIC
AND A PURPOSEFUL LIFE

KEN DYCHTWALD PH.D.

AN UNNAMED PRESS BOOK

Copyright © 2021 Ken Dychtwald

All rights reserved, including the right to reproduce this book or portions thereof in any form whatsoever. Permissions inquiries may be directed to info@unnamedpress.com. Published in North America by the Unnamed Press.

www.unnamedpress.com

Unnamed Press, and the colophon, are registered trademarks of Unnamed Media LLC.

ISBN: 978-1-951213-31-2

Library of Congress Cataloging-in-Publication data available upon request.

This book is a work of nonfiction.

Cover Design by Robert Bieselin
Designed and Typeset by Jaya Nicely
Manufactured in the United States of America by Versa Press, Inc.
Distributed by Publishers Group West

First Edition

To Casey and Zak
May your futures be filled with love, health, hope, big dreams,
grand adventures... and purpose.

CONTENTS

PART IV: BEING IN THE ROOM WHERE IT'S HAPPENING

PART V: SELF, SUCCESS AND PURPOSE RECONSIDERED

PART VI: ELDERHOOD

RADICAL
CURIOSITY

INTRODUCTION
WHAT SCARES ME ABOUT GROWING OLD

Eventually you will reach a point when you stop lying about your age and start bragging about it. —Will Rogers

For more than forty years, as a psychologist/gerontologist and CEO of Age Wave, I've dedicated a lot of my career to investigating how people, especially boomers, relate to becoming elders. Meanwhile, in my personal life, I got married and had children, watched both of those children leave the nest and make lives of their own. I have been in the presence of both my dad and then my mom as they passed away. I celebrated my sixty-fifth birthday and then, during COVID, my seventieth. Gliding along at the speed of life, it turns out I have become an elder myself.

Sometimes, when people see a picture of a younger me from one phase or another, they comment on how much fun it is to get a glimpse of who I "used to be." However, I still am those younger versions of Ken Dychtwald—all of them. In fact, I've discovered that growing older hasn't been a Lego-like replacement of "young" Ken figures with increasingly older versions. Instead, all of these younger selves are still very much alive and thriving, layered and integrated over the years into a fuller, more experienced, wiser, and more complex human who continues to grow and evolve. Through this lens, I have come to appreciate that aging is not necessarily a process of decline, loss, and diminishment. Quite the opposite: while there is definitely loss and suffering to be grappled with, the journey to and through elderhood seems to be a continually fascinating and unfolding journey of the flowering and flourishing of life.

This book began as an effort to gather many of my key life lessons and stories, especially the ones that reveal and reflect the truths and values I hold most dear. And yet, as I worked on it, it evolved into something more. I noticed that I'm able to keep those past versions of myself alive in my present self, thanks in large part to the way that I've lived my life, something that I came to recognize as *radical curiosity*. Supported by my memories and some (often wild) experiences, the lessons in this book may also serve as a guide for your own journey, as long as you are open to it.

Because I wrote so much about aging when I was young, people today occasionally ask me how the experience of growing old feels to me—and whether it's different from how I characterized it when it wasn't yet personal. It's one thing to cite a statistic, you know, such as "83 percent of people age sixty-five and over have at least one chronic health condition." But to be near when close friends and loved ones have gotten knocked to their knees with illness—or to begin worrying about my own or my wife's age-related scary stuff—is intense, and impossible to imagine before you get there.

I've continually found myself banging into other people's attitudes as to whether aging is a good or a bad thing. Once when Morley Safer was getting set to interview me for a segment on *60 Minutes*, he told the New York studio crew, "Ken Dychtwald has talked to more people about aging than any human being in the history of the world." In truth, it isn't a black and white issue. I've wondered, Is aging something to be embraced or conquered? Should we be "pro-aging" or "anti-aging"? Marketers are busy shaming people about their aging bodies in order to persuade them that they'd be happier if their skin, hair, weight, and faces were "younger." Gray Panthers such as Maggie Kuhn implored people to be proud of their age. I have repeatedly found myself confused as to whether people are even talking about the same thing when they use the word "aging." With some reflection and untangling of ideas, I have come to believe that there are four different flavors of aging—and that much of the confusion comes from conflating or confusing them. Here's my attempt at clarification and how I currently feel about my own aging process while still fully immersed in my ever-challenging journey of life.

Chronological aging is dependent only on the passing of time. Inexorably, we become a day older each day. We are not alone: the same is true for trees, frogs, and even the sun. This is not to say that with each passing day we humans become more or less happy, more or less beautiful, more or less aware—simply one day older. In chronological time there is no absolute relationship between age and happiness, beauty, or knowledge; there is only the steady ticking of the clock and the continual accumulation of minutes, days, and years. So, twenty-five years after our birth, we become twenty-five years old; fifty years after our birth, we celebrate our fiftieth birthday, and so on. One other potent aspect of our chronological age is that it anchors each of our lives to a particular era and moment in time. For example, although I turned fifty in the year 2000, that I was born fifty years earlier in 1950 says a lot about who I am and how I might see myself and the world. If I had been fifty in the year 1279, I'd for sure be a lot different. And last, you don't start aging on your sixty-fifth birthday. It's not a process reserved for "old" people. You began aging when you were conceived.

Psychological aging is the normal developmental process of growing up while migrating through the various experiences and transitions of our lives. Hence, the baby becomes a child, who then becomes a teenager, who then becomes a young adult, and so on until she eventually becomes an elder. Some people also view maturity as a time when the deepest aspects of one's spiritual self ripen and blossom. While spiritual aware-ness doesn't always emerge with the passing of birthdays, it is frequently the case that the more years and experiences one has and the more lessons learned from those experiences, the more opportunities for spiritual devel-opment.

Then there's our *aging-related social roles.* This aspect of aging is a bit fickle and tends to shift around as demographics, cultural trends, fashions, fads, and lifestyles alter. For example, in colonial America, people were seen as acquiring great perspective and authority as they grew older. By age sixty, an individual might feel as though he had arrived at a powerful stage in life, a time to assume the role of family head, take charge of community decisions, and enjoy the fruits of a long, full life. That's the way aging has been viewed in many parts of the world throughout history. However, as America became more industrial and urban, this modern-ization began to maniacally elevate the look, feel, and mind-set of youth, which significantly diminished the importance of elders. Soon, the older one became, the more he or she was viewed as "over-the-hill" or irrelevant. In this recent youth-dominated era, growing older has largely come to be viewed as socially negative, and many people therefore wish they were still young, or don't want to be thought of as "old" no matter what their actual age.

In the mid-1990s I had the good fortune of getting to know legendary feminist Betty Friedan after the publication of her book *The Fountain of Age*. We were paired as co-keynoters at a variety of conferences from the American Society on Aging to CBS Television's producers, directors, and scriptwriters. As we were getting to know each other, one night over dinner I asked Betty what her purpose was in writing *The Feminine Mystique* back in 1963. She explained to me that she felt the time had come when women should no longer be measured by the metric of men—either how well they could please a man or how they might compete with men generally. "Women," she said, "should be measured by the metric of women." When I then asked what her purpose was in writing *The Fountain of Age,* she said that elders should no longer be measured by the metric of youth. "Who knows," she reflected. "Maybe in the decades ahead, elderhood will once again be appealing, even aspirational." We raised our glasses of wine and toasted that possibility.

Physical aging is probably the one dimension of the aging process that no one, other than teenagers, looks forward to. And for good reason. When we think of growing older physically, we usually view the process like a climb up Mount Everest. First there's the ascent: with each step the view is grander as one moves closer and closer to the peak. Then, on the descent, with each step the experience diminishes and one is farther and farther from the peak and closer and closer to the end. So, after around the age of fifty, most people think of physical aging as fraught with steady and cumulative loss—loss of health, sexual potency, beauty, coordination, strength, and vitality. While the rate of physical aging can be sped up as a result of a toxic or unhealthy lifestyle, we now know that it can also be slowed down—never stopped but slowed down—through things like regular exercise, maintaining a healthy body weight, proper, mostly plant-based nutrition, sufficient rest and relaxation, and stimulating social engagement. The concern over physical aging is certainly not just a modern phenomenon, and in many ways the entire history of civilization has been a constant struggle against the forces of physical aging and toward the ever-elusive "fountain of youth."

*

Where am I personally with each of these dimensions of aging? It's a mixed bag. I like to think that I've not just been having birthdays but instead, in *Star Trek* fashion, I've been circling the sun seventy times, and it's been quite a fantastic (and sometimes maddening) journey, filled with surprises, romance, money troubles and triumphs, and the love of my family. So chronological aging is okay with me. I definitely aspire to psychological and spiritual maturity, and as I age, I feel a far greater sense of perspective than when I was younger. Every now and then I even notice some buds of wisdom trying to bloom. I also feel far more appreciative of all the people I love and the friends I've made and the work that I've been fortunate to do.

And physical aging? Going forward I'd like to physically age as slowly as possible! I think my lifelong commitment to bodymind wellness and healthy living has been paying off somewhat, and I'm doing pretty well. But I definitely don't have the body or vitality I did when I was young. I've got an artificial shoulder. I've gained some weight, and I don't sleep as well as I used to. And even though I haven't eaten meat for more than thirty years and have been working out and also doing yoga for fifty years, I have to work diligently to manage my stress, high blood pressure, and high cholesterol. When I look in the mirror, I realize that I look older than ever before, but I actually like this look and particularly my gray hair. I've worked hard for that. All in all, I'm proud of my years and I feel I've earned my elderhood.

The truth, though, is that even for a guy who's spent a vast majority of his waking hours helping others imagine the best way to age, there's a lot that scares me about getting old. I'm frightened of something happening to my wife, Maddy, or to my children, my brother, or my close friends. And I'm frightened of something happening to me. I'm particularly scared of suffering. The idea of losing a part of me, or not being functional, or losing my mind terrifies me. I watched my dad go blind from macular degeneration a decade before he died at ninety-three. I watched my dear mom be decimated by Alzheimer's disease over the course of twelve increasingly agonizing years. I've seen people put into institutions and treated in horrible, demeaning, degrading ways. I'm also scared of being tossed to the sidelines or being a burden on my family. As you get older, you can't help but confront these things, and I've begun to realize—as a guy who likes to stride through life with a certain amount of boldness— that I'm actually frightened of *being frightened*.

When I turned sixty, my good friend Danny—who is ten years younger than me—asked me how aging looked from my new vantage point. Without thinking, I said, "Like a game of dodge ball." Because yes, I have seen bad things happen to good people—including good people who ate healthy diets, had loving relationships, and lived purposeful lives. It seems that by making healthy choices, you can turn the odds in your favor as you age, but you can't seal the deal, and that uncertainty frightens me. I'm very frightened of ever being a burden on my family. I have seen so much emotional and financial hardship among older men and women and the struggle of so many their caregivers. I'm scared about one day finding myself damaging the lives of my wife and children. I'm also frightened of being tossed to the sidelines. I have seen a lot of aging men and women who have become kind of irrelevant or just out of touch. I've also seen a lot of older people make themselves irrelevant by being unwilling to relate to modern times. I don't want either of those things to happen to me.

Last fall I spoke at a conference at which actor Harrison Ford was also a presenter. During his session, Ford—an outspoken environmental activist—stimulated the audience by proclaiming that young people all over the world should plant millions of trees to help save the planet. It struck me that he didn't challenge the world's older adults to go out and plant a million trees. We may have aches and pains, but it's not something we can't do—in fact, many of us have more time and resources to do it. Why would Ford, an active and engaged elder to be sure, not hold his own peers accountable? When I brought it up to him in a private meeting later that day, he admitted he hadn't even thought of it. To see older men and women planting trees in whose shade they would never sit would make an entirely different statement. Or even better, maybe old and young people should plant trees together. We both smiled when he responded, "Ken, I had never thought of that. What a great idea!" Elders, even icons such as Han Solo, are being conditioned to "pass the torch" and step to the sidelines, for no good reason.

I am increasingly convinced that we need to keep our curiosity engines running, by being more invested in being "useful" than "youthful." We never stop growing up, and rather than turning ourselves into "back in the day" Disney rides, we must continue to stand up tall and be loving and concerned for all people in the world who are grappling with fear, loss, trauma, poverty, and inequality in their communities—especially during Covid-19, which is raging as I finnish this book. We can both share and teach "perspective," and we can be society's elders—in the grandest sense of the word. But we have to be interested. We have to be curious.

When I passed sixty, I found myself occasionally measuring my life not from my starting point but from the finish line. That was a truly interesting switch. I began to wonder, How many more times will I tell my Maddy that I love her? How many vacations with Casey and Zak have I got left in this life? What more can I accomplish? Can I become a wiser, kinder, better version of myself? What will be my legacy? How will I be thought of after I'm gone?

At the end of the day too there's now a sort of lurking fear about whether I'll be ready to embrace the final chapter when the final chapter comes. Having been with my dad and then my mom when they died, and having also experienced the deaths of my father-in-law and my mother-in-law, I'm now at peace with the idea that there is an end point to this life. If I reach forward, I can even catch a glimpse of my final moments, when I'm dying. I imagine that there will be a swirl of feelings as I see the brushstroke that was my life and judge it. And there could be the realization that my relationship with my body, which has always been very high-spirited, is coming to an end. But I imagine that the really hard part will be saying good-bye to my wife, Maddy, and to Casey and Zak. And then there's the curiosity about who and where I'll be in the next instant—which excites me.

Which gets us back to radical curiosity. If there has been one pull-through theme throughout the journey of my life, it is this. Radical curiosity has fueled my early interest in self-awareness and then ongoing self-discovery. It drove me to try to untangle the threads of human potential. It angled me into people-oriented professions and also propelled my attempts at entrepreneurialism. Curiosity has driven my thirst to see, touch, and feel other cultures all over the world—hence my love of travel. It has caused me to probe the underworld of success as well as failure. It has driven me to seek out teachers of all stripes, from hippies and Hells Angels to professors to presidents, from whom I have managed to extract many valuable—and teachable lessons. And it has allowed me to appreciate both the differences between us and the divinity among us. Most significant, it has allowed me to stay close to my family, to come alongside my parents through their suffering, and to continually learn deep lessons from my children.

Radical curiosity is a way to approach the world that is primarily driven by the desire to know and understand more about yourself and the world at large. As I was writing the stories of my life, I saw emerge what I believe to be the main characteristics of radical curiosity:

- Perpetual openness to self-discovery—we never stop "growing" up.
- A relentless interest in the diversity of the people of the world (put another way: having both an open mind and an open heart).
- Ambition with integrity: while plowing or dancing forward,

remaining mindful of your values, and living by then—regardless of what siren songs might attempt to distract.

• The desire to always seek to learn and to teach what we know, and then go on to learn something else. It includes a mantra: *Breathe, learn, teach, repeat.*

• The willingness to allow for pauses in life—they sometimes provide the opportunity for reevaluation, reprioritization, cocooning, and even, sometimes, rebirth.

• Respect for death as a part of life, not simply its end. It provides the ongoing time beat for just about everything.

Without a doubt, this radical curiosity has made boredom an infrequent visitor in my life. Now it has motivated me to stitch together my stories from the journey of my life to see just what kind of tapestry they form. Needless to say, I sure am curious which chapter(s) and lesson(s) will be your favorite(s).

PART I

THE SORCERER'S APPRENTICE

Who are you?
·
How will you untangle yourself from the grip of
your parents' expectations?
·
How do you discover your truest self (again and again)?
·
Will you find love and will you be lovable?
·
What inspires your curiosity?
·
Will you be happy?
·
What do you really believe about life, death and God?

METAMORPHOSIS

Be yourself; everyone else is already taken. —Oscar Wilde

When I'm lost, I usually ask for directions. One way or another, I feel a bit lost much of the time. This can be a complicated existential equation because as a husband, father, employer, author—and by some standards an expert in aging, longevity, psychology, and several related fields— there is the presumption that I know who I am, what I'm talking about, and where I'm heading. And yet, with each turn around the sun, while I do feel a bit wiser from time to time, I have also come to more fully appreciate how much I still don't know, and how much more I have to learn and make sense of. So I often seek guidance from folks who might be able to help me get where I'm trying to go.

When my dad passed away in the fall of 2013, not only was I dealing with waves of grief over his passing but I also had to come to terms with the presence of his absence—sort of like how I imagine an amputee might miss a limb. My dad had been a constant in my life—just a phone call or plane ride away. I always knew that if I asked, he would find a way to make himself available (in his own unique and opinionated way) to listen to me, give me advice, try to get me to switch my political views, or, most often, just shoot the shit.

Even though we continually butted heads about politics, prejudice, and the media, there was not one instance in my entire life when he wasn't there for me when I truly needed him. I vividly remember a weekend in 1971 when I rode my motorcycle from Allentown, Pennsylvania, to visit my folks in their new home in Springfield, New Jersey. At that point I had already tuned in, turned on, and dropped out, grown my hair and beard, started wearing an earring, and cultivated many viewpoints about life that were far more "alternative" to ones he strongly held. He must have thought I had lost my mind—while I believed I was finding it.

Late that Saturday night, my mom had gone to bed and he and I were arguing about something or other. He started barking at me with criticisms and nasty comments about my life and friends. I squared off with him, nose to nose. I felt, You don't know who I am—you don't get me! I don't even remember exactly what we were fighting over, but I do remember it's the closest I'd ever come to telling him to go fuck himself and punching him in the face. So that things wouldn't get completely out of control, I turned on my heels, went to the bedroom, and slammed the door. Feeling I had to get out of there and not wanting to confront him again in the living room, I jumped out the bedroom window. Okay, it wasn't that high—maybe six feet above the ground. It was adark and rainy winter night, and all I had on were my jeans, a T-shirt, and a trench coat. With sheets of rain pouring down, it was going to take me about two hours to ride my motorcycle back to my apartment in Pennsylvania.

As I careened down the highway, I was crying and furious. I was thinking, Fuck you—I'm going to do what I'm going to do with my life. The road was wet and slippery, and riding the motorcycle was a harrowing experience. Finally, at around two in the morning, I pulled off Highway 78 at the Fifteenth Street exit in Allentown. I took the back road to my apartment. Exhausted, I parked my motorcycle in front. Although it was pitch-black, I noticed that there was a car way down at the corner. It was moving slowly, but the lights weren't on. As I walked across the street to get to my apartment, I looked at this car as it was turning around. It was my dad. He had followed me all the way to Pennsylvania to make sure I was safe, and now he was silently turning around to drive all the way home.

When he died in October 2013, I missed him emotionally, viscerally, spiritually. If my daughter, Casey, did something really cool at work, or my son, Zak, sent us a note from his adventures in China, I immediately wanted to call him and tell him about it—but he wasn't there. It wasn't that I wished he was immortal or even that he had played that much of an active role in my or my family's life in his final years. I simply realized that he had always been a powerful magnet on my compass, impacting my sense of true north and slightly distorting (often for the better and sometimes for the worse) nearly all of my life's navigations. While I felt liberated by no longer being judged by him, parts of me grew more uncertain. I realized that no matter how self-determined and grown-up I believed myself to be, I was reliant to some extent on his point of view and, yes, when it came to me, his approval. Perhaps I'm like other ambitious or driven people: while a big motivational force for me has always been to make a positive impact on the world, another part of me has never known how much is good enough, what it should take for me to feel satisfied with my efforts, and who ultimately measures me.

In the months after my dad died, when I lay in bed at night taking stock of myself, I felt as though big tectonic plates were moving around very deep inside of me, causing everything to shift. When I was young, I had no idea who I was, but something in me pushed me to find out. Now, once again, I was feeling disoriented. My father's death had fundamentally changed me, and I was no longer sure who I was.

I decided to seek out some help. I've always been somewhat of a seeker, and I was intensely curious to know my psychological DNA more deeply than I had ventured before. I first reached ⟨ ⟩ to gifted psychologist and mindfulness teacher Dr. Jim Bramson an⟨ ⟩ weekly meetings—navigating around my travel schedule⟨ ⟩ ⟨sim⟩ultaneously, I sought out the wise and imaginative sto⟨ ⟩ ⟨G⟩olden, with whom I scheduled sessions every other week, ⟨ ⟩ ⟨yea⟩r so. Why two different people with different talents? ⟨ ⟩ of parallax, I suppose. Both men provided a safe, open-⟨ ⟩ me to explore the inner workings of my plot line.

During those many intense, self-reflective, and self-evaluat⟨ive ses⟩sions, I dove way down into my mind and soul to catch and release ⟨ ⟩ stories of my life, while trying to comprehend why they happened and what they might teach me—and, possibly, others. I relished this kind of curiosity- driven self-exploration. With today's go-go and tech-connected lifestyles, taking regular time to remember which path you're on and where you're trying to go can be invaluable. I hadn't kept a journal since the 1970s—it was required as part of my psychology graduate program—and most of my writing and speechifying had been about subjects such as aging, demography, marketing, longevity, and health care. Keeping a journal was a kind of internal adventure, a chance for a more authentic self-expression. Much of the content for this book emerged during these sessions.

In one of my meetings with Jim Bramson we discussed the work of Joseph Campbell, author of *The Hero with a Thousand Faces* (whom I had the good fortune of learning from when I was at Esalen), which explores how myths and stories can shape our views about so many things. For example, most psychologists know that "The Ugly Duckling" is not really a story about waterfowl but rather about the transition from awkward youth to self-confident young adulthood, "Cinderella" is about the dream of finding one's true love, and "Little Red Riding Hood" reflects fears of sexual abduction. And "Snow White and the Seven Dwarfs"? I have no clue what that's supposed to be about! Jim asked me if there was any famous fable or story from a movie that I identified with. Without any hesitation, I responded, "'The Sorcerer's Apprentice' in *Fantasia*."

"Why is that?" he asked.

I explained that throughout my life, I had always related to the Mickey Mouse character in that intense and complicated story. When I was a little boy, we lived across the street from a movie theater. Sometimes on Saturday my mom would take my brother and me to see whatever was playing. One day we saw *Fantasia*, and the incredible combination of animation and music blew my little mind. Later, when I was in college, there was a classic movie festival on campus and *Fantasia* was featured. Again, it blew my mind, but as an adult I paid more attention to the psycho-spiritual story it was revealing. Then after I moved to California it was playing as part of a Disney collection and I saw it again. And again it blew my mind. (Truth be told, I downloaded it last night and watched it again. Yep, it still blows my mind!)

I am particularly taken by the Mickey Mouse character—the sorcerer's silly but aspirational apprentice. While hoping one day to be a grand wizard himself, he has the mundane job of filling buckets with water, carrying them down a bunch of steps, and putting them into the sorcerer's cauldron. As the scene opens, the wizened old wizard is focused on a big book in front of him, which looks to Mickey to be the grand book of magic. Then the powerful sorcerer removes his hat, sets down his wand, and leaves his chamber. Little Mickey impishly takes the sorcerer's place, puts on the hat, and examines the book. Raising the magical wand and turning the pages in the book, he starts to wave his hands just like he's seen the sorcerer do.

As his untested and unrefined magical powers awaken, he causes a broom that's lying against the wall to come alive, grow arms, and then carry the water buckets. *Slosh, slosh, slosh.* He falls asleep and envisions himself at the top of something like Mount Olympus, waving his hands while the waves are crashing high above the cliffs. He then reaches farther up to the heavens, and the stars come alive. In his dream he's become the master of the universe. With classical music thundering in the background, Mickey wakes up and is shocked to see the broom running amok. He takes an axe and tries to stop the out-of-control broom. Instead, his axe breaks the broom into thousands of pieces, and each one animates into another broom with arms and buckets of water. He's lost control, and the sorcerer's chamber is being flooded by an army of living brooms carrying buckets and buckets of sloshing water.

When the sorcerer returns, he sternly takes stock of the mess his ambitious apprentice has created and immediately takes back his hat and his wand. With a skilled wave of his hands, he calms the flooding and makes the water recede. To add insult to injury, the sorcerer takes the broom from his misbehaving apprentice, whacks him on his backside, and sends him on his way.

After I explained all of this, Jim asked me how I related to the scene and why I thought I'd picked it. "Well," I said, "I've spent much of my life as a student of human potential with a desire to make magic in the world, and I've sought out powerful teachers to help me learn how. So I identify one hundred percent with the apprentice's aspirations. I have at times found myself setting things in motion that went out of control, so I also really relate to the mayhem that Mickey unleashed." Bramson asked for an example. I explained, "In the 1990s, instead of just creating one Age Wave company, I got carried away and tried to create six at the same time. I bit off far more than I could chew …"

"Okay," Jim said, reflecting. "You love that movie and that scene, and you feel that's your story being told?"

"Yes, that's right," I said. "In fact, if you were to visit my home office or my corporate office, you'd see a little statue of Mickey Mouse as the sorcerer's apprentice on both of my desks. He's my spiritual icon, and he has been for as long as I can remember."

I asked Jim if he had asked many of his other clients to pick a movie or fable that they related to, and he said he had. Had anyone else had chosen *Fantasia*? "Nope," he said. "But let's try to unpack that one…"

LEAVING A LEGACY
VALUES AND LIFE LESSONS

I am what survives of me. — Erik Erikson

I've often been surprised by how much my professional interests have either collided with or been midwifed by personal reflections and actions. For example, in 2005 I oversaw my company Age Wave's first national study about how people felt about leaving or receiving an inheritance and how they might want to live and leave a legacy. We initially asked focus group participants, "What does an inheritance mean to you?" and "How do you want to pass your inheritance on to your children and grandchildren?" Guess what? Nobody wanted to talk about inheritance, and the initial focus groups were a failure. The participants complained, saying, "It's too uncomfortable a subject. Inheritance has to do with divvying up the loot. It's about burying me before my time. It makes me uneasy to even think about."

Feeling stymied, I said to the focus-group moderator, "Try changing the word from *"inheritance"* to *"legacy."* Ask people, 'Would you like to leave a legacy? Would you like to receive a legacy?'" To our delight, the floodgates opened. Everyone was eager to share a wide range of feelings about what they were hoping to leave behind for their children, grandchildren, and the world beyond family.

When we sent our questionnaire to survey how thousands of people related to either giving or receiving a legacy, we were captivated by what emerged. First, we discovered that there were four key pillars to legacy, some more important than others. One pillar had to do with the desired disposition of any wealth or real estate that had been accumulated. This mattered quite a lot to both the givers and the receivers but not nearly as much as the other three pillars.

Next on the hierarchy of importance was "possessions that have emotional value." We came across a thought-provoking study that had been done at the University of Minnesota, called "Who Gets Grandma's Yellow Pie Plate?" The title said it all. Most families have possessions that hold great value to family members, even though on the open market they're not worth very much. For example, my brother, Alan, had been so close with our grandfather Max that when Max passed away, of all the grandchildren, Alan received Max's ring. I don't know if this ring was worth very much, but to Alan it was. I have never seen Alan without this ring on. Similarly, someone might appreciate owning their mom's piano or their dad's baseball glove. On a grander scale, the family elders might have owned a cabin by the lake in which many memories were shared and there's no desire to sell it and divide the cash. Rather, the heirs might want to keep the cabin as a family heirloom to be shared and enjoyed with future generations.

Even more important than money, real estate, or possessions with emotional value, the third pillar of legacy was "instructions and wishes to be fulfilled." Here's an example. My mom and dad had the wonderfully good fortune of being in love and married for seventy-one years before my dad passed away. He had become blind in his last ten years from diabetes-related macular degeneration, and my mom had Alzheimer's, which over a twelve-year period decimated her memories and ability to function. In his later years, my father asked my brother and me to come visit with him in Florida. On that special trip, our dad insisted that we spend a full day allowing him to tell us all his wishes for how he wanted our mom—his beloved wife—to be cared for after he died. He didn't want her in a nursing home, and he didn't want her to ever feel alone or frightened. He didn't want her to ever be cared for by unkind people. And he wanted us to spend whatever might be necessary so that our mom could always feel secure and loved. Alan and I agreed to all of that with both respect and honor—we loved our mom so much, we would have done it even if he hadn't asked. When my dad passed away, Alan relocated from New Jersey to live with our mom. As a long-distance caregiver, I tried to support them in every way I could to make sure that she remained in her own home and that she received the best home care from the kindest aides. Alan definitely did the heavier lifting, but we made every effort to work as a team. By carefully outlining his instructions and wishes regarding our mom, our dad showed great respect for her, for us, and for our family bond. He also appeared to feel a certain amount of peace of mind having us look him in the eye and promise him that we would honor all his wishes.

From this study we also learned that the single most important pillar of legacy people wanted to leave—and, incredibly, that younger people wanted to receive—were "values and life lessons." I don't mean, "Dad, did you go to Woodstock?" Or "Mom, what's your favorite snack food?" It's the deeper stories that matter most, the ones that reflect core values and important life lessons. The ones that answer questions such as "What do you hold to be true?" "Who and what do you love?" "How do you discern right from wrong?" "How do you feel about religion?" "Do you believe in God?" "What do you believe about your role as a parent, and what was your experience as a child?" "What do you feel about your work, your life, your impending death?" "What can we learn from you?"

Inspired by the research and motivated by my dad's passing, I decided that I absolutely needed to write this book— maybe just for my kids, but maybe for a wider readership too.

FROM NEWARK TO BIG SUR

LEAVING KENNY BEHIND

Life can only be understood backward. But it must be lived forward.
—Søren Kierkegaard

Travel back with me to my youth. I grew up in in the 1950s and '60s in a hardworking, middle-class community in Newark, New Jersey. During my first five years of life, we shared a duplex with my grandparents, my mom's parents. My grandparents were simple folks of Russian Jewish stock. Neither had received much education, but they worked hard for everything they had. He was a car mechanic, and she was a homemaker. What mattered most to them was their family. They had two sons, two daughters, and ten grandchildren, and we all got together nearly every Sunday in their modest home to play, laugh, and eat a home-cooked meal.

Then, thanks to GI home loans, my dad placed a bet on himself and moved us to a lovely four-bedroom home in the Weequahic section of Newark. This new home was one block away from our grammar school and three blocks from the high school. And we were still only a couple of miles away from my grandparents—a short bike ride. We had a driveway and a backyard with enough space to install a basketball hoop on the garage. My brother and I were in heaven. In our home we had one black-and-white television set with four working channels: ABC, NBC, CBS, and and later PBS. In my teenage years, on most Sunday nights we'd pile into our family car to drive to Uncle Marty and Aunt Ethel's house to watch *The Ed Sullivan Show* in color. These relatives were the only people we knew who owned a color TV at that time, and it was thrilling to watch. In our home, we had two telephones: one was downstairs on the wall in the kitchen, and the other was upstairs in my parents' room. My parents shared a car, and my brother and I had bicycles, which was how we got everywhere we wanted to go. We didn't have much, but neither did anyone else. I had a great crew of friends, and every day—rain or shine—we played in the streets or in the playground after school. Our rules of the road, our code of ethics, came from living in a fairly homogenous, tightly knit community. My parents and grand-parents shared the values of their neighbors, taught me "right" from "wrong," and habituated me to the proper pleases and thank yous. In the Boy Scouts we were taught to be "helpful, friendly, courteous, kind, obedient, cheerful, thrifty, brave, clean, and reverent." Given that I still remember those attributes fully and in order, I guess that had an impact! In our mostly Jewish neighborhood, everyone was trying to make some-thing of themselves. My father was a fiercely hardworking guy who wanted to be successful. For him, work wasn't about "finding his bliss," it was about being a responsible husband and father. His dad had skipped out on him, his brothers, sister, and mother for almost ten years during the Depression. In contrast, my dad wished to be a reliable family man. He wanted our family to be living the American dream. Neither of my parents had gone to college, but neither did the parents of most of my friends. There wasn't a need or desire for excess; if anyone had it, we certainly weren't being exposed to it. The kids on Dick Clark's *American Bandstand* coming out of Philly looked and acted a lot like my Weequahic friends, who were a cross between the characters in *Grease* and *Diner*. The Cleavers and other families on TV seemed a lot like ours, maybe a little better off, although the parents were more placid and doting than mine. I should note that all the happy families on TV at the time were white, although some had a black maid. For all the idealism of the era, these were fiercely and ignorantly racist times. In retrospect, our parents, the so-called Greatest Generation, sure didn't like people of color very much.

Our parents weren't all that involved in our lives, and they weren't supposed to be. Did my folks ever go to school and meet with my teach-ers? No. Did they help me with my homework? No. Did they come to my basketball games or tennis matches? No. I do think they attended my high school graduation, but they didn't throw any big celebration afterward. My dad worked ten to twelve hours a day, and that was what he did. In addition to her nearly full-time job in my dad's retail clothing business, our kind and wonderful mom also tended to our home and made sure my brother and I felt loved and supported. We were kids, and being kids was what we did. While I liked school somewhat—I remember a few terrific teachers, named Sadie Rouse, Ed Truman, and Phil Egeth—the very best part of growing up was my friends. I had a crew of great ones: Larry, Jeff T., Jeff R., Bobby, Paul, Herman, Kenny, Mike, Gordon, Jon, Ken, and many others. And a short bike ride away lived our cousins Jan and Ira and all their Hillside friends. The Weequahic girls were mighty—Fern, Rita, Paula, Beth, Barbara, Betsy, Fran, Carol, Joan, Nancy, Debbie, and Linda. We all loved playing almost any kind of game and riding our bikes until it got too dark to see.

Nearly all the guys wanted to be on one sports team or another. Many of the girls hoped to be cheerleaders. If you got into a fight, you wanted to not get beaten up and you expected your friends to back you up. Come Saturday night, everyone wanted to have good dance moves and maybe slow dance with your girlfriend or boyfriend. I went steady when I was fourteen with my first girlfriend, Fern Polinsky, who was pretty, a cheerleader, and had a great personality. Fern's father was a kosher butcher, and her mom, like many moms of the day, didn't drive but rather took the bus anywhere she needed to go. In high school there was some hugging, kissing, and feeling around here and there, but no one was having any sex. Fern wore my ID bracelet for almost a year.

As a teenager, I played by the rules. I was a normal, reasonably well-adjusted kid and a very conscientious student—getting all As throughout high school. I was also a pretty good athlete. I was captain of the tennis team (there weren't many tennis players in urban Newark), and we all played a lot of basketball. Our Jewish Community Center (JCC) basketball team—comprised of many of my best buddies—won the state tournament, then the regional, then we took first place in the national championship. Competitive team sports were, without a doubt, the master narrative and favorite part of my growing-up years. Given that I was also on the high school math team, you could say I was a scholar-athlete kind of kid, but with plain vanilla dreams. My intent was to become an electrical engineer or physicist, fall in love, get married, have children, and live in a house within a few minutes of where my mom and dad lived.

While I was in high school, our community was declared to be "culturally deprived," which made us eligible for a Title I grant. I didn't really feel culturally deprived, but I guess with the levels of poverty and illiteracy in the area, that's how we were categorized. The folks in charge of Title I programs arrived at a solution worthy of Sacha Baron Cohen: every student in my high school received their very own copy of *The Brothers Karamazov* by Fyodor Dostoyevsky. That night when many of us gathered in the school playground to play basketball, we laughed when we noticed that the garbage dumpster was overflowing with fresh copies of *The Brothers Karamazov*.

The rules of life were simple—almost two-dimensional. There definitely wasn't a lot of talk about personal feelings or identity, self-actualization, discovering your passion, or mental health—none at all, in fact. I didn't do much deep thinking about anything. No one I knew did. The most famous person from our neighborhood, Philip Roth, was a decade or two older than me. When he first achieved fame as a writer and storyteller, it was with a book about a guy who masturbated all the time.

There were several undercurrents in our lives during those years, realities that were felt but seldom discussed.

First, there was the absolute belief that if you worked very hard, you might one day achieve some success and, perhaps, your own version of the American dream. We saw that all of our parents were devoted to this principle, but especially our dads. While our moms unquestionably over-saw our homes, our health, our school life, and our friendship networks, it was the dads who left home every morning and tried to make a buck, which in postwar America was both difficult and beckoning.

When I was a child, my dad worked as an "installment dealer." He and three other guys—I think their names were Harold, Bernie, and Irving—had a warehouse where they stored stuff such as pillowcases, blankets, and clothing. Each of the men had what looked like a milk truck, and every day they would drive around neighborhoods and try to sell things to people out of their trucks. Since their customers would pay them on an installment basis, my dad and his partners would come back to their homes or apartments once a week or month and collect a few dollars until the item was paid off. It was a rugged hustle, and my dad's dream was to have his own store. He took a big risk and opened a modest little flea market storefront on Bergen Street in Newark that he called Bergen Bazaar. Then he then took an even bigger risk when he and our mom opened a much bigger and nicer modern clothing store in Elizabeth called the Dress Rack. At that point I was a teenager, and I can remember his excite-ment when the store did so well that he opened another and another and another. He and our mom—and then my brother, Alan—became a formidable team, and my dad turned his dreams into quite a success—enough to put my brother and me through college and ultimately pave the way for a relatively comfortable later life for him and his wife and now business partner, our mom. What a dazzling display of inventiveness and willpower, marketing ingenuity, and a massive work ethic. Bravo! But he wasn't alone; in nearly every house in our neighborhood, there was a dad trying to make something of himself—as a car dealer, a taxi driver, a baker, a butcher, a gas station owner, or a retailer like my dad. For their generation, who came back from the war with nothing, the old-fashioned work ethic was alive and well.

Second, when I was growing up, some of my friends' parents had tattoos on their forearms. You'd be at their houses, and you'd see their dad with sleeves rolled up, fixing a broken pipe, or you'd see their mom washing dishes and their forearms had numbers that had been tattooed onto them by the Nazis. They had been in concentration camps and survived. People whispered about how some of the women had been raped and abused and terrible things were done to the men and millions of Jews had been gassed and killed while the world looked on. This was the 1950s, the first generation after Hitler, so being Jewish was filled with anxiety, pride, and fury. The grown-ups in my neighborhood didn't talk about any of this. Later in my life, I saw movies such as *The Pawnbroker* and read books such as Viktor Frankl's *Man's Search for Meaning*, and I came to realize how traumatized some of the adults in my neighborhood were in that period.

While there wasn't much of a belief in God (how could there be a God, with what had just happened in the Holocaust?), my Jewishness made me a member of a tribe, which, it occurred to me, was a proud tribe to be in. If somebody called you a kike, you had full authority to punch them in the face.

The third undercurrent had to do with the ongoing anxiety of the Cold War and the worry that the "commies" in the Soviet Union might drop nuclear bombs on us. Nearly all of our dads had recently served in the military and were not keen on doing it again—or having their boys be shipped off to war. And even though the Soviet Union had been an ally against Hitler, they had become the new enemy. Some of the families—like mine—created makeshift bomb shelters in their basements and stocked them with food, water, and a radio so that if something horrible happened, we could retreat to our little hideaway under the house. In addition, I can vividly remember the duck-and-cover drills we went through as young high school students when the air-raid sirens went off every few weeks. We trained repeatedly to either stand facing the wall or crouch under our wooden desks and thereby be protected from the force and heat of a thermonuclear device. Brilliant!

The fourth undercurrent had to do with the dramatic shift taking place in the racial makeup of my community. When I began Weequahic High

School, my freshman class was 90 percent white. On my first day of high school, the city government created a new ruling that said if you lived in Newark, you could attend any school you wished. The sociology of my neighborhood changed instantly. By my fourth year at Weequahic, the freshman class was 90 percent black. My friends and I integrated relatively comfortably with the new kids. We played sports together, did homework together, and got on with the business of being teenagers together. With Motown music coming alive from our sister city, Detroit, and everyone wanting to be cool like the Temptations or Supremes, it appeared—at least to us—that integration was a normal part of life. Who would I have most liked to be, Pat Boone or David Ruffin? David Ruffin, hands down (maybe with a bit of Elvis mixed in). Perhaps we were innocent, or naïve, or ignorant, because my friends and I were unaware of the deep racial issues brewing in Newark and across America. The Newark riots exploded shortly after my final days in high school. Weeks later there was a full-artillery Sherman tank in the street directly in front of my home. The next month my parents fled to the suburbs.

The fifth undercurrent was that many of our parents deeply wished that their kids would grow up to become something more than a car mechanic or a shopkeeper. They hoped we would go to college and one day have a professional career. In truth, this aspiration was more geared to the boys than the girls – who were expected to become moms and housewives, although that was soon to change. The self-improvement bug sure bit me, as I imagined that I would become an electrical engineer or physicist. Why? Because when I was in high school, where I was an honors student, I went to one of those vocational testing places—at the Stevens Institute—and they told me I had a strong aptitude for math and the sciences and that I should therefore be an electrical engineer. Not having any clue as to who I actually was or what the world actually had to offer, I figured, okay, then that's what I'll be.

Since neither of my folks had been to college, I didn't have much per-spective or insight about this path. I just figured I'd go and get a degree, get started on a career, and hopefully have a good life. And so I went to a fine engineering school at Lehigh University in Bethlehem, Pennsylvania. I partly went because they accepted me on early notice, and it was a good school, and also because I could be on a bus to get home for a visit in around two hours. During my first two years, I jumped whole hog into science. In truth, I didn't enjoy it very much. I didn't particularly like the classes, the homework, or the professors. I was pretty good with my slide rule, which was clipped to my belt, but in the 1960s, science simply didn't captivate me. Living in a dorm and then in a frat house—on an all-male campus with our sister school, Cedar Crest, a half hour away—we had a truly stilted social life. This while in the larger world the sexual revolution was awakening and protests to the Vietnam War were erupting everywhere. I got drunk on most weekends and tried pot, but my state of mind remained relatively plain vanilla and middle of the road.. Overall, my grades were fine, and I was making progress toward adulthood, albeit feeling somewhat uninspired.

In my junior year I had to take some electives. My curriculum advisor suggested I take a social science course to round out my engineering and physics training, so I wandered into a psychology course being taught by a cool young professor (every campus had one). It was 1969, and I honestly didn't know what psychology was. The professor, Dr. Bill Newman, had recently graduated with his PhD from Stanford, so he'd been living in the San Francisco Bay Area, although he had grown up in Brooklyn. At that time, before the Palo Alto peninsula became Silicon Valley, it was the home of Ken Kesey and the Merry Pranksters, Jerry Garcia, and a whole new drug-fueled bohemian culture. Dr. Newman was smart and hip, very unlike my physics and chemistry professors, who were quite square. The course was titled The Psychology of Human Potential, and from the first lecture, it absolutely blew my mind. It was based on the idea that human beings have extraordinary capabilities, vast mental, physical, and even spiritual potential, and that we were only tapping into maybe 5 percent of it. There was also the suggestion that our modern educational and physical training programs were quite pedantic and designed to activate only a tiny portion of our capabilities. This point of view completely turned me on and excited my imagination more than anything I had ever encountered. It occurred to me that there was a multicolored world out there, yet I was trapped in the black-and-white anteroom. The first textbook of the course was *The Varieties of Psychedelic Experience* by psychologists Masters and Houston, and the second was *Psychotherapy East and West* by philosopher Alan Watts. The third was *Toward a Psychology of Being* by breakthrough "self-actualization" thinker Abraham Maslow, and the fourth was a book by Dr. William Schutz called *Joy*, about the exaltation one feels when one breaks free of restrictive and confining patterns. All these books were recently written, filled with big ideas, and, for me, mind-boggling.

As I dug deeper and deeper, I learned that there were ancient therapies and practices such as meditation, tai chi, and yoga that could unleash these potentials. I learned about many emerging new approaches, including bioenergetics, Rolfing, Feldenkrais, encounter groups, and Gestalt therapy, that were designed to loosen mental and physical constraints and liberate people to live a bigger, grander version of their possibilities. I immediately starting practicing beginner's yoga and meditating. I also gathered some of my electrical engineering friends to build simple biofeedback equipment with which we attempted to alter our brain waves while in sensory-deprivation chambers. I went to the library and started gorging on everything I could find that probed the search for human potential: Ram Dass's *Be Here Now* (a Xeroxed copy of the manuscript), P. D. Ouspensky's *In Search of the Miraculous*, Alexander Lowen's *The Betrayal of the Body*, and Hermann Hesse's *Siddhartha*, to name a few. Over my life, I have heard people tell stories of their awakening sexuality, or their discovery of their personal passion for playing the piano, or even their realization of God. For me, then, it was like my previously quiet volcano of curiosity had exploded. Who am I? How does my mind impact my body? Do I have any superpowers? If so, what are they? Does my brain contain all of my mind? Is there a God, and if so, what's his or her plan? Am I reincarnated, and if I am, what other lives have I lived? Are humans done evolving? Evolving to what? What is my purpose? Do I have a destiny? Questions poured forth unrelentingly. I had never really experienced angst before, but I was swimming up to my eyeballs in it now. I knew that I had to find answers.

I couldn't help but notice that in the human potential authors' bios it would say, *Alan Watts is a teacher at the Esalen Institute* or *William Schutz left Harvard to be a teacher at the Esalen Institute,* or *Fritz Perls teaches workshops at the Esalen Institute*. The pursuit of human potential became my singular focus, and I just couldn't get enough of the real deal in Bethlehem, Pennsylvania. I decided to drop out of Lehigh and go to the source of this revolution— California, specifically, the Esalen Institute perched atop the mysterious cliffs of Big Sur. This decision surely didn't make my mom and dad happy. They thought my mind had become unhinged and they were losing their fair-haired, all-American boy Kenny.

Some of my friends thought what I was doing was very cool, while others thought it was totally stupid. For the very first time in my life, I honestly didn't care what other people thought I should do. In some eerie way, I felt my destiny was calling to me, and I responded.

There was nothing in my life up to that point—absolutely nothing—that would indicate that I would drop out of college and go off to California in search of human potential, cosmic magic, and purpose. I had not been a rule breaker or a renegade in any way. Something was changing deep inside of me as I heard the siren's song of new adventures both in the world and inside myself. It was time for me to shed my current life and leave Kenny behind.

It's important to note that there is a difference between knowing you want to change or grow and understanding who you are. As a young man, I didn't have any idea who I was. I didn't even know it was a question. Most people didn't. But somehow I knew I wanted to figure it out. Curiosity without self-knowledge can be really harmful because it's aimless... and that is part of youth. You make mistakes. You fuck up. Your anxiety can overwhelm you. Radical curiosity seeks to understand the self, and as you get older, you do it more intentionally, as I did in seeking out various therapists and storytelling coaches, but you don't give up on yourself. You can always change. You can always evolve. After my dad died, you could say I was just as lost as when I was twenty; I just had more evolved GPS resources—and a greater willingness to ask for help—for finding a way back to myself.

So I sold everything I had and cut into my bar mitzvah money and the meager savings I had accumulated from my summer jobs to pay for the workshops I was going to take at Esalen. I imagined that five months at Esalen would be kind of like a semester at college. So, very innocently, I signed up for five months of nonstop workshops.

A LEAP OF FAITH

*Look up at the stars and not down at your feet. Try to make sense of what
you see, and wonder about what makes the universe exist. Be curious.*
—Steven Hawking

When the day arrived for me to fly west, I said good-bye to my family. My
brother, Alan, who was three years older than me and a straight arrow,
was bewildered by the whole thing. My mom was, as was her nature,
encouraging but nervous. When my dad said good-bye, he broke down
and sobbed—something I had never seen him do before.

I took off from Newark Airport, bound for San Francisco. I had never
been farther west than Pennsylvania. Upon landing, I had only to begin
walking through the terminal to be immediately entranced by the Summer
of Love look, style, and attitude that made California feel so completely
different from New Jersey.In contrast to the gray suits and harried feeling of
Newark airport, I was immediately entranced by the bell bottoms, flower
prints, and summer-of-love look, style, and attitude that made California
feel so completely different than New Jersey. There were so many young
people, and they were so attractive. With my backpack and my guitar,
I walked outside into the sunlight onto Highway 101 and put out my
thumb to hitchhike into San Francisco. I was struck by the quality of the
light. It's what I have, for the past half century, loved the most about
Northern California. It was so bright and clear that everything looked
sharper and more colorful than I had ever seen. Even the shadows had
shadows within them.

Back then, hitchhiking was one of the ways you got around, made new
friends, or found places to crash for a while. The driver of the car or truck
would flash you the peace sign, slow down, open the door, and you'd be
off. It was a bit like a mobile Burning Man. But on that day, in that spot,
I didn't get a ride—I got arrested. Within minutes. Apparently, you were
not allowed to hitchhike on Highway 101, and the police were convinced
I was a runaway. At the station, the police called my parents. You can
imagine their alarm. But after assurances by my parents that I was in fact
free to go where I wished to go, I was released, no time served.

Fortunately, Esalen had a van that would pick you up in the city. When the minibus arrived, I was immediately in a different world. Inside were two women and an older man. Soon enough, I and my new friends were on the way through the gorgeous terrain where the soaring mountains meet the Pacific Ocean along the rocky cliffs of Coast Highway. I kept the window open so I could feel the cool ocean air. And it was a ride unlike any I had ever taken. As you pass Monterey Bay heading south, all of a sudden an unending cascade of massive mountains rises up to your left, while the highway begins to lift you above sea level on the precarious edge of a winding cliff to your right that plummets to craggy rocks and the tempestuous Pacific Ocean below. Having grown up near the Atlantic, with its flat beaches and pulsing shoreline waves, I could not believe the primitive strength and beauty of the Big Sur Pacific coastline.

For the next hour there were countless hairpin turns, each one revealing a panorama of the Santa Lucia Mountains meeting coastline more incredible than the one before. All along the route we spotted tourists who had precariously parked their cars on the narrow shoulder to snap a few breathtaking photos, and hippie boys and girls thumbing their way to who knows where. Out at sea, we could catch glimpses of whales breaching. At one point the van driver whispered over his shoulder to his spellbound passengers, "This is why it's called God's country."

And then, about fifty winding miles south of Monterey, on the ocean side of the road, a modest wood sign (which still exists today) that we could have easily missed, declared ESALEN INSTITUTE / BY RESERVATION ONLY.

We had arrived. I had arrived.

As the van pulled down the nearly vertical driveway to reveal an Eden-like campus with a sumptuous vegetable garden unlike anything I had ever seen, I might as well have just landed on an alien planet. We all jumped out to register in the Esalen office, staffed by beautiful hippie women and men. Around the fourteen-acre property gorgeous rock formations were swarmed by flowers, a great hall served as a communal dining room, a spectacular canyon with waterfalls contorted among cypress trees, and, of course, a natural hot spring was filled to the brim with naked folks laughing, playing, or staring out across the ocean.

(Fast-forward many years: Maddy and I are watching one of our favorite TV shows when its protagonist arrives on Esalen's mysterious cliffs, seeking answers to his own inner turmoil and to his curiosity about where pop culture is heading. Turns out that the last episode of *Mad Men* sends

Don Draper to Esalen, an end point that is actually a beginning. Draper's arrival takes place in exactly the same year and season when I was first there—although I don't recall meeting him at the time!)

That first day, I found my way to my shared room and unpacked. I ate alone in the cafeteria, mesmerized by the truly amazing sunset over the Pacific. Soon after, I walked up the hill to a funky building where I'd be joining my first workshop, It was an "encounter group" led by Dr. William Schutz, the Harvard professor who had dropped out of academics and invented encounter groups. Schutz had gravitas at Esalen. He had recently published his controversial book *Joy*. And with the popularity of the 1969 movie *Bob & Carol & Ted & Alice*, which playfully spoofed one of his Esalen workshops, Will Schutz appeared on *The Tonight Show Starring Johnny Carson* many times demonstrating trust exercises with other guests and declaring the need for everyone to get open and honest and tell the truth about what they were feeling. During this antiestablishment period, fueled on the one hand by antiauthoritarian political protests and on the other by the sensuality and freedoms being espoused by a new era of sex, drugs, rock and roll, and mind expansion, Schutz and many others felt it was a time for a new psychology.

In addition to having taught traditional psychology at Harvard, Schutz had recently trained with Ida Rolf to become a Rolfer. Because he and Fritz Perls both lived and taught at Esalen, Schutz picked up many of Perls's Gestalt therapy insights and techniques. He was also fascinated by the work of Wilhelm Reich, Moshe Feldenkrais, and J. L. Moreno—and he combined all those different modalities into a new kind of therapeutic dynamic, which he called an encounter group. Depending on how you looked at his approach, it was either a brilliant synthesis of numerous mind-body therapies or a zany, touchy-feely mash-up—or possibly both.

The encounter group movement aimed to achieve personal openness, honesty, and realness by stripping away the façades, unpeeling the armor, and uncoiling the usual defenses. No need for pretense or cover-ups: if you're hurting, be hurting. If you're angry, be angry. If you're deeply sad, let it out. If you're jealous, talk about it. Before then, most psychotherapy was done one-on-one for an hour or so in the privacy of a therapist's office. And it could take years for a breakthrough to happen.

Encounter groups busted that wide open. First, let's remove the privacy and make therapy into a group thing. To be sure, that was a wild idea. Some of the impetus for that came by way of AA recovery groups and from drug rehab programs such as Synanon. In England, T-groups and sensitivity training were becoming popular. Second, let's use these groups to break people out of their uptight, middle-class lives of the 1950s and'60s, where everybody was trying to keep up with the Joneses and people weren't willing or even able to share their true feelings. That was a key theme: Aside from your thoughts, what do *you feel*? "What do you *really feel*?" the group leader would ask. And most people would respond, "What do you mean? What is a *feeling*?" The idea was that you can know yourself more truly if you are in touch with your feelings.

Psychotherapists around the world were fascinated by these intensive new modalities, and they flocked to Esalen to experience them and see what the fuss was about. Due to extensive media coverage, New York intellectuals, Hollywood creatives, and midwestern ministers alike found it interesting. A writer might be in her office in Weehawken, New Jersey, working on a screenplay one day and then the next day be flying to California, to be in a room with twenty strangers—all of whom would be getting down into their raw issues, no holds barred. Directors, actors, all manner of artists, and voyeurs flocked to these sessions because they resembled the techniques being used in actor training. You know, "Feel what it's like to be a sexually promiscuous woman with schizophrenia," or "Feel what it's like to enraged by fear and jealousy." It was believed that there was a truer version of one's self buried under the armor, under the façade. People came to drop out, turn on, and tune in.

Encounter groups were not for the faint of heart. Group sessions would start after breakfast and usually run until midnight; on some days they'd keep going right through the night. They might last for days or even weeks. You could never be sure what good or bad news might surface and how it might resolve. And in the early years, many of them were done in the nude.

Back to my first evening at Esalen. Dinner was over, the sun had set, and it was eight o'clock on a Friday night in early September 1970. I was twenty years old. A few months before, I had been an engineering student at all-male Lehigh University in Bethlehem, Pennsylvania. I took off my sandals and entered the workshop room, which was filling up with men and women. The room was carpeted, and there was no furniture other than colorful oversized pillows arranged in a tribal circle. I took a seat-pillow, looked around, and suddenly felt very, very young. People were forty, fifty, seventy years old. Being the early moments of the hippie era, most of the guys had muttonchop sideburns and bell-bottoms, and the women were braless and adorned with assortments of beads and headbands.

The group leader, wearing a Harry Belafonte–style dashiki, introduced himself not as Dr. Schutz or Professor Schutz but simply as Will. Then with no further pomp, circumstance, or introductions, he invited us to "stand up and silently walk around the room and touch people wherever you wish and look into their eyes." And that's exactly what everyone started doing. Before I knew it, I was being touched in exploratory ways on my face, my chest, my thighs, and everywhere else by both women and men.

Fifteen minutes into that, Will said, "Okay, now I want you all to go outside the door, remove all your clothes, and then come back into the room and find the person to whom you're least attracted and sit in front of them and tell them why." *Do what?* I was terrified. This is fucking nuts! I thought. What the hell have I gotten myself into? I thought of walking out the door and worming my way back to New Jersey. But my curiosity got the better of me and I steadied myself. This sure could be interesting, I said to myself.

That was the first time I saw seen a group of strangers nude. Other than being naked in a locker room after gym classes or on intimate occasions with girlfriends, and the few minutes an hour before at the baths, I hadn't been exposed to nudity. That was plenty jolting all by itself, if disappointing, because most people were not nearly as good-looking naked as they were fancied up in their clothes. And I'd never been around old people who were naked. It was scary. Is that what happens to the body with age? Yikes. Look at those saggy old ball sacks. Is that what a mastectomy looks like? Being nude with a group of adult strangers felt totally weird to me.

That was my first thirty minutes in a personal-growth workshop. It only got wilder from there.

That night I learned that nearly everyone had signed up for this one workshop—and then would be returning home a week or so later with the intention of digesting what they had experienced and learned. That was the way people engaged personal growth workshops – one at a time with lots of time in between to make sense of the learning. I was completely ignorant about the depth and intensity of what we were about to encounter in others and ourselves. But I wasn't going home after this workshop. I was about to immerse myself—again and again, from Sunday to Friday,

Friday to Sunday, Sunday to Friday, Friday to Sunday—for the next five months, during which I would witness/experience/uncover/remember heartbreaking loss, debilitating grief, painful sadness, mean-spirited hatred, terrifying fear, raw disgust, tantric sexuality, empathetic joy, and both the oddness and beauty of human individuality.

The idea of it now seems bizarre—and maybe it was bizarre then too. Regardless, over the next five months I learned that in this new world of psychology-meets-emotions-meets-the-body, we hold fears, we hold trauma, we put on façades, fake smiles, and stylish clothes as we all attempt to make the most of our lives—usually with mind, body, and feelings somewhat disconnected. The speculation was that this absence of alignment is at the source of much mental and even physical dis-ease. So, in encounter groups, with "Let's get naked and express our real selves," the idea was that the process could bring people to a point of openness from which they can discover their fears and learn to talk about feelings, hopes, and dreams that are deep and significant.

Everything about my first encounter group was otherworldly for me. As the days unfolded, some people cried about an illness they were grappling with, and others vented anger at an abusive parent or partner. Others shared their passions, some dealt with the sadness of losing a loved one. Everyone let down their guard, and we all grew closer, more open, more at ease with ourselves. It was touching and, in many ways, quite magical. We got to "see" everyone else and let them see us as well.

At the end of the first week, a few hours after saying good-bye to my newfound friends, I was joining another workshop with a whole new cast of characters, this one was titled "Sensory Awakening." It was led by Bernard Gunther, who had just published *Sense Relaxation: Below Your Mind*. The theme of that group was learning to feel again in a hard-driving, highly uptight world. The first day, we each held a stone in our hand for many hours and then described the experience while the rest of us listened. Then we'd each wander off and find a flower, smell it, and study its petals. Later we were advised to quietly sit for hours and fully observe all the colors of the sunset and the sounds of the waves. On another day somebody would slowly bathe your feet in warm water, while across the lawn a flute was playing. To me there was nothing abusive, nothing sexual in this course. It was simply learning to feel the world with all our senses again. We also experimented with synesthesia—feeling sounds, tasting colors, smelling ideas. I thought, Wow, this is a different way to feel embodied. Other than exhilarating sexual sensations I had enjoyed from time to time with girlfriends, and the pain of breaking bones while playing sports, I'm not sure I had ever learned to feel with all my senses.

After a few hours soaking at the baths, taking in the ocean below the cliffs of Esalen, I got dressed and had some dinner, and then my next week's class would begin.

This next workshop at Esalen was entitled The Passionate Mind, led by master yoga teacher Joel Kramer. Although I had already been practicing yoga for a year or so, Kramer's approach was both athletic and super-natural—in an era when yoga hadn't yet broken through into the main-stream. First, his asanas were propelled by his extraordinarily slow and deep breathing, and he could do just about everything with his body I had ever seen in any yoga book. I was absolutely mesmerized. Second, he focused half the workshop on jnana-yoga, which is the yoga of thought and problem solving. And third, he described and introduced us to the "edge"—that zone of expression/effort/resistance where most growth occurs. This became a core philosophy for how to engage change for me, which I'll discuss further in later chapters. I came away from that group convinced that yoga wasn't physical exercise but rather a path to a deeper mind and a more integrated self. Why hadn't I been exposed to any of this in all my years of physical education in grammar school, high school, and college?

Then I joined another intense workshop: Gestalt Dream Analysis led by Dr. Jim Simkin. People had come here from all over the world to have every ingredient of their most troublesome or wondrous dreams—characters, colors, sequences, and outcomes—revealed as elements of their unconscious mind.

From that I rolled into a wild workshop focused on dealing with madness led by Esalen co-founder Dick Price. A brilliant and charismatic Gestalt therapist and former mental patient at Agnews State Hospital, Dick had a level of grace, intensity, and insight I had never encountered before. These sessions were focused on the idea—recently proposed by R. D. Laing in *The Divided Self*—that all of us have regions of craziness and psychosis buried inside. Dick wanted us to think of the workshop room as a safe place to let these demons and angels out. I could write an entire book about that workshop alone.

The tendency toward nudity in certain workshops, while at first in-timidating to me, also instigated some early moments of deep learning.

Observing many people abreacting deeply held feelings, I was able to notice how emotions impacted physiognomy: how they breathed, how they held their shoulders, how they moved their hips and legs, how they gestured when emoting. Over the weeks and months, as I watched people with strikingly different backgrounds work through similar issues, it began to occur to me that there were patterns to how people embodied their minds. Had these sessions been dressed and in a therapist's office, there wouldn't have been very much to notice. But in this Gestalt/ encounter/psychodrama/yoga laboratory, I began to realize how feelings influence the flow of our energy, which influences our movements, which over time shapes the musculature, posture, and flow of our bodies.

Next was an entire weekend workshop conducted 100 percent in silence, which was a real bear for chatterbox me. Then another led by Dr. John Lilly on altered states of consciousness. Through intense breathing exercises, meditation walks, and other techniques, Lilly introduced us to his latest maps of human consciousness.

During all of these workshops, I wasn't a spectator, I was a very active participant. I cried, I laughed, I convulsed, I let go, I regurgitated, I fought, I got made fun of, I discovered senses I hadn't known existed, I felt feelings I didn't know I had, I hallucinated, I portrayed people's demons, I listened to people screaming about life's unfairness, and I even primal screamed a few times myself (who would have known that deep inside the plain vanilla kid from Jersey there was so much rage?).

What made the largest impression during these months of workshops was how many people had been wounded or damaged in their lives; and how many were hoping that these new therapies might unburden them of their trauma. I was naïve, having enjoyed a youth and upbringing that was generally safe and secure. Witnessing firsthand the depth of other people's suffering, how badly they had been bruised along the way, was jolting. I was shocked by stories of sexual molestation. I was saddened to encounter folks who had lost a loved one to tragedy, illness, or mishap. And I ached when I learned about the suffering that so many people had lived through due to the dishonesty of folks or groups they had trusted. Notwithstanding co-founders Murphy and Price's stated interest in exploring the frontiers of human potential, people were showing up at Esalen as if it was a modern-day Lourdes, hoping simply to be healed. Many were helped. Many weren't. These months of "encounter" with folks of all ages and narratives exposed me to an interpersonal underworld that I hadn't known existed as a happy kid in the neighborhoods of Newark, where I had been living by the Boy Scout code.

My Esalen experience went beyond the workshops. I was also volunteering alongside community members in the sumptuous organic vegetable garden, washing dishes while dancing to the Chambers Brothers, and taking nature hikes high in the mountains of Big Sur. With three or four different workshops going on each week, the lodge and campus were always populated by an interesting cast of characters—fellow seekers, numerous celebrities, and many potential playmates (remember, this was the free-love era). A great deal of cross-fertilization happened at the meals and also at the natural mineral baths perched on the side of the cliffs over the Pacific. I loved to soak in the baths, particularly at night. As the stars rotated around the sky, I joined in some of the most interesting discussions I had ever heard—and did a lot of listening. For example, I remember sitting in the baths one night while Princeton religious scholar Sam Keen was engaged in an intense discussion with Hector Prestera, a physician who dropped out to become an acupuncturist, and Dr. John Lilly, who had just done breakthrough research on dolphin brains and interspecies communications. They were discussing their views about whether the human mind could experience cosmic consciousness. It was eleven o'clock at night when the discussion began, and I sat there and listened to them explore one another's views about this vast subject until the sun rose in the morning.

As I had more of these experiences with so many remarkable people, a narrative was emerging. It was the idealistic and hopeful notion that humanity might be at the brink of an extraordinary evolutionary jump, that we were going to see kinder people. We were going to have richer relationships. We were going to understand our bodies in a way that would help us be healthy and vibrant and orgasmic and beaming, that we would see people less superficially and more deeply, and from all of that would come a new psychology, and new medicine, maybe even a new humanity.

Like an unfolding symphony, one workshop and discussion led to the next. As many parts of my body, mind, and spirit became activated, I thought this was what it must have been like in Paris after World War I, when great artists of the Lost Generation communed in cafés and salons. Maybe this was one of those moments when imaginative, well-intentioned people came together to think and talk and share and dream and ideate. Alongside that, I felt as though a somewhat different version of me was emerging. Who am I now? I wondered. What becomes of my former life? And What is my role in all of this?

Near the end of my five months of back-to-back workshops, one of my roommates at Esalen was a brilliant young man who was an undergraduate at Yale. He explained that he was getting independent-study credits for his week at Esalen. I wondered if I could do that retroactively at Lehigh. I wrote a letter to the deans, saying, "I've just finished a full semester at Esalen Institute, and I'd like for that to be considered as fully accredited education, as this is the cutting edge of psychology and medicine." My psychology professors and department chairman all supported my request. And amazingly, the deans approved it, which allowed me to return to Lehigh, finish up a few assignments, and graduate along with my class.

While in that final semester at Lehigh, I applied to and was accepted into a special doctoral program at the Union Graduate School, part of the Union for Research and Experimentation in Higher Education"—an innovative new consortium of more than thirty colleges and universities. This further distressed my parents, as they had hoped that I was done with my "alternative" interests and would somehow find my way to either Harvard or Stanford. Union Graduate School, needless to say, was not a traditional university experience. I would be allowed to travel to different universities as well as nontraditional schools and centers around the world to complete a doctorate on the "psychology of the body"—and be the first person in the world to do so. This was a perfect fit for me, but it came at a personal cost. My parents were disappointed, worried, and feeling left behind. At the same time, there was nothing I could do about it without sacrificing what I knew was right for me. I would have to trust that they could appreciate that.

MY DAY WITH THE ANGELS

In my life I've experienced many terrible things,
several of which actually happened. —Mark Twain

In the late summer of 1971, when I was twenty-one, I had just finished up at Lehigh and I had decided to experience America the slow and dreamy way: on the road.

A couple of years before, I had seen *Easy Rider*, and I fully believed the myth of the studly, solitary, mysterious explorer, though perhaps not the means. I needed a few more creature comforts than a chopped-down motorcycle would offer. Instead, I had a sturdy green Ford Econoline van fitted with a mattress and a small refrigerator, stocked with apple juice and trail mix. My modest worldly possessions were also on board: a typewriter, my guitar, a few changes of underwear, some T-shirts and sweatshirts, and a couple pairs of jeans. I figured I would camp out as I wandered across this vast country, with California my ultimate destination. I allowed myself a full year for this hippie-styled walkabout—or, more accurately, drive-about.

Since many towns I'd visit had universities in them, I hoped that from time to time I could meet people and crash in their apartments or communes. I also had a few college friends scattered here and there whom I expected to look up along the way. I began in Vermont at the start of fall, when the air was growing crisp and the leaves were turning magnificent colors. As the leaves fell in New England, I set myself in motion southward. I slowly followed autumn all the way down to the Carolinas, and then I kept going to Florida, where I crashed for a couple of weeks to enjoy the warm air and fun surf. Then I turned my van westward and worked my way to Columbus, Ohio, because a friend of mine from high school was in college there and had said, "Hey, if you come through, you can stay at our place."

The university town was crackling with energy and intriguing people, so I wound up staying almost a week. For gas money, I worked as a substitute elementary teacher for a couple of days—usually math or social studies, but sometimes I just brought my guitar and led the classes in folk songs. I perused the AAA map—remember paper maps?—I saw that Saint Louis, Missouri, was about 450 miles due west on Highway 70. One of my former professors, Dr. Frank Wuest, had relocated there to head up the psychology department at Saint Louis University. He was a great man with a terrific family (I have to admit that I had a crush on one of his stepdaughters, who I heard was staying in Saint Louis for a while). He was also an excellent blues harmonica player, and therefore someone I could play music with. I imagined that they'd have an extra bedroom or maybe just a spare mattress in the basement on which I could crash for a bit, while getting to wander around this city with the highest concentration of stained-glass windows of any city in America—or at least someone had told me that.

On the morning I was leaving Columbus, a fierce snowstorm began that quickly upgraded into a blizzard. I braced myself for what would likely be a difficult eight-to-ten-hour ride. As I was turning onto the freeway, I saw two oversized guys hitchhiking on the side of the on-ramp. Hitchhiking was commonplace then, and as I worked my way across America, I picked up lots of guys and girls with whom I'd share some time and gas money. That morning, although it was freezing cold, I noticed that neither of them was wearing gloves and they were both clinging to their long coats for warmth. Since they didn't have backpacks or suitcases, I assumed they were a couple of local farm boys. I thought I could benefit from some pleasant company to help pass the time. The snow was swirling as I hit the brakes and pulled my van over so them to get in. "You guys need a ride?" I asked.

"Yeah. It's freezing out here. It's fucking freezing," one of them said.

"Well, come on in and warm up," I offered.

The light-haired one—who was massive, maybe six feet five inches and around three hundred pounds—quickly opened the front passenger door and got in. The other guy was wearing a long leather coat and was darker-complexioned with very long jet-black hair and a very long, bushy, jet-black beard. He got in the side door and took the seat behind me. Thinking they were probably headed to Springfield, Ohio, the next major town down the road, I welcomed them into my van and told them to warm up, dry off, and enjoy the ride.

As they warmed up, I said, "Hey, my name's Ken."

The huge guy to my right said, "Hey. My name's Bull, and this here's Whop."

"Hi, Bull. Hi, Whop, glad to meet you. Where are you guys going?" I asked.

"LA," Whop said.

"Really?" I said. "You don't have any bags or anything. You're traveling pretty light."

Bull turned to face me, and as his steely blue eyes checked out my van, he said, "We were just in a big fight in Tampa and had our motorcycles stolen. Some of our buddies were badly beaten up and are in the hospital there. One was beaten to death. We're going back to LA to get new bikes, gather up our gang, and then we're going to head back to Florida and settle the score."

Who the hell did I just pick up?

A few minutes later Bull took off his long, snow-soaked trench coat. Underneath it he was wearing a denim jacket with the sleeves cut off, and crisscrossing his chest and back were large chains. As he turned to his right to whisper something to Whop, I could see HELLS ANGELS imprinted on the back of his jacket. I almost shat my pants. A few minutes later Whop removed his leather overcoat to reveal a similar Hells Angels outfit, with both chains and a shoulder-holstered gun. It struck my hippie-wannabe self like lightning. Oh my God, I thought. I have just picked up two for- real Hells Angels, and they need to go to LA. Thinking they were going to either steal my van and throw me out the door or worse, kill me, steal everything I owned, and leave my body by the side of the road, I took a deep breath and said, "Cool. But I'm not going to California. I'm only going as far as Saint Louis."

"No problem," Bull said with a weird smile. "You got any food?"

"Just my trail mix and some apple juice," I said, and pointed them toward the refrigerator.

After guzzling everything I had, Whop said they hadn't eaten since the fight and were starving and that I should pull over for some more food if there were any rest stops ahead. For the next while, we drove along without talking—I'm not sure whether I even continued to breathe. Then we spotted a sign announcing a Howard Johnson's restaurant a few miles ahead.

"You have any money?" Bull asked.

"Some," I said.

"Pull over and let's get some food," Whop demanded.

As I, Ken Dychtwald, a twenty-one-year-old, science-fiction-reading, yoga-practicing, eight-years-since-being-bar-mitzvahed aspiring free spirit from Newark, New Jersey, walked into Howard Johnson's restaurant with two deadly-looking Hells Angels, I was thinking about calling out for help or slipping a note to the waitress saying I was being abducted. But I simply wasn't clever or quick enough to pull that off. Instead, while everyone in the restaurant stared at us, we three sat down at a booth and ate lunch. And what did we do? We talked about our lives. Mine was likely the least interesting story. "After studying physics and engineering, I switched to psychology, I have been trying to make sense of my relationship with my mom and dad, blah, blah, blah, find myself, blah, blah, blah." From these two men, I learned that there was a core philosophy to being a member of the Hells Angels. What's the purpose of life? It was all about riding and partying and getting high and getting laid. Period. It was straightforward. They had rules of living. Since that week I had been struggling to interpret the hidden meaning and metamessages in Herman Hesse's *Narcissus and Goldmund*, their code of life sure seemed uncomplicated. Also, while inhaling their second round of cheeseburgers, they explained that if somebody was on your side, you would lay down your life for them. If anyone ever crossed a friend or gang member, you would retaliate: an eye for an eye. That, they explained, was why they were going all the way across the country to assemble their gang and then they were all going to ride all the way back to Tampa and take out the gang that had fucked with them.

"How many guys are you going to ride back to Tampa with?" I asked.

"A couple of hundred," Bull said. They would be organizing a small army. I was living in a world where things were far fuzzier for everybody. And since I was a part of the "Make love, not war" cohort, the idea of beating someone to death because they stole your bike seemed a bit extreme.

There at HoJo's I was kind of listening, but I was mostly frightened. I couldn't help thinking that I was going to get murdered by these guys before the day was over. I paid the bill and we all got back into my van and started heading west. When we were nearing Saint Louis, Bull asked, "Where are you staying? Can we stay with you?"

I said, "I've got this old professor who lives here with his wife and his teenage daughters."

"Can we come?" Bull pressed.

I thought about it for a second and said, "You know, I just don't think it'd be cool."

There was a very long silence. "That's okay," said Bull. "Just let us off when you turn off the highway."

Right before we got to my exit, Bull lit up a joint and we passed it around. I told them I had enjoyed my time with them. Whop said, "Hey, man. We appreciate the favor. We get that you're on the road to find yourself. You're a good guy. You'll see. Things are going to turn out okay."

Bull added, "And, hey, if you ever make it out to LA, if you need a lady or if you want to get high, find us. We'll pay you back for how you helped us today. For sure."

That day I wasn't exactly Margaret Mead exploring the culture of Samoa, but my brief time with the Angels gave me a glimpse into another culture, a counterculture, a violent rebel counterculture that I'd had no experience with before, other than in the movies. I don't think I have ever encountered anyone else along the way who had such a clear code of living. It was illegal but straightforward. It was criminal but righteous. It was Neanderthal but totally rooted in loyalty.

DECLARATION OF INDEPENDENCE
A LETTER TO MY MOM AND DAD

One day in retrospect the years of struggle will strike you as the most beautiful.
—Sigmund Freud

Bull had said I was a good guy. And in the Esalen workshops, lots of people seemed to like me. But who exactly was I? During this time on the road, I was reflecting on that question, which was less about labels of good and bad and more simply about understanding who I was. I had no idea. But it was bothering me. And it was the unconscious beginnings of radical curiosity. Because one of the most important things to be curious about in life is yourself.

Alone, on the road, I felt I was losing touch with my family. I missed them and could only imagine how they were coping with the "new" me. While I wasn't really clear about why I had to leave and venture out on my own, I knew for sure that it was something I must do. My parents couldn't fathom my wish to do roam around the country, pursue a non-traditional graduate degree, or head back to California —and it seemed to be breaking their hearts. In their occasional letters my mom kept asking me when I'd be coming home to live near them, and my dad wanted to know if I'd soon be ready to work in one of his women's clothing stores. On Tuesday, October 24, 1972, I wrote a letter back to my parents. I realize now I wasn't just trying to explain to them what I was doing, I was also trying to explain myself.

Dear Mom and Dad,

I am writing from the Woodstock Conference Center in Woodstock, Ohio, where I am starting the month-long orientation colloquium to kick off my doctoral program. Not counting advisors and professors, there's around forty other graduate students here—from all over the world and all walks of life, with interests in everything from helping orphans in Kenya to managing civil unrest in Mississippi. Can you believe I'm the youngest person in the program? But we do have something in common. We're here to learn more about how each of our graduate studies will unfold in the years ahead. I know you're still upset with me for choosing this non-traditional path. I know how important it is for you and our family that I make something out of college. That said, I am absolutely committed to human potential related research. It's the most interesting and stimulating thing I know. Since Esalen, it has been on my mind all the time. The focus of my degree is going to be on the relationship between the mind and body, about which I am endlessly curious. And so, at the recommendation of numerous people I respect, I chose Union Institute. By studying with experts and leaders in my field from throughout the world, I am going to shape a body of work that is truly unique. Tonight, I'm sitting behind my new electric Smith Corona typewriter making notes to myself and friends and it just hit me that I should take the time to tell you all of this. How else would you know?

These past months as I have been driving alone from Maine to Florida, and then across the Deep South before aiming back, over and up through the Midwest to Ohio, I have had a lot of time to think. Maybe more than I've ever had. And being away from all of my friends and relatives has been really disorienting—but I think it has caused me to think more deeply about myself than I ever have before. There are several things about me that I'm coming to understand. First, I am an explorer and I am really curious about nearly everything. I like to find things out for myself. I have many questions regarding my own life and the lives of others that I have chosen to ask, and I will not rest until I have found the answers to these questions. Underneath it all, I believe I am a seeker of knowledge; I am a searcher for excitement; I am an explorer of the unexplored. I expect that, in some form or another, I will always continue to be this way. Maybe I take on more than I can handle, and maybe, sometimes, I even drive myself to the point of emotional overload, but I don't think that my persistent curiosity is bad. Instead, I'm thinking that it may turn out to be one of my strongest attributes.

I know how much you both love me and how much concern you have for my life. I appreciate this and I love you for it. Still, please respect that I have to live my life for my own needs. Even if you can see the foolishness or wrongheadedness of certain things that I do, please don't deny me the right and opportunity to learn for myself. All in all, I guess that I am telling you that I need to grow up my own way in my own time. While I am doing this, I will need your love and encouragement, although I don't know how we'll handle this being so far away from each other.

When I left New Jersey months ago, you both were very worried. The way I feel now is this: I have a long life ahead of me. Hopefully we will spend a large por-

tion of that life together, but I don't really know. I have got to search out a place for myself that will be a fit for my own needs and likes, hopes and dreams. It looks like the next step will involve me going to California and studying with either Dr. Carl Rogers at the Center for the Study of the Person in La Jolla or back at Esalen in Big Sur with Dr. William Schutz. I will be leaving this graduate school colloquium on Friday and driving west.

I hope that I have not upset you with this letter. I don't mean to. I guess that I am asking for your support and encouragement, even if I am doing something you don't fully agree with. I am going to do what I feel I must and I'm willing to pay the consequences or reap the rewards—depending on the outcome. Please know that I miss you and love you deeply and not a day goes by when I don't think of my wonderful mother and father and how much you have given me. With much love,

Ken

On one level, this was a declaration of independence, from my past and the expectations of my parents. On another, more profound level, this was the moment where I began to see—and understand—who I was. Since then, I haven't ever stopped learning about myself. There is no expiration on self-discovery.

ENVISIONING THE BODYMIND

See me, feel me, touch me, heal me.
—Pete Townshend, from the rock opera *Tommy*

As part of my Union Graduate School program, I returned to Esalen and Big Sur for another two years of study and teaching—and thousands more hours of encounter, psychodrama, tai chi, Rolfing, bioenergetics, Reichian energetics, meditation, massage, shiatsu, the Feldenkrais method, Gestalt therapy, and a variety of yogic practices with prominent teachers such as Alan Watts, Joseph Campbell, Michael Murphy, Gregory Bateson, Baba Ram Dass, Joel Kramer, John Lilly, Bernard Gunther, Dick Price, Moshe Feldenkrais, Ida Rolf, and Chungliang "Al" Huang. I also continued learning from Jean Houston, Swami Vishnudevenanda, Carl Rogers, and others.

One of the first workshops I took when I returned was being led by Drs. Hector Prestera and William Schutz. I was fascinated by its title: Bodymind. The term was new to me, and it suggested a simple recognition of the interrelationship of body and mind.

In this workshop, which ran for seven days with ten to fifteen hours of therapy sessions per day, Schutz and Prestera combined encounter with psychodrama and Rolfing. Schutz, whose workshop I had been so impressed by two years earlier, was a psychotherapist, and Prestera was an internist, but they were both also recently trained as Rolf practitioners. This was one of the first times that two influential teachers from diverse backgrounds joined together to pool skills and talents regarding the bodymind in an experimental therapeutic setting.

What this meant for us as participants was that in addition to the usual encounter work, focused on interpersonal sharing and processing, we would explore the ways in which each of us animated our own body in relation to our unique characters and emotional histories. Right off the bat, Schutz asked our group, "Is anyone dealing with any recent loss or trauma?" A troubled-looking woman in her mid-forties raised her hand

and explained that she was still struggling with the loss of her dad, who had died several years before. She missed him dearly, and because she was out of the country when he passed, she hadn't gotten home in time for the funeral. Her sadness and guilt were entwined and were, in a sense, strangling her. Schutz said, "We're going to stage a funeral right here, right now, if that's okay with you."

"Yes it is," she said.

"Who in this room would you pick to play your dad?" asked Schutz.

She pointed to a man in our group who in some way reminded her of her dad, and Schutz said, "Please ask him if he'd be willing to play this role, and if so, help him lie down like he's in a casket. And who might be able to play your mom?"

She immediately turned to an older woman in the group and said, "You remind me a little of my mom." Then she looked at me and said, "You can be my brother. He's kind of an asshole, and he's always trying to prove he's better than me." And to someone else, "Please be my cousin."

And so, with specific direction from the woman and the group leaders, we all proceeded to act our parts. What ensued was powerful. Holding her deceased dad in her arms, she told him all the things she had wanted to tell him, and she began crying when she shared how much she had always loved him. Although she had been very buttoned up when she started, when she professed how much she missed him her chest began to heave and she began sobbing profusely. Then, all of a sudden, other people in the room started sobbing. I guess that inside all of us there's a well of sadness over the death of a loved one. We were using improvisational drama to go beyond words and activate a wide range of feelings. And since most participants were nude, it was quite a lot to take in. Through this facilitated psychodrama, nearly everyone let go of some sadness and we all wound up feeling both lighter and closer. By the time everyone had commented on their experience, it was after midnight. We all hugged, said good night, and went off to our rooms and cabins to sleep.

The next morning Prestera and Schutz integrated Rolfing into our therapy circle. Rolfing was a newly crafted system of deep myofascial massage developed by biochemist-physiologist Dr. Ida Rolf. She had carefully put together a system of ten therapeutic sessions that were aimed at allowing the body to not only release chronically held traumas and patterns but also to assume a more healthy and integrated position with respect to itself and gravity.

That morning, twelve of us found ourselves sitting in a circle around one of the group members who was completely naked and was being Rolfed slowly and simultaneously by both Schultz and Prestera. This middle-aged, fit-looking man was being encouraged to let go and express himself and his emotions in any way he wanted during the Rolfing ordeal. Because the massage work is deep, the Rolfee may experience pain. As Prestera's and Schutz's hands moved over and into his body, he responded with some defiant screams, sobs, and even laughter, as feelings and memories seemed to be coming up from nowhere. But they weren't coming from nowhere— they had been trapped in his body. I had absolutely never seen anything like this before.

As the days passed and our stories emerged, we began to feel one another's pains and pleasures with a great deal of openness and sensitivity. Since we were all completely naked throughout the group sessions, there was nothing covered up. It was especially interesting to me to note how each of us responded to certain aspects of another's ordeal. It reminded me of the first time I learned to tune a guitar. I was amazed to find that when I struck a particular note on one string, if there was another guitar in the vicinity, the same note on that guitar would vibrate too, even though I hadn't touched it. In very much the same way, it seemed to me that each of us was tuned to a variety of notes and chords (feelings and attitudes), and when these vibrations were struck in our presence, we resonated.

Each day three more of us were Rolfed as part of the group ritual, and each day I watched as different group members responded to the process in a unique fashion. Since the number one Rolfing session—the one being practiced in our workshop—was a standard procedure, most variation in response was due, it seemed, to the physical or mental state of the individual being Rolfed rather than to variations in pressure or movement on the part of the Rolfer. My observations now went far beyond what I had begun observing back in 1970. I began to notice that some similar stories were being recalled and abreacted by different members of the group. What was even stranger was that these similar stories came up when the *same* parts of *different* Rolfees' bodies were confronted. For example, feelings and memories of being left and neglected repeatedly appeared when a Rolfee's chest was being released. When the upper back was worked on, the muscular confrontation was repeatedly accompanied by strong feelings of rage and anger. Rolfed jaws released sadness; Rolfed hips released sexuality; Rolfed shoulders seemed invariably to tell stories of burdens and stressful responsibilities. The crazy idea occurred to me that the body was like a multidimensional circuit board: when certain switches were triggered, similar stories and experiences emerged from the same body parts belonging to different people.

At first this didn't seem possible. I was having a hard time buying the notion that emotions were somehow stored in the body and that there were general patterns by which they stored themselves. Yet as each day passed and I watched more and more deep emotions being released and worked through, this possibility seemed less and less unreasonable. I became fascinated by the body as a storehouse for feelings and memories.

While studying everything from yoga to tai chi to dream analysis with Esalen leaders, I chose to apprentice myself to Schultz, who agreed to serve on my graduate committee, and Prestera, who was writing *The Body Reveals* with Ron Kurtz and agreed to become a mentor to me. I got to watch them Rolf dozens of different people. In addition, I was in encounter group therapy, some of which was done in the nude, for more than one thousand intense hours. This allowed me to observe hundreds of bodies in the process of interacting and emoting in a manner that no traditional psychotherapist could have witnessed. As before, I wasn't a bystander— that would not have been tolerated. Encounter, Gestalt, psychodrama, and other therapies were invasive, confrontative, and intense. I was fully engaged and involved. Sometimes it was exhilarating, and other times it was really rough. Week after week, I'd be sitting in the group meeting rooms watching people deal with psychological and emotional issues, and I couldn't help noticing what was happening in their bodies. Somebody might be talking about an incredible anger they felt toward their father, and I'd see the way the musculature in their back and shoulders held them tight. Then two weeks later, while in another workshop, I observed someone else basically going through the exact same thing— with the same back and chest structure and ailments. One day a group member would be talking about the death of their mom, and I'd notice the way their breathing was trapped in their abdomen, and I'd see that pattern over and over again in other groups with other people.

In out-of-session discussions with group leaders, it was mentioned that when Freud was doing his pioneering work, his patients would be fully clothed, and they would lie down on his couch and talk about their feelings. This was an utterly different laboratory for observing the mind and body at work. We realized that the odd combination of New Age interests,

Big Sur's isolation and natural setting, the coming together of countless different therapies and research modalities, and a post-Woodstock acceptance of casual nudity gave us a theater to observe people's body-mind patterns in unprecedented ways. And I was right in the middle of it all.

During that period I heard that a very special workshop was going to be held at another growth center, this one named Kairos, located near San Diego. The five-day workshop would be led by two legendary figures, Drs. John Pierrakos and Alexander Lowen, both former students of Dr. Wilhelm Reich. Based in New York City, they were the co-founders of the modern field of bioenergetics and had come to the West Coast to mix it up with what was happening on the other side of the country. It was to be attended by around a hundred leading psychotherapists and researchers interested in the intersection of the mind and body. Although the workshop was sold out, there was a last-minute cancellation, and I grabbed it. I hitchhiked from Big Sur to San Diego, unpacked my knapsack, and joined the program.

On the first evening of the workshop, John Pierrakos peered out at the room through his rose-tinted, Coke-bottle glasses and asked if anyone was willing to strip naked and stand in front of the room. Having just spent months in that mode, I thought, What the hell? I quickly raised my hand and said, "Sure." As I stood in front of everyone, Dr. Pierrakos stared intently at my body, as did everyone else in the room. He circled me and examined the texture of my skin and circulation and the overall quality of my musculature. Then he backed up a bit and squinted at me so that he could more easily "read my aura," as he explained to the group. I must admit, the aura reading idea seemed like voodoo to me.

Then, as though he was describing the prime cuts on a steer, he proceeded to interpret what my body revealed about me. He told me—and the group of professional students—about my relationship with my mother as well as my father. He described my general attitudes about life, love, sexuality, and identity. Then, with remarkable accuracy, he discussed the sorts of relationships I would seek and the way I was inclined to deal with them. For a finale, he told the group what my major personality strengths and weaknesses were and what frightened me. To my astonishment, everything he said, every observation he made, every description he offered, was entirely accurate.

How could he do this? How could my body be so expressive of my inner self? How could my life history be revealed in my posture and the shape of my muscles? Did my mind create my body, or did my body create my mind? And how come I had never heard about any of this before my journeys to the West Coast? I had taken a few psychology courses by that time, but they were all about rats in a maze, patterned behavior, or neurotic thoughts—little about the mind's many connections to the body. And having been a medical patient from time to time during my growing-up years, I'd never had a doctor ask me questions about my emotional history when assessing the state of my body.

During the days that followed, both Pierrakos and Lowen read everyone else's bodymind with similar precision. In their many lectures during that workshop, I learned that their work was an extension of the pioneering insights of Dr. Wilhelm Reich, a student of Sigmund Freud who developed theories about what he called body armor. He believed that when people go through a trauma or difficult experience in their lives, they take it in, and related parts of their body react in terms of either ease and flow or conflict and tension. Depending on the intensity and/or frequency of the experience, these tensions can become chronic and turn into a kind of protective body armor. Reich postulated that throughout our entire lives, our bodies develop various pieces of armor plating, which both protect us and lock feelings in, while also keeping many feelings out. Depending on the nature of the experience, the armor might be in the thigh or it might be in the groin. Maybe in the chest. Or the shoulders and back. Just as a young tree may twist and grow around the rock it is embedded in, our bodies twist and grow around the emotionally driven holdings in our body. Looking at all these twisted humans, I found that it made sense. Further, Reich believed that when energy gets blocked somewhere, it becomes like a river that's been dammed. For example, if you block a flowing stream, the water is going to get stuck, stop flowing. Here's a simple example. If a child growing up has a need to cry, the crying expression might begin in the gut, then move up through the chest, then flow through the throat and jaw, often showing up as a quivering in the jaw, before releasing from the mouth and face. If for some reason the child is told, "Don't cry," the crying process gets stuck. The next time the child is told not to cry it might get locked again. The time after that, it might get locked and stop. By the time the child is seven or eight, crying doesn't come easily. Instead, the energy and the experience unconsciously become locked in his jaw, throat, chest, or stomach—depending on where it's been getting cut off.

Then, as an adult, if the person feels a need to cry, instead of the emotion naturally flowing out, the individual will just tighten his gut or squeeze his jaw or whatever. Usually this tightening moves out of his conscious experience. I observed this in both bioenergetics and Rolfing, when some people's jaws were released and rivers of tears came crying out. Imagine that a person is angry and feels the rage flowing up into her arms and then it's stopped. Or what if someone is feeling like he wants to run away and instead he freezes up? Or how about someone who wants to express love but is denied? These feelings don't necessarily just evaporate. I wondered if they became embodied. I wasn't alone in this enquiry. These kinds of questions were beginning to be asked by both doctors and psychologists around the world. And they were seeping into popular culture.

Dr. Fritz Perls was another heir to Reich's work. He founded modern Gestalt therapy as a means toward more fully integrating the mind and body, thoughts and feelings, through conscious attention. Perls had lived at Esalen but, unfortunately for me, had passed away several months before I first arrived in 1970. He had postulated that people develop body attitudes and armor as a result of unresolved conflicts, unsatisfied needs, drives, inhibitions, abuse, trauma, et cetera. The conflicts become a state of tension, of dis-ease. If you hold a state of dis-ease for a period of time, it will become frozen. And then it becomes unconscious.

Another popularizer of Reich's teaching was Dr. Arthur Janov, famous for creating primal therapy. He was also famous for treating Beatle John Lennon. Reflecting about being trapped within his own body armor, Lennon sang, "Till the pain is so big you feel nothing at all." Similarly, in the Who's rock Opera *Tommy*, young Tommy is witness to the murder of his father by his mother's lover, who then demands that he lose all memory of the entire occurrence. In response, Tommy becomes deaf, dumb, and blind and remains so until later in his life when—after a fantastic collection of experiences—he releases the trauma, sheds the emotional armor, and regains full sensory functions.

Many of the bodymind therapies of that era, from encounter, to Reichian energetics, to Gestalt and to psychodrama, were trying to free up the feelings, and reintegrate the whole person. It was a radical departure from both traditional psychoanalysis and traditional allopathic medicine.

During those years the workshop rooms became living laboratories for me, in which I would watch the bodymind in action. With a passion that verged on fanaticism, I made mental notes to myself about what sorts of people were shaped in what ways. Conversely, I would look at the physical makeup of those who were in a Gestalt session or were being

Rolfed and try to imagine the sort of memories and blocks that would be released by the therapeutic intervention. I was often spot-on. Just as the mind reflected the body, the body reflected the mind—if you could decipher its language. As the months passed, I found that my feelings and observations were leading me to develop a psychosomatic system that accounted for the direct relationships between particular feelings and beliefs and the shape, energetics, and flow of particular body parts and regions. Was I too young to be trying to make sense of all this? Yes. In fact, at twenty-two, I was almost always the youngest person in all these workshops, without enough training or education to comprehend much of anything I was seeing. But then again, I didn't have any medical training or background as a psychotherapist to get in the way of observing what was manifesting. My youth, ignorance, and inexperience may have worked a bit to my advantage, as I didn't have an entire body of perspective to set aside.

Making this the thrust of my doctoral studies, I compiled insights from Lowen's writing and overlaid it with Reich's and then integrated ideas from Perls and Schutz. A complex pattern of relationships between our minds and our bodies emerged. For example, the left side of the body— corresponding to the right side of the brain—was more involved in the feminine aspects of one's self, while the right side of the body was more driven by the masculine forces. The top half of the body seemed to be oriented toward socializing, outward expression, and manipulation, while the bottom half was more oriented toward privacy, grounding, stability, and support. The feet and even the shape of the arches reflected how one grounded oneself emotionally, while the thighs often reflected personal will or strength. The way the pelvis was tipped—downward or upward—often correlated with how one activated or blocked sexuality, while the abdominal regional was the storehouse for deep feelings. And on and on. By studying everything I could get my hands on, I began to craft a master map of the bodymind.

Then my studies and investigation were impacted by an entirely other universe of views. Someone offhandedly gave me a copy of *The Serpent Power*, by Sir John Woodroffe, in which he explained the realm of kundalini yoga. Although I had been diligently practicing hatha-yoga for several years, the kundalini perspective on how the mind is embodied was new to me. The central idea of kundalini yoga is that within the spine, in a hollow region called the canalis centralis, is an energy conduit that the Hindus called *sushumna*. Along this conduit, from the base of the anus to the top of the head, flows the most powerful of all psychic energies, *kundalini*. On either side of this canal are two additional energy channels. One is called the *ida*, which originates on the right side of the spine, and the other is the *pingala*, which begins on the left. These two currents are believed to correspond to the male and female life forces said to coil upward around the spine like snakes, crisscrossing at seven vortexes, called chakras or energy wheels. I devoured Woodroffe's book as well as every other book about this subject I could get my hands on, from Gopi Krishna's *Kundalini: The Evolutionary Energy in Man* to Carl Jung's *Psychology of Kundalini Yoga*. Apparently, way before the Reichians and Rolfers, and long before Maslow had imagined his "hierarchy of needs," within ancient Hindu literature existed a model of the body, mind, and spirit in which each chakra was concerned with very specific aspects of human behavior and development.

In addition, there seemed to be a progression in the ascending locations of these chakras, sort of like Maslow's hierarchy but grander. Armed with these new ideas, I intensified my yoga practice to around four hours a day as I tried to personally "feel" each of the chakras and the behavioral neighborhoods that lived within my own body. As I moved very, very slowly through my extensive set of asanas each day and paid careful attention to how my mind shifted in relation to each region, I was consciously exploring my own inner stories.

Like a jigsaw puzzle coming together, when I overlaid the Kundalini model with that of Reich, Lowen, Schutz, and Perls, what did I find? They matched!

Then, at the ripe age of twenty-three, while sitting under the stars in Big Sur, I decided to try to write a book about this new model of mental and physical health and personal growth. My intent was to distill these converging understandings into a common framework with a common language. Feeling that I was on the brink of some revolutionary insights, and propelled by youthful excitement, I hoped to unleash a new era of both psychotherapy and medicine. It was a key manifestation of radical curiosity. In a moment of reflection after an intense period of learning, I saw that I had something to give back. And while I may not have been saying it explicitly to myself at the time, a mantra came alive for me, nurturing my soul: *Breathe, learn, teach, repeat.*

I struggled to cultivate and explain this new conceptual framework. I was hoping to not just put out my own ideas and observations but to integrate

Reich, Gestalt, Rolf, Feldenkrais, and the whole kundalini notion of the chakras in a fashion that had not quite been done before. But I couldn't figure out how to organize the book. Maybe by East/West? Lowen versus Freud? Love/hate? Illness/wellness? Then one day I had a visualization that resolved all my confusion. Why not present a discussion of the human bodymind using the physical and energetic body as the referent from which to share my ideas? I'd start at the feet and the need for grounding and survival and wind up at the crown chakra and cosmic consciousness.

For the next two years, while I worked at the SAGE Project during the day (to be explained in a little while), my evenings and late nights were spent writing *Bodymind*, which served as my doctoral dissertation.

RAVI SHANKAR AND THE IMPORTANCE OF BEING IN TUNE

Those who believe in telekinetics, raise my hand. —Kurt Vonnegut

One day in Big Sur we heard through the grapevine that there was going to be a special night of meditation and music at the student center at the University of California, Berkeley. Former Harvard professor Richard Alpert had changed his name to Baba Ram Dass after a mystical experience in India and was going to give a speech about enlightenment. Then Ravi Shankar, the great Indian sitar master (who George Harrison of the Beatles had begun studying with and emulating), was going to perform. At Berkeley my friends and I followed the crowd into a big open room in the student union and we tried to position ourselves near the small stage that had been set up in front. As was the style in that era, there were no chairs, so hundreds of people were sitting or lying on mats and sleeping bags and pillows. Everywhere you turned there were shaggy hairdos, bell-bottoms, love beads, and exotic earrings. Many folks—including me—were sitting in one yoga position or another. Back then nobody knew quite how you were supposed to sit or stand to appear like you were on the path to enlightenment, but everybody was trying their best. Likely too, nearly everyone was stoned, geared up for a rip-roaring consciousness-raising (or altering) experience.

First, a bearded and ponytailed Ram Dass came out onto the stage and seated himself cross-legged on a simple meditation cushion. With eyes closed, he breathed deeply, meditated a bit, chanted for a while, and then began his captivating, wandering, fascinating, New Age spiritual speech about "being here now" and the cycles of reincarnation. He closed by telling us that enlightenment required much practice. To illustrate just how much practice, he said, "Imagine a mountain that's six miles deep and six miles high. A small bird has a silk scarf in its mouth and flies back and forth across the mountaintop, the scarf gently brushing the mountain surface. As many passes as it would take the bird to wear the mountain to the ground, that's how many lifetimes of meditation practice it takes to become enlightened." The stage was modestly set for three musicians. Ravi Shankar appeared first, a handsome and graceful man with his sitar at his side. He was accompanied by the renowned Ali Akbar, who would be playing the sarod. Akbar was beaming with an otherworldly smile and presence. And there was another person, a much younger man, whose name I don't remember, who would be playing the tabla. The audience was psyched and ready to be taken to another galaxy.

Then, Ravi Shankar began to play. The energy in the room jolted. But he paused right after hitting his first few notes and looked around. Then, to my astonishment, he stopped performing and began to slowly tune his sitar. While I believe that there are around twenty strings on a sitar, only six or seven of them are played—the others are drones. He was tuning and tuning and tuning. The other musicians closed their eyes and were just sitting mindfully on the stage. This went on for maybe half an hour, and because we were all so geared up, that felt like a very long time. It seemed like everyone's highs were wearing off a little bit, and the crowd was settling down.

Finally, Shankar looked around, took a peaceful breath, and launched into an absolutely mind-boggling performance. The music was piercing, penetrating, haunting, and fantastic. It lasted for about an hour, and everyone seemed completely spellbound. When the musicians finished, they took their humble bows to our enthusiastic applause. Then, little by little, everyone gathered their belongings and stepped outside into the beautiful California night. Wow, what a high. What an experience.

As fate would have it, about three weeks later back in Big Sur, the word went out that Ravi Shankar and his fellow musicians were going to be staying at Esalen for a few days to rest and recharge. When I heard the legendary musicians were going to perform an impromptu concert that night for a small group in the Esalen lodge, I made sure I could attend. His wonderful Berkeley concert was still fresh in my mind, and the chance to hear Mr. Shankar again and maybe interact with him in Esalen's intimate setting energized me. As he ate dinner that night in Esalen's lodge, surrounded by friends and fans, I slid my way into his table to join him and have a salad. The conversation was respectful and lively, and he seemed to be completely open to answering anyone's questions. I got up my nerve and asked him about the Berkeley performance I had attended a few weeks ago. Did he always take that long to tune up? The sitar master studied me, so I continued: "Clearly there was more to it than just tuning your instrument, Mr. Shankar. But what was it?"

"Well," he said, finally, "I was not tuning my sitar. I was tuning the audience."

Immediately I thought back to ideas I'd had during my recent Rolfing sessions: human beings had notes and chords (feelings and attitudes) that could resonate with one another. It wasn't so far-fetched to believe that Shankar could reach them through his sitar. It was a major learning moment for me, one where my curiosity gave me the courage to ask what may have been regarded as a silly question. Because of Shankar, I realized that regardless of what kind of communicator you are—whether it's a musician or storyteller or stadium announcer—it's not enough to have something to say. You also need to understand the energy of your audience, to understand the collective group's emotional state and use it to get your story across. In many ways, for a world-class communicator of any kind, the audience *is* your instrument.

THE PROS AND CONS OF APPEARING NAKED

Only those who will risk going too far can possibly find out how far one can go.
—T. S. Eliot

With prodding from older friends and teachers, many of whom were published authors, I sent my *Bodymind* manuscript out to more than a dozen publishers. In fact, I had submitted the manuscript to two different editors at Pantheon. Like most of the others, one of these editors rejected it, sending back a terse note saying the book was both silly and unpublishable. I was beginning to think that at twenty-seven I was perhaps not ready to become a published author myself. Then the other editor, Ursula Bender, replied. Along with an enthusiastic acceptance letter came a contract and a ten-thousand-dollar advance.

As we approached our publication date, I realized that I'd need body sketches in the book and the sketched models would need to be naked. For example, if I was talking about tension in the buttocks, how could I properly describe it if I didn't show what it actually looked like? Similarly, to explain the implications of the forward or backward rotation of the pelvic bowl, I would need to show what this looked like. Likewise, when describing how feelings got held in the chest, I'd need to show a chest or two. Of course, these sketches of nude models had nipples and genitals and pubic hair. While this wasn't a medical book with medical drawings, it was intended to illustrate the way people were embodied—and that needed to be done with drawings that revealed the body unobstructed by clothing, nothing more, nothing less. I didn't see it as a big deal; these were not meant to be sexy. Naked is who we are.

On the first page of *Bodymind*, I say, "I am standing naked before a room full of men and women of all ages." A sketch of a young me standing naked was supposed to be on the front page. This revealing, yet innocent sketch was complete and ready to be inserted, but at the last minute Ursula my editor at Pantheon Random House, decided it was a little too risqué to show a young author standing naked for all the world to see.

I pushed back and said, "Come on now, aren't you being a bit too New York uptight? If I'm saying, 'I'm standing naked,' I'm revealing myself to the reader, 'Here I am.'" Other popular holistic books of the era, such as *The Well Body Book* and *The Massage Book* had nude drawings throughout, as did *Bodymind*.

However, my editor and her committee concluded, "Sorry, we're not going to use a drawing of naked Ken on page one." At the time I felt they were making a mistake, but I've since come to more fully appreciate the thin lines separating radical curiosity, openness, and recklessness.

*

I still treasure the lessons learned during that period of my life—the shedding of clothes, façades, and armor was liberating—and maybe just as many species of snake will regularly shed their skin to be reborn as a better and more beautiful version of themselves, we all might feel more alive if we did something like this from time to time—either literally or figuratively. In a way, I now feel proud of the courage it took (in truth, it seems a bit like foolishness too) to be willing to publicly put myself in an exposed and vulnerable position. However, I also now realize that if my publisher had not made that last-minute decision, and if that naked drawing of me had appeared in the book, my identity and credibility would have been influenced quite a lot by that picture. For the sake of myself and my family, I'm glad that didn't happen.

PART II

ENCOUNTERING THE PARADOX

Why doesn't school prepare you to grapple with life's big decisions?

·

What is your life's path and how will your life be best lived?

·

Which teachers or role models have got the best guidance and lessons for you?

·

To what extent should you be following your parents' path?

·

How important will love and parenthood be for you?

·

How do you learn to live your life on purpose?

·

Are you a teacher or a student—or both?

DESTINY KNOCKS

It's not whether you get knocked down. It's whether you get up.
—Vince Lombardi

It was 1974 and I had been living in Big Sur for several years—while also working on my doctorate in psychology and starting to write *Bodymind*. I had a little cabin just north of Esalen that I rented for $150 a month, which I could barely afford by teaching workshops at Esalen and other growth centers. It was a dump, but I loved it. It was nestled in a redwood grove right alongside the Big Sur River. Since I had read *Siddhartha* several times by then, and like many of my peers was hoping to become enlightened as soon as possible, living next to a flowing river seemed a perfect fit. My place was located about an hour south of Monterey, right before you got to the Big Sur post office. To get to it, you had to cross a tiny bridge on the west side of Highway 1, secured by a locked gate. Once you crossed the bridge, the dirt road opened onto miles of protected forest, streams, and hiking paths. Up and over the mountain, you'd find yourself looking out at a truly magnificent coastline of craggy cliffs and picturesque sunsets. Although mine was a beat-up little house, the setting was spectacular, and the property private, secure, and cozy. I dreamed that I would stay there for a long time—maybe forever.

There were no cell phones of course, and there was no television reception in Big Sur. The only radio access we received was late at night: Wolfman Jack, who played great music and howled a lot, beaming out of LA. Because there was almost no technology in that era, I filled up my time with learning, reading, writing, playing music with friends, meditating, thinking, daydreaming, hiking, doing yoga, having fun, and lots of sex. This was a window in time, after the introduction of birth control pills but pre-AIDS, when "Make love, not war" was more than a slogan—it was a lifestyle. It was a beautiful and crazy era. During that relatively carefree period of my life, I did two hours of yoga each morning before going to study and work at Esalen and then did another hour of yoga in the afternoon and often another hour of very deep asanas at night. I weighed about 150 then. (That would be 50 pounds ago!) My hair reached halfway down my back, and I had a beard and multiple earrings. If you would have met me then, you would have thought I was a displaced Jersey boy who was trying to be a skinny California yoga guy. And I guess that's what I was.

I drove the half hour to Esalen almost every day, training there with various leaders, teachers, and authors in the fields of psychology, yoga, bioenergetics, psychodrama, sensory awareness, meditation, and tai chi. At twenty-three I was also co-leading workshops, and my youth made me somewhat of a novelty. What I knew, perhaps more intuitively than consciously, was that teaching was a path that led to more learning, as long as you were passionate about what you were teaching. As my experience writing *Bodymind* would show me in the coming years, the process of *Breathe, learn, teach, repeat* was cyclical but not redundant. I wanted to keep learning *new* things. I wanted to keep growing.

I wasn't the only one. So many people had become interested in self-actualization, personal growth, and mind-body practices that there was an explosion of what were called human potential "growths centers." There were catalogs featuring all of the programs at all of the growth centers throughout the United States and even worldwide. Since Esalen was considered to be the mother ship and model for this movement, if you were on the Esalen faculty and willing to travel (as I was), you could spend your entire year orbiting through these centers run by like-minded souls. There was the Gestalt Institute of the Rockies, run by Beth Prothro and her husband, George Dovenmuehle, in their living room. There was one in Miami called Cornucopia and one in Boston run by Jack Canfield, who would go on to author *Chicken Soup for the Soul*, and his then wife, Judy; another in New York called the East-West Center, and another, named Anthos, run by Bob Kriegel, who would go on to write *If It Ain't Broke … Break It!*, and David Schiffman (both of whom became luminaries in the field). In San Diego there was Kairos, in Denmark there was Skovly, and so on. So, while anchored to Esalen and Big Sur, I also flew all over the world, spending as many weeks as I wanted leading workshops in these growth centers. I also spent several weeks each year at the Siva Ananda yoga retreat on Paradise Island in the Bahamas, which charged a whopping twenty-six dollars a day for a cot in a shared room or tent, two vegetarian meals, and four hours of yoga training alongside other seekers. This center was run by Swami Vishnudevananda, whose *Complete Illustrated Book of Yoga* was the north star of yoga practice in the West.

And yet, at the end of each adventure, I returned to my cabin in the woods, which I rented from a guy named Jan Brewer, who owned a number of properties in the area. I had never met him, as he was believed to be living in New Zealand. I simply sent my monthly rent checks to the post office box of his property manager. Word was that Brewer was quite an odd character: movie-star handsome, certifiably crazy, and considered a violent outlaw by anyone who knew him. Remember that back in the late sixties and early seventies Big Sur was a wild "multicultural" mosaic. You had the bikers (principally Hells Angels), gypsy-style wanderers, hippies, and movie stars hiding out, and many outlaws—ex-cons, lawbreakers, and renegades of every sort. And of course, the Esalen community within Big Sur was populated by professors, revolutionaries, belly dancers. It was a strange universe of artists, seekers, and crazies. For me, after a straitlaced upbringing in urban New Jersey, it was a psychedelic fairy tale, and I loved it. Every night as I watched the stars rotate around the sky, I thought, Why would I ever want to leave here?

Then one day, at around five in the morning... *bang! bang! bang!* I shot up from a deep sleep on my mattress on the floor and trudged naked to the front door. Standing in front of me was a guy with a very bad mood written on his face. He resembled a young Clint Eastwood, if you imagined Clint Eastwood having dropped a very toxic tab of acid. I was thinking, Who is this guy, and how did he get through the gate and onto my property?

He barked, "Hey, are you living here?" It seemed like a rather dumb question, but I didn't think it wise to point that out.

"Yeah," I said. "I am. Who are you?"

"Get out," he barked, then raised his voice and declared, "I'm Jan Brewer. I own this property, and I want you out now!"

I said, "You've got to be kidding me."

Brewer reached under his vest and produced a gun from the holster hidden beneath, which he pointed at my head. He said, "You're leaving."

I asked, "At the end of my lease?"

"No, now."

I looked into his eyes and realized that he was not fooling around. Then I looked at his gun and said, "Okay. I guess I'm leaving right about now."

Moving his gun closer to my face, he said, "You have until sunrise."

During the next hour, in a panic, I speedily loaded my clothes, typewriter, diary, and guitar into my van. I had lived in my van before—during the time I had spent wandering across America—and figured I could live in it again. By the time the sun came up, I no longer had a place to live. Over the next months I tried with no luck to find another place to rent in Big Sur. I considered moving back to New Jersey or Pennsylvania, or maybe Colorado or Florida. I crashed at Big Sur friends' homes and campsites for a while, but things just didn't feel right. In truth, I was rattled.

So I asked some friends for advice. "What should I do?" One of the people was the remarkable Dr. Jean Houston, who was on my graduate committee and became a very influential person in my life. Jean was—and still is—a brilliant philosopher, author, teacher, and storyteller. In many ways she's bigger than life.

Jean said to me, "Kenny"—she always called me Kenny—"it's time for you to leave Big Sur. Your time is up. You've got the training. You've got the skills. Now it's time to do something *big* with all of that!" What I had been building was a sort of fluency in all the newly popular therapies and a few ancient ones as well. I could teach yoga. I could lead encounter groups. I could conduct Gestalt and psychodrama sessions. I could do these so-called alternative therapies, and I somewhat understood them. Jean was a selfless connector—one of those grand human beings who bring people together— just because she loved doing so. I used to wonder if she wasn't a gift to our world from some advanced race of beings who wished to create connec- tions in order to improve our species. She said, "You need to meet my best friend, Dr. Gay Luce, who recently moved from the East Coast to Berkeley."

"Okay, why?" I asked.

"Well," she said, "Gay wants to start the most amazing human potential project that has ever been created, and you should be working with her and her collaborator, Eugenia Gerrard."

I drove up to Berkeley to meet Gay Gaer Luce, who lived in the Berkeley Hills. She was twenty years older than me. She had been a well-respect- ed researcher-writer working at the National Institutes of Health and had dropped out to move to the San Francisco Bay Area, where she believed the future was unfolding. She had written several books, and one, titled *Body Time*, about biologic rhythms, had really caught my attention. Her live-in boyfriend was a wonderful man named Erik Peper, who was creating what would become the National Biofeedback Society and had bold ideas about the relationship between the brain, mind, and body.

I met with Gay, and she was just so full of life and so smart, a grand woman. She explained her dream that, rather than these weekend personal-growth workshops or evening lectures focused on one thing or another, this was going to be an all-in, comprehensive, yearlong self-actualization curriculum with a pilot group of participants who would meet for a half day each week and also have one to two hours per day of personal-practice assignments. Gay introduced me to her collaborator, Eugenia Gerrard, who was in her mid-thirties and was trained as a family therapist. She too was a spectacular human being.

I was so curious about the project that I found a place to crash for the next several weeks (on the floor of astrologer Shirley Leitch's apartment in Berkeley) as Gay, Eugenia, and I began to conjure up something special. Gay knew a lot about mind-body types of psychotherapy, and I was going to contribute yoga, Gestalt, and psychodrama. Eugenia had a deep interest in co-counseling and using breathing techniques for stress management and healing. In addition to ourselves, since Northern California was brimming with consciousness types of every stripe, we imagined we could invite many renowned teachers, from Erik Erikson (adult development) to Robert Monroe (astral traveling) to Elisabeth Kübler-Ross (death and dying), to provide special sessions. We were surely naïve, idealistic, and enthusiastic at that moment, but we imagined that we could weave together both ancient and new therapies, techniques, and experiences, and put a group of people through it for an entire year—at the end of which they'd be, you know, next level. Because we three had read and liked the science-fiction book *Childhood's End*, we joked that if what we were going to try worked, our participants would become an advanced version of the human species.

I was young, jobless, and homeless, and this all seemed totally exciting to me. I thought, Well, here we are at the beginning of 1974 and Berkeley's kind of cool. It's not Big Sur, but it sure isn't Newark either.

We formed a study group and were joined in our envisioning by some truly fantastic people, such as Ken Pelletier, the young psychologist and medical student who was writing the pivotal book *Mind as Healer, Mind as Slayer*; Dr. Len Duhl, who had been JFK's personal psychiatrist; Dr. Stanley Keleman, who was transforming the pioneering work of Wilhelm Reich into what he was calling Core Energetics; and Dr. Erik Peper, with his biofeedback. Several members of our study group were friends with Stewart Brand, who lived across the bay and had just conceived and published a radical retailing/consciousness idea that he called the *Whole Earth Catalog*. Stewart was so intrigued by what we were trying to do that he provided our group with five thousand dollars so that we could file as a not-for-profit.

As we were filling out the paperwork for our project, we realized we needed a name. What are we going to call ourselves? The Human Potential School? The Mind-Body Collective? Consciousness University? We were just trying out all these hokey names, and someone—I think it was Gay—said, "What about using the word 'holistic'? None of us had ever heard that word. She explained that there had been a South African philosopher named Jan Smuts who had used the word maybe fifty years earlier. Okay, holistic what? "How about 'holistic health,' and we can be a 'council'—building off of the American Indian idea of a group of leaders?" We loved it. But how do we spell it? I thought it should be spelled w-h-o-l-i-s-t-i-c ... because it would be based on the idea of bringing different ideas together into a whole. Gay, who at the time was a board member of the Nyingma Institute, a Tibetan Buddhist center in Berkeley, preferred that it be based on 'hol' as in "holy-istic." So that battle raged for a little while, and we ultimately landed on the Holistic Health Council.

It was time to learn something new. I decided I would move to Berkeley and begin a whole new chapter in my life. I was going to be one of the three founders and co-directors of the world's first Holistic Health Council. Although we didn't have any money and had no prospects for funding at that time, we were going to be transforming people in ways nobody had ever done. I found an apartment in Berkeley behind a Chinese restaurant, signed a year lease, and couldn't have been any more sure of myself.

But then, *boom*. Gay's mom, Fay Gaer, an absolutely lovely and kind-hearted seventy-five-year-old, suffered hypertension that was making her woozy. Frustrated with traditional Western medicine, Gay started doing biofeedback and breathing therapies with her mom, and she swiftly got better. So out of left field, Gay said, "Let's fill our human potential school with old people!"

I responded, "Old people? What are you talking about?"

Without hesitation, Gay went on. "Let's try biofeedback, tai chi, yoga, meditation, psychodrama, art therapy, and journal writing. Let's see if we can use these techniques to help older men and women feel more alive than they have felt for years! Who knows, maybe we'll create a revolution in the way the world thinks about aging—and possibly transform medicine too. And let's change our name from the Holistic Health Council to the SAGE Project."

I thought, That's a weird idea. How do I feel about old people? I like my grandparents a lot. I don't have a problem with old people. They're all right, but they're definitely not as appealing to me as young people. Do I really want to base my career on old people and aging? I don't think so. So I said to Gay, "I'll tell you what. I'm going to help you and Eugenia set up the program blueprint—that will be both challenging and interesting. It should take a few months. But then I'm out of here."

We put the word out, and a diverse group of elderly people started signing up. Our pilot group had twelve participants, and the first year we conducted all our meetings in the living room of Gay's house in the Berkeley Hills. Before I knew what hit me, I was sitting on a pillow in a circle, not with good-looking, playful hippie chicks or dudes, but with grandmas and grandpas with arthritis, canes, ostomy bags, and cancerous skin.

But *everything* changed for me when they began sharing their stories, hopes, and fears. At that point in my life—like so many others—I was searching not only for transformative therapies and practices but for wise guru types. Not that I necessarily wanted to follow one. I thought of myself as a student in search of greater awareness. And that the keepers of these insights would be famous professors, experts, authors, or swamis of one sort or another. It had not occurred to me that regular, everyday older people could in fact be the true holders of wisdom.

I didn't leave the SAGE Project after a few months. In fact, I had the honor of working for the next five years with Gay and Eugenia as our idealistic little project expanded in scope and number of participants, received funding from the NIMH, and became the model for hundreds of courses, programs, clinics, and schools worldwide. All of this while the holistic health field rose up like a volcano from the multidisciplinary study group in Gay's living room.

Thank you, Jan Brewer, for knocking on my door, holding a gun to my face, kicking me out of my (your) house, and opening the path to my destiny. Although I never saw him again, I heard that Jan Brewer died a violent death while serving time in prison for some crazy misbehavior a few years after our encounter.

LEARNING PERSPECTIVE
FROM THE ELDERS

*There is no passion to be found playing small—in settling for a life
that is less than the one you are capable of living.* —Nelson Mandela

In 1974, during the early months of the SAGE Project, our elder participants were opening up about nearly every aspect of their lives during our
weekly group sessions. We sat in a circle on pillows or on couches in Gay
Luce's expansive living room with a huge picture window overlooking
the San Francisco Bay. We'd begin each session with a quiet meditation,
and then everyone would say a bit about how they were feeling, whether
they did their journal writing and yoga practice during the week, and
generally how the SAGE process was unfolding for them. Everyone was
encouraged to be open, honest, and nonjudgmental. Although they were
of all shapes, sizes, religions, and races and from all walks of life, there
was definitely a sense that we were all coming together like a kind of
modern tribe. Then during each session we would focus on some new
aspect of mind-body well-being, such as nutrition, management of stress,
spirituality, or caregiving. For a complete portrait of the SAGE Project,
Gay wrote a wonderful book called *Your Second Life*, which I highly recommend.

I was struck by how, rather than being uptight about sharing their
stories, the SAGE participants were eager were to make sense of the lives
they had lived—knowing and respecting that they were in their last innings.
Although I had been in countless therapy groups and late-night discussions in my years at college and Esalen, I had never heard more interesting
reflections than from these almost strangers, most of whom had never
been in therapy or participated in anything like this before. I'm not exactly
sure why, but I became particularly interested in how they viewed and
described the lives they were wrapping up. Since I was so entranced by
what I saw to be the beginning of my adult life, I wondered how they
viewed life from a point close to the end. As they were attempting to
make sense of their experiences, to use the word "nostalgia" would be

both trite and wrong: there was perspective; there was insight; there was wisdom. And most of all, there was an ability to see the topography of their life journeys with dazzling clarity.

Gay, Eugenia, and I were largely just making up discussion questions and therapeutic interventions as we went along, and our participants seemed game to try just about anything. So I made up an assignment. I said, "Hey, everybody, here's a couple of sheets of graph paper for each of you. For next week's session, draw a horizontal axis along the bottom of the page. On one end put year one, on the other end, put year one hundred. Give it some thought, but during the week, please chart on the graph the experiences you've had—or will have—with your life from birth to death."

"What do you mean?" they asked. "What's down? What's up?" "What are we measuring and charting—our health, our feelings, our success at work?" "What color pen should we use?"

I said, "You decide what's important and chart it any way you want."

In our next group session they were eager to explain their charts and also see what other people had done. Everyone's charted drawing was different, as lifelines rose and fell, flatlined and spiked. But the explanations were incredibly revealing, and there was a lot of common ground. Vivian explained her largely steady and flat chart as a reflection of her life, which she felt she lived without peak experiences. She cried when she described decades in a loveless marriage. Herb chimed in that he had worked his whole life in a job he hated, until he retired and found that he really enjoyed volunteering, as reflected in his happiness and lifeline rising after age sixty-five. Mac, when explaining the occasional spikes in his chart, could remember a handful of wonderful, sexy weekends in a life otherwise devoid of pleasure. Evy smiled as she pointed to her fifty-second year, when she divorced her husband and got remarried to her high school sweetheart. Ralph was effusive when he explained a highly purposeful period of his life when everything seemed to be flowing wonderfully, until his wife died unexpectedly of a heart attack, and then for the next five years he had a downward spiral of loneliness and depression.

It was apparent that these older men and women could look back at their lives and, relatively easily, see that there were high points and low points, happy periods and unhappy ones, with sometimes lasted for decades, sometimes just days. Together they discussed the fact that the high points of their lives were not nearly as frequent or long-lasting as they had imagined they would be when they were young (my age). Frances told us that when she was young and had married her husband, George, she believed they were destined for a wonderful life—just like in the movies. However, she explained, after a few years she realized that George was a jerk, with all sorts of bad behaviors from drinking too much to regularly lying to her and their kids. There were health-related realizations as well. Herb was battling lung cancer, and it was clear to him that his long smoking habit had caused it. Elaine had always loved being outdoors in the sun but was now tormented by recurring skin cancers. Several of our participants were really overweight when they started our program, and they could see the connection to the heart problems and diabetes they were grappling with. Some of our elders were struggling financially, and they bemoaned not having saved more during their working years. And since several of our participants were grappling with loneliness, they could also track in their life charts the period when friends either moved away or died and they hadn't replaced them with new friends. There were also the exhilarating moments or decades of being in love, experiencing something new, enjoying caring friends, having fun, laughing, or working in a career that was nourishing, rewarding, and/or purposeful. At one point in this discussion, one of our elder group members, Vivian, proclaimed, "Ken, when it comes to how people change and shift as they become older, I believe in the 'Moreso' philosophy!" Imagining that Moreso was a French philosopher, I asked her if she could say a bit more about that. She wryly responded, "If you're a jerk when you're young, you'll be more so when you're older!" All the group members roared with knowing laughter.

That afternoon everyone was so immersed in this rich exploration that no one wanted to leave, so we got some pizza and continued until long after the sun set. They reflected that because there was so much small talk in their lives, they loved this chance to go deep and examine truly interesting and important issues. What evolved was a heartfelt and profound discussion among our elders about how they would have lived their lives differently if, when they were young, they could have understood what they now saw so clearly. There were many comments like "I should have married the person I really loved instead of the one that my parents preferred" and "I wish I had worked at something I cared about, rather than stayed with the shitty job I had for so long." Also "I should have spent more time laughing and less time worrying." "I should have cared for my body with more respect to have allowed it to go the distance with more energy and health." "I should have moved to a different area as soon as I realized that, on my salary, I couldn't afford the life I was living." And "I shouldn't have spent so much time with friends who really weren't friends." The biggest wallop I personally received from these reflections was from the men and women who were childless. Clyde shared, "I wish I had had children. To be approaching the end of my life knowing that there's no more biologic lineage and just no child to miss me and remember me... there is such a big hole in my heart."

Then, to build on this overall theme, I asked the group to bring in pictures of when they were in their twenties, thirties, and forties. In the photos the women were vibrant and stylish, some were sexy, and all were beautiful in their own way. Similarly, the men looked athletic and handsome, and since many had served in the military with pictures from that era, they often appeared quite courageous. Most astonishing, all the men and women were young! I know that sounds absurd, but it occurred to me that when young people see old people, most unconsciously assume that they were always old people. We look at their gray hair or stooped shoulders or untrendy attire and think this must be kind of how they have always been. But when I looked at the faces in the pictures, it was obvious that the young people in the pictures were not old-people-in-waiting. Albeit with different hairstyles, they looked like me, Gay, Eugenia, and all our friends. And when I looked from their pictures to their wrinkled faces, I realized that in their minds, they were still those young people, just older versions. They were us, downstream.

Here's what struck me like a bolt of lightning. First off, unlike them, at twenty-four I didn't have enough life yet to chart—three-quarters of my graph was a blend of wishful thinking and abstract murkiness. Second, with their long view gained through seven, eight, or nine decades, they could clearly see the patterns of their lives, which elements made them happy and gratified and which didn't. Third, because most of us ramble through our lives, only to one day discover that somehow we've become old, how fascinating it was to collectively explore which choices—psychological, social, physical, financial, and spiritual—these men and women felt they should have made along the way, if only they'd known then what they knew now.

If you're going off on a camping trip and you're going to take a complicated hiking trail, there's some value in talking to other hikers who have just finished the trail. While there should always be room for experimentation and discovery, there's also value in getting counsel and suggestions from those who have been down the path before. This way you can learn where there were danger zones and scenic stops and fresh water. And while you are free to disregard their counsel, these experienced hikers can inform both your preparation and your actual journey. Watch out in the valley, as there are rattlesnakes, and make sure to load up your water containers by the stream before climbing up the mountain—and whatever you do, don't miss the sunset over the gorgeous waterfall! You may never see anything like it again.

One of our group members commented, "Every teenager should take a mandatory course in healthy, successful, and financially secure aging—and maybe retirees like us should be the instructors." We all applauded that idea.

That entire week, I couldn't sleep. I sat up every night and reflected on how many young people—and maybe even people of all ages—were hoping to live happy, healthy, loving, successful, and enlightened lives. But we didn't ever talk to people who were just finishing the journey, who have lived their lives with ups and downs and learned massive lessons along the way. This is one of the unintended consequences of having the young and the old socially disconnected. Instead, to seek out wisdom or life tips, we read self-help books and listen to forty-five-year-old self- proclaimed "experts" who may have meditated for a few years or taken some courses in college and think they know something. I thought, We're making a big mistake. We should be listening carefully and deeply to our elders. As the years unfolded and these kinds of discussions became a standard part of all our SAGE groups, with almost identical outcomes and insights, I was becoming increasingly aware that in our youth-obsessed culture, nobody was listening to older people.

From these experiences, my identity in the SAGE Project flipped 180 degrees. Although I continued to try to do my best as a teacher of practices such as yoga and psychodrama (with far less pretention), I mostly became a student of aging. My teachers were the older men and women all around me—and they were so eager to share. As I worked to distill the core lessons about life that my elder SAGE friends were teaching, there emerged a kind of duality—a paradox—with which I struggle to this day.

They taught me that on the one hand, life is a very long and windy road and you can't be in such a hurry that you miss the sweet moments it offers. Slow way down, celebrate every triumph, and take your time to savor each moment of every day. On the other hand, they all said, "Snap! Life is over like that!" Do you think you can put off what you really want to do or who you really want to be for some later date? Wrong. The next thing you know you'll be eighty-four, and you'll be sitting in a circle like this one, filled with regret, looking around the bend to the end of your life. Do everything you want to do mindfully, here and now, and do not waste a second on things or people that don't matter.

People sometimes ask me why I live my life so intensely. It may be because that's the way I'm wired. However, when I look back at my life before and after these powerful discussions, I believe my intensity is because of what I learned from my elder SAGE friends—and my openness to their lessons. I was taught to both savor each and every morsel of my life but also to live it fiercely and with purpose, like it will be over in a flash—the paradox.

I was given a gift. Way before I knew what life's questions would be, these elders shared many of the answers. I pass this gift along to you. Why wait until you're old to learn how to live life on purpose?

OUT OF THIS WORLD

When I let go of what I am, I become what I might be. —Lao-tzu

Back in the day, as I was straddling the worlds of human potential and aging, there was a lot of public curiosity about how psychedelic drugs could unleash your mind to greater awareness and an expanded sense of self. Harvard professors Timothy Leary, Richard Alpert (later known as Ram Dass), and Ralph Metzner were championing their use, and everyone was reading books such as Aldous Huxley's *Doors of Perception* and Carlos Castaneda's *Teachings of Don Juan: A Yaqui Way of Knowledge*, which offered tantalizing glimpses into expanded consciousness. And so many of our musical heroes, from the Beatles to the Grateful Dead to Blind Faith, were being wildly influenced by newfound psychedelia. We could hear it in their music and see it on their album covers. Think: *Sgt. Pepper's Lonely Hearts Club Band*!

During those years, while massively curious, I was never a heavy drug user. Sure, I smoked a fair amount of weed to get high, have fun, and try to decipher Dylan's brilliant yet esoteric poetry or the meaning of a Beatles album. I tried cocaine a bunch of times, took a handful of wild and crazy LSD and mescaline trips, and loved sexy, dreamy Quaaludes when they were available. I never thought of myself as an aggressive user of these substances, but I had lots of friends who were. Instead, I thought of many of these drugs as possible perception expanders that had a place in the pursuit of human potential.

It was while living in Berkeley that I became curious about a drug named ketamine. A number of Esalen-related consciousness explorers such as Drs. John Lilly and Hector Prestera had been experimenting with this non-psychedelic pharmaceutical. Ketamine is a powerful dissociative anesthetic that allows the mind and central nervous system to go on functioning while it completely turns off the rest of the body. How is it different from the usual sedatives? Most others turn off the mind too. I had heard that with ketamine, when all of the normal sensory and physical experiences evaporate, the mind is free to experience out-of-body, astral traveling. While hard at work writing *Bodymind*, I read Aldous Huxley's *The Doors of*

Perception. I was fascinated by the proposition that our minds, rather than reveal the universe to us in all its glory, instead work hard to filter out more than 99 percent of it, so as not to overwhelm us, thereby allowing us to live somewhat normal, practical lives—but miss out on quite a lot of splendor.

Although ketamine was a legal sedative and was primarily being used as a horse tranquilizer, a handful of folks were using it for spiritual explorations. Some progressive psychiatrists were thinking about using ketamine with older and near-death patients in order to let them experience a controlled, altered state of consciousness, which they believed paralleled an ego death or body death. By directly experiencing this kind of loss and coming out feeling okay, perhaps folks would be less fearful of dying. There was growing evidence that people who had had so-called transcendent experiences—either due to surviving trauma or through spiritual practices or psychedelics—seemed to be much less fearful of death and more alive in their present state as a result. Ketamine was believed to be more conducive to this sort of experiment than something like LSD, because it was non-psychedelic and it its dosage was easier to manage precisely.

The ketamine stories were intriguing, but I hesitated to try it. As with all drugs, there are a lot of unknowns and there also tends to be both abuse and/or exaggeration on the part of the users. Although their ketamine-induced astral travels later became the story line (modified a bit) of the popular movie *Altered States*, Lilly and Prestera had been taking ketamine often and in very large doses, frequently submerged in Samadhi tanks, which Lilly had invented. They both looked pretty burned out to me.

After much deliberation, I reached out to a highly respected Harvard-trained psychiatrist, whom I'll call Dr. R. He agreed to take me on a ketamine trip in his home. First he conducted a full medical exam to make sure my system, and my heart in particular, was healthy enough for what I was about to undertake. We had several therapy sessions in advance so that he could get, in a sense, the lay of the land inside my head. I wondered if Lewis and Clark were so deliberate in preparing for their explorations.

The following is my exact account as I wrote it in my journal in November 1974.

Yesterday, after careful deliberation, I had my first (and only) ketamine experience—and it was a whopper. On Wednesday evening at around sunset, Dr.

R. welcomed me to the small guest cottage beside his secluded home in the hills of Berkeley. Wearing loose-fitting, comfortable clothes, I laid down on a comfy mattress on the floor. Dr. R. covered me with a light blanket. The room was dark. There were no sounds present: no stereo or radio. After I settled in, Dr. R injected sixty milligrams of ketamine into my butt. Within minutes, the most amazing experience of my 24-year life began.

How can I describe such a thing? How can I try to recall some of the places and insights I experienced when many of them had little to do with the me, who is now describing them, and the frame of reference of where I traveled had very little resemblance to the normal world we inhabit? How can I talk about a travel experience that can't be described in terms of three- or four-dimensional coordinates?

Let me first just provide a bit of a backstory about the nature of what I experienced. Normally, it seems, our brains spend most of their energy focusing on their relationship to our bodies and their relationship to our material (non-spiritual) world. So, we identify a lot with our egos, our personalities, our physical health, our ambitions, and fantasies of past and future experiences. With ketamine, most of these connections and objects of consciousness simply drop away.

The ketamine was injected. As I rested on the floor trying to relax, I took some deep breaths. I was nervous. I wondered, "What's going to happen next? Will I be okay? What will I experience? If the normal physical world evaporates, will I experience access to the pulsating cosmos like the mystics report? Or will I just nod off? Who will I be when this trip is over?"

As I was lying on the floor, the first sensation brought on by the chemical was that my body was growing very, very heavy. It quickly became very hard to move any part of my body. My observing mind (the one that talks to me all the time) watched these changes and I played with my muscles to see and feel just what was happening. I was amazed at the swiftness of the changes. I began to focus on the "here/now" and almost immediately became aware that my physical body seemed to have a great deal to do with my "personality" because I felt it too was growing heavy and dissolving into the floor. By personality, I mean all my perceptions, beliefs, aspirations, fears, tastes, looks, and ambitions that collectively define what I normally think of as "me." I began to notice that my mind was paying less and less attention to analyzing what was happening in terms of how it related to the human being who is Kenneth Mark Dychtwald in America, planet Earth, 1974. Instead, I was increasingly present in the here/now experience while nearly all of my objective observer—and the physical world—faded away.

After a short while, my body got so distant from my point of awareness that it seemed to evaporate, but not in a bad or frightening way. I felt liberated, joyous almost. Instead of sending attention and consciousness off in a variety of directions, my consciousness focused more intensely than ever. My brain surged with an incredible quantity of energy, which allowed me to experience what "is" in a less temporal or corporeal way. In so doing, I felt myself to be shifting from a self-conscious centipede to a single point of consciousness in four dimensions.

Mind you, I was not evaluating this because the part of me responsible for judging and rating experiences had dropped away. In fact, I was losing all judgment of good and bad. It struck me that these material world-based evaluations may not be real. Maybe they're just constructs we individually and collectively create in order to navigate our lives? I had also lost my concern for reporting my experiences to myself—as I had always done. I simply engaged more fully in the experience of experiencing. I felt both calm and fully alive and ecstatic. In reflection, I'm not sure if I was feeling ecstatic because my usual dependency on self-confirming feelings had dissolved. Or was I for once feeling what really "is" and what really "is" is ecstatic?

As the drug's effects deepened, I was noticing the absolute hugeness of what was swirling around me, but I didn't feel the need to categorize any of it on a personal level. As I glided further and further in this direction, I encountered feelings that had to do with death. I truly felt like my personal ego was dying— not my essence, but maybe my ego and maybe my body. At first, I experienced a sensation that might be called fear. But these shifts in consciousness catapulted me into a position where I looked at what death was for me. Who was dying? Who is Ken Dychtwald? What is Ken Dychtwald? What dies? Who dies? Who cares? As my life flashed before me, I swiftly reviewed my thoughts and feelings regarding what I had believed about death. And soon I began to detach even from them. Imagining that I actually was dying, I thought of all the people who would be affected by my sudden death, which troubled me. I didn't want to make anyone sad. But with every second that passed, I continued to separate. When it was clear that I had nearly completely died already, I said to myself, "Let go, let go, let go." I instantly had the feeling of magically falling slowly backwards over and over again. The room, the Berkeley Hills, the earth fell away as I found myself joyously tumbling through space. Incredibly, at that point, my consciousness seemed to be able to direct itself anywhere at all within time and space. I could send the universe spinning off to the left or right, or in and out simply by allowing it to go that way. Time was just one more dimension that I could direct myself to move around in. This was okay. This was far better than okay. I experienced it all with a sense of wonderment, with respect, with awe.

Then I made another quantum leap in consciousness. My sense was that physical reality—the earth, moon, sun, stars, galaxies, people, me—as I had come to know and depend on it, was still definitely there and present but that there were also many other realities that were at least as real as that one. I began to directly experience these other realities. It was absolutely majestic. I felt like I was pulsing in a multiverse of colors, flows, sounds, and sensations. I could feel myself as pure energy, rippling and changing shape with each new wave of contact. The network that is me and that was tied into my usual reality let go of itself, and I found myself experiencing the others very vividly.

I continued to let go, and it seemed to me that these other realities were not substantially physical but instead were more subtle, fluid, and energetic—what some might call spiritual. As the ketamine coursed through my body, elements of my personality danced in and out. Embodied moments of self-reflection were few and when the trip was most intense, they were nonexistent. I wasn't feeling feelings; I simply was them. It was wonderful. I was being made love to by myself and my relationship to all of these forces.

At that point, something very powerful happened that was so multidimensional that I can't get much of a grasp on even explaining it. All the movements, colors, and sounds I was seeing, hearing, and feeling began to gradually converge in very much the same way as I suppose my consciousness was converging. The inter-meshings and galaxy-wide syrupy swirls of energy grew more intense, and then, suddenly, everything got brittle and exploded into trillions and trillions of stars. I was witness to a universe being born.

The next thing I was aware of was massive godlike beings, forms, or intelligences in my presence. They were ancient and powerful "star-makers." They weren't bearded, sitting on thrones or carrying tridents. Nor were they holding court over a piece of earthly real estate. Instead, they were massive—bigger than galaxies, loving, and powerful non- physical beings. I was humbled, utterly in awe. At the time, this realization was clear as day; now it seems harder for me to grasp. I cannot remember ever being in the presence of anything so huge and majestic. It seemed to me that, guided by these "star-makers," I flew through the galaxies being formed as I watched over the course of thousands and thousands of years. Somehow my "self-aware" consciousness then completely let go at this point and I cannot recall anything that happened with the stars after this. I guess I simply merged with them.

Now, I still have very faint memories of what these elements of life looked and felt like, and I am reminded that in hundreds of unremembered dreams, I have encountered these beings before. I stayed in this place for a long, long time while all the rhythms danced and swirled. I cannot remember ever being so awed by the splendor of anything like I was then. The only feeling present was pure bursting love and there was no thought, just white light. I experienced a joyously happy aliveness that verged on being folded inside out.

Then I began to lose some of the thrust of the experience, and I became aware of myself becoming aware. My thinking, evaluating, choosing brain began to reappear, as I was returning slowly to being Ken Dychtwald, man of Earth, November 8, 1974 coordinates.

Along with these impressions, a variety of evaluative perceptions returned. I was sorry to be leaving this ecstatic space. I wanted more. Why did it have to end? I had been with the cosmic gods—and now what? As I was reconstituting, I somehow latched onto thoughts and feelings regarding my elderly grandfather Max who was pretty sick back in New Jersey. He appeared to me and I felt my love for him. He was unclothed and his essence was radiating that special presence that made him so uniquely godlike in his own special way. I looked at him for what felt like years and allowed myself to observe all of him that I had known: the Max Siderman who loved Clara Siderman, who drove a Chrysler, who told stories, who had a pacemaker in his chest, who was the father of my mother, and on and on. But it also occurred to me that all these elements were just shells and the real essence of my grandfather was eternal. Here was a handsome, beautiful, cosmic being temporarily inhabiting a shell, living on a planet that was also a shell. This was okay. I was engulfed by my love for him. My arms reached out to him and he drew me to his heart. We embraced for eons as we lovingly drifted together through the vastness of space. As we held each other close, he told me the specific date his physical body was going to die and asked me to look after his beloved Clara when he passed. Then we were joined by my grandmother, and she too revealed her essence to me. And then we all embraced. My God, what a deep and profound connection that was. It sounds odd when I try to write about it, but it wasn't odd at all. It was sublime. From there I immediately found my father and mother in this non-physical realm and we all embraced and swirled through space. In them I felt myself. I loved my parents as they are myself as much as I am them. My parents are God. Maybe we're all God?

While I was feeling overwhelmed by what I had just experienced, I then realized I was starting to return to normal consciousness. My mind began to race, my body began to sense, my thoughts became evaluative. Like when an elevator on the 73rd floor plummets down to the ground floor, I felt myself zooming inwards from a thousand dimensions, aiming at the coordinates that are me on Earth—now. I eventually came back to feeling like 24-year-old Ken Dychtwald lying on the floor at Dr. R.'s house having just had a drug induced trip. I felt totally overloaded with thoughts and memories and questions. If I am back to normal—what is normal anyway? I felt both overwhelmed and underwhelmed by the pressure and responsibilities of the coordinates I was inhabiting.

Realizing that eons had not passed in Earth time like it had felt to me, but that I had probably been in this semi-coma state for several days, I opened my eyes and saw Dr. R. sitting nearby.

I asked him how long my trip had been. "Twenty minutes," he said. "And how was it?"

"Cosmic, magical" was all I could say. And it was.

As the years have unfolded since this cosmic trip, I have never forgotten what I witnessed and experienced. Did I encounter the essence of cosmic life, or did my imagination have a field day? I don't know. Perhaps when the time comes, and my body dies and my nonphysical essence gets poured back into the multiverse, I can compare notes. One thing I do know for sure: my grandfather Max died on exactly the date—January 15, 1975—that he told me he would when we were swirling together in the cosmic soup.

GRANDMA CLARA'S STORY

My greatest skill has been to want little. —Henry David Thoreau

After my grandfather passed away, my grandmother Clara—who had never learned to drive and was only modestly literate—became increasingly withdrawn. Because she was such a good soul and loving grandmother, and because my work on the SAGE Project had made me curious, in the fall of 1977 I decided to spend a week in New Jersey, bringing with me an old-fashioned reel-to-reel video recorder and microphone in hopes that she'd be open to allowing me to interview her. My grandmother had never spoken much; in truth, she had usually deferred to my grandfather in social situations.

When I arrived at her apartment, she answered the door with her lipstick on, her hair coiffed, and wearing full jewelry, as though she were attending a bar mitzvah. I told her she could relax and dress more comfortably, but no, she said, she wanted to look her very best. Even though I'm not sure she ever understood what my video recorder was, some deep part of her knew that I had come to take her portrait, to capture her story. What follows are a few excerpts from those days of interviews.

Ken: All right. First of all, how old are you?

Clara: Well, that I wouldn't know. Because when I was born my mother passed away and there was no record of me.

Ken: Where were you born?

Clara: In Elizabeth, New Jersey.

Ken: Do you figure you're over seventy?

Clara: Oh, yes.

Ken: Do you figure you're over eighty?

Clara: That I don't know. Around that age, I think.

Ken: Where did you live when you were a little girl?

Clara: I was raised in the orphan asylum in Elizabeth, New Jersey. I stayed there quite some time. And then when I got a little older, whoever took me in, I boarded with them whether it was an aunt or a stranger or a... I don't know. I boarded with everybody.

Ken: What kind of girl were you?

Clara: I was a very good girl. I helped everybody, and wherever I boarded I helped them clean the house and wash the floors and clothes and whatever. You know, I done a lot of housework.

Ken: What do you remember about those years when you were boarding with people?

Clara: Well, I remember I went to work when I was eleven years old. I worked at the Central Stamping Company from seven in the morning until six at night. I worked there until I got married.

Ken: What was your life like back then?

Clara: Well, we had no electric lights. We used to burn kerosene lamps, and we had no gas stoves. And the bathroom was about a block away from the house. You had to use the lantern to go out there at night. In the winter we'd dress up warm and go. And we used to wash clothes by washboard, and there were no bathtubs, nothing. Everybody would take a bath in a round galvanized tub. They'd put it in the kitchen, and you'd take a bath and you'd walk out and the next one would walk in and take a bath, and that's how we lived. And when I was a little girl, I used to go on the railroad tracks to pick coal that fell off the trains, because that's what we burned in the stove. We couldn't afford to buy coal, so we picked up pieces on the railroad.

Ken: How old were you then? Were you very little?

Clara: Oh, I was a little girl. In my bare feet. Half the time we didn't have no shoes, and I remember that I was never sick. If anybody got a cold or they were sick, we would take a teaspoon full of kerosene oil. You know what that is? We would take kerosene oil, and we'd use that for the cold. And if you had an infection, we would take baking soda. We never went to a doctor, and if you did it was only a quarter.

Ken: Do you think people were happy?

Clara: Yes. They were very happy. We were happy with what we had. You never heard gossip or things like you hear today.

Ken: Did you have a lot of boyfriends when you were growing up?

Clara: Well, I could have had a lot of boyfriends, but I didn't bother too much with them. Once a week we went to a dance down at Saint Aloysius Church. That's all there was, dancing, once a week. And then my brother watched very carefully over me and watched who I went out with. And I had to come home early—by eight o'clock. You know, I kept very early hours. And then I met Grandpa.

Ken: How did you meet Grandpa?

Clara: I had a girlfriend named Sylvia, and one time she says to me, "Would you like to meet my brother?" I said, "Okay, bring him over."

Ken: How old were you then?

Clara: It must have been about nineteen. Something like that, I don't know. Like I said, I never knew exactly how old I was. And she brought him up and I used to play piano, you know, and when she brought him up, he came up with two brothers to see me the first time. I was playing "You Made Me Love You and I Didn't Want to Do It." That was my lesson for that week.

He was an automobile mechanic then, and that was equal to a doctor. He was the head mechanic at the Motorcar Company, and so he was very special. He also did extra work fixing things for people at night. He liked me right away, so he made a date with me for the following Sunday.

He came over and he took me for a ride on his motorcycle. He asked me if I could cook. I said, "Sure, I can cook." Then he made a date with me for the following week, but he couldn't keep it because him and two fellas rode their motorcycles to Connecticut, and he had an accident. He was broken up pretty bad, so he was in the hospital for about six months. I thought, "Well, I was out with the guy once and liked him. I might as well go to visit him." So, I went to visit him, and I brought him soup. When he finally came out of the hospital, the first thing he did was come and see me … on crutches. Then, he started coming to see me every night, and he fell in love with me.

Ken: And were you falling in love with him?

Clara: I didn't like him at first, but I thought maybe he'd make a good husband. Then one Sunday afternoon he invited me to his parents' house for dinner. After we had dinner, he handed me an engagement ring. I didn't know whether to take it or not. I didn't know whether I liked him or not. But I took it anyway. The next day, he drove me down to the corner of Springfield Avenue and Belmont Avenue. There was a candy store there where we all used to go and have sodas. We went in and we had an ice cream soda and then we took a walk down two blocks where there was a furniture store. In the window there was a dining room set and a living room set. He said, "Let's go in and look at it." I said, "Well, I'll go in and look at it with you." So I went in and looked at it and he bought it. He paid the man some money and told him, "I'll pay you off so much every week because I'll be getting married soon."

So, I thought, "Well, now I've got the ring and I got the living room set and I got the dining room set. I might as well get married. I might as well like him." Sure enough, about six months later we got married. And after that we got a six-room apartment for eighteen dollars a month. It was a nice apartment … a little expensive, but nice.

Ken: Did you continue working after you got married?

Clara: No. I quit a week before. Grandpa wanted me to quit, so I quit.

Ken: What kind of man was he then?

Clara: He was a very good man. He didn't smoke. He didn't drink. He didn't play cards. He was a good husband and we had good children. He was never cranky, and he was always satisfied. Whatever I done was satisfactory, and he liked my cooking. All he knew was working hard, and every nickel he made he gave to me. He never questioned what I spent, or how I spent it. If anybody in the family needed anything, I was the first one to help them. Had he lived three more months we would have been married sixty years.

Ken: Do you miss him a lot?

Clara: I certainly do. I don't go anywhere because I miss him very, very much because we never had an argument. Not one argument. We never had a fight. We were always happy, and whatever he earned, I made do, you know, and we were very, very happy.

Ken: What do you miss most about him?

Clara: Well, I miss every part of him, being in the house and taking care of him and cooking his meals and taking care of him.

Ken: How does it feel to be alone after having been together for so many years?

Clara: Very, very bad. Very bad. I don't go anywhere outside of sitting in the yard or go to the children, you know, like that's all.

Ken: Did you love him a lot?

Clara: I certainly did.

Ken: How did Grandpa feel about you?

Clara: Well, he was in love with me.

Ken: How did you know?

Clara: Because he always told me. He always told me how much he loved me and that he couldn't be without me, and he loved me very dearly. We used to sit and watch television, and when the number would come up, we'd get up and dance the two of us. We'd get up and dance right here on the floor. Whenever there was a good music on the television. "The Anniversary Waltz" or different ... whenever they'd play nice music. We'd get up and he'd take me in his arms, and we'd dance.

Ken: Did you like that?

Clara: Sure I did! I'm a girl, ain't I?

Ken: He told you he loved you all the time?

Clara: All the time till the night that he passed away.

Ken: What happened that night?

Clara: Well, we sat on the chair, on this chair here, and he says, "I want to tell you that I love you very dearly all these years," and he was very happy that we lived happy and if he'd ever done anything out of the way to please forgive him, and I should always know that he loved me dearly, and after that he went to the hospital and that was it. I miss him so much ...but I dream about him sometimes.

Ken: In your dreams how does he appear? Does he say anything?

Clara: Yes. He tells me that he's all right, that he still loves me.

Ken: When your time comes, how would you like to be remembered?

Clara: That my four children liked me—and my grandchildren and great-grandchildren, that they all loved me.

Ken: You think everybody will remember you for a long time?

Clara: I don't know. Maybe they will or maybe they won't.

Ken: If there's a message you'd like for all of us children and grandchildren—to live on twenty, fifty years from now—what do you want us to learn from you that we can continue doing?

Clara: To be good, honest, respectable and live happy with your families like I've lived happy with my husband!

Ken: What do you think about all this? What do you think about what I'm doing with this camera and microphone? Why do you think I'm asking you all these questions?

Clara: I don't know, because you want to remember me and you like me, right? Because you love me.

Ken: I do love you.

Clara: And I love you, too. From the minute you were born, I loved you. And find a nice girl and get married and I'll love you double.

From this experience, I learned that my grandmother was very wise and very straightforward and, of course, that she loved me. When she expressed her life values that she wanted to pass along to us—"to be good, honest, respectable and live happy with your families like I've lived happy with my husband!"—they were simple and uncomplicated. In the years since, I have learned that very few people take the time to sit down with their grandmas, or their parents, or their friends and allow these special folks to tell their story. Having such an exchange on video, versus just a photo album, makes a massive difference. When I watch the filmed interaction between my grandmother and me, I can still smell her homemade soup, feel her good-naturedness, and see the twinkle in her eye.

LEARNING FROM
"THE BEST"

Find out who you are, and do it on purpose. — Dolly Parton

In the 1980s, with the arrival of cassette-tape players in cars (replacing eight-tracks, but far before CDs, DVDs, podcasts, or the Internet), more and more people began to purchase audio self-help learning programs they could listen to while commuting to work. Usually there was a six-tape course, with each tape/module lasting around twenty-five minutes—which, handily, was the average commute time. The leading publisher in this audio-learning space was Nightingale Conant, based outside of Chicago, which produced an unending stream of self-help learning programs in conjunction with best-selling authors and sought-after motivational speakers. Since I was conducting seminars on bodymind, wellness, and peak performance, they reached out to me and commissioned me to produce a six-tape set, entitled *The Keys to High Performance Living*. It was fun to do. I recorded the six sessions in a studio, got them edited, and then sort of forgot about it.

However, as a regular buyer of Nightingale Conant programs, I wound up on several of their targeted databases as the kind of guy who was interested in many self-improvement subjects. So when a new program was released that might be up my alley (according to their database, which tracked my purchases), I usually received a direct-marketing brochure for the tape set and an offer to purchase the program in one of those customized form letters we all were getting used to receiving in that era.

While I was conducting seminars on bodymind, holistic health, wellness, and peak performance, I had overloaded my life with more pressure and complexity than I felt I could handle. My exercise regime was faltering, and I had gained weight and was having trouble sleeping. Then one day I received a brochure in the mail from the president of Nightingale-Conant, Dave Nightingale, which read:

> **Dear Mr. Ken Dychtwald:**
>
> *Do you feel you have lost control of your life? Are you suffering from too much stress? Are you finding it harder and harder to stay on your regular fitness program? Are you struggling to balance your work and family responsibilities? Do you feel that you are not achieving your highest potential?*
>
> *If so, then* **Dr. Ken Dychtwald can help you!** *In his new six-tape program, this well-known expert on high performance living will help you solve all of your problems and take control of your life again.*

What? This letter was indicating that if I was out of control, then I could help me.

Although I didn't buy the six-tape *Keys to High Performance Living*, this existential message from me to me seemed strangely like a very good idea. After all, when most of us feel like we're losing control, we probably don't need some "expert" to tell us what to do. One of the nice things about growing up and growing older is that most of what so-called experts can teach you, you've already learned. The real challenge is often less about knowing what to do and more about doing what you know.

HOW WILL YOU USE YOUR LIFE?

Develop enough courage so that you can stand up for yourself,
and then stand up for somebody else. —Maya Angelou

I was on a lecture tour through Denmark in 1978. As the California author of *Kropbedvisthed* (Danish title of *Bodymind*), I had been invited to give a series of lectures on holistic health, aging, and self-awareness, thanks to the book's unexpected Scandinavian success.

Boarding the plane for the long flight from San Francisco to Copenhagen, I was feeling proud of myself for taking such a big leap into the world. Except for my dad's stint in the army, no one in my family, including me, had ever been outside of the United States. As I deplaned in Copenhagen, I was instantly captivated by the look of the Europeans—their dress, their style, the way they carried themselves. I thought, I've really done it. I'm in a foreign country. I'm in Scandinavia, I'm in Denmark. However, as I proceeded to walk through the vast terminal, my eyes were taken by a fantastic mural across an entire wall. I could see that it was some sort of map, but I had no clue what it was a map of. I stopped walking and stared. Is it abstract art? Is it something prehistoric? And then, with a shock, I realized that what was I looking at was a map of the modern world, but one in which Denmark was at the center. I laughed out loud. It had never occurred to me that the center of the world was not a fixed location known as the United States. My frame of reference was jostled, and I hadn't even left the airport yet.

Reporters were waiting for me when I landed in Copenhagen. My book was in the window of bookstores throughout the city. In this faraway place, I was being hailed as something like a celebrity. The fame was new to me, and I didn't mind it at all.

I began returning to Denmark each year to give speeches and present workshops, and together with my Danish friend Jesper Juul we created the Bodymind Institute of Scandinavia, which lasted more than a decade. On one of these visits, I received a call from the offices of Denmark's renowned octogenarian geriatrician Esther Mueller, who was a highly respected physician and philosopher in her home country. Dr. Mueller asked me to lunch. Wow, my life was really taking off! I loved it. I was flying high.

Dr. Mueller and I met for lunch in a charming, quiet restaurant and proceeded to have a pleasant conversation about my journey to her homeland. We exchanged the usual small talk. Soon enough our conversation turned to professional concerns and issues. She wanted to know about my insights and research on preventive health, aging, and human potential. I was interested in her views on healthcare and medicine in Europe. Honestly, even though I barely knew what I was talking about, I yammered on. Then Dr. Mueller brought me back to planet Earth as she jolted me with a pointed question. "Ken, you're obviously smart and ambitious," she started. "You have a keen interest in what will become a hugely important field as the global population ages. You have a hit book and can command a fair amount of attention through your lectures. What I want to know is this: How do you intend to use your life?"

I wasn't sure what she meant. "You mean in terms of what I'm going to make of my career?" I asked.

"No," she said.

"Do you mean in terms of the books I may write?"

Again she answered, "No."

Perhaps something was lost in translation. What did she mean?

"Ken, how will you *use* your life?" she repeated.

I was just thirty. My mind was stuck in concerns over my emerging career, newfound Danish celebrity, and hopes for a creating a family one day. How would I use my life? I was going to make some money and hopefully have a wife and a couple of kids, I said to myself. Yet I knew she was trying to get at something deeper, but at that time I didn't really understand the meaning of her question.

I fumbled for an answer and ended up telling her, "I'm not sure. I'll have to see where my career takes me."

We finished our lunch and then parted ways, and I couldn't help but feel that I'd seemed shallow in my approach to life and that it had disheartened her. Her question—how will you use your life?—haunted me for many years.

PART III

CAUGHT BETWEEN
THE TAO
AND THE DOW

What do you prioritize? Love of life, love of yourself
and/or love of another?

·

How willing are you to sacrifice your aspirations for
your partner's comfort and aspirations?

·

How do you balance your work and your family on a daily basis?

·

What does money mean to you?

·

Is untapping your potential a matter of accepting who you are,
or striving for a better version?

·

Is the spiritual idea of life—to work hard and seek abundance
or let go and enjoy emptiness?

·

How much is enough—and how will you know?

THE BEST DAY(S)
OF MY LIFE

*He now felt that he was not simply close to her, but that he did not know
where he ended and she began.* —Leo Tolstoy

When I was growing up in Newark, New Jersey, there was a beautiful
suburb not too far away named Short Hills. I didn't have much interaction
with the kids from that community, and they didn't bother much with our
group, as we lived on the "other side of the tracks." But I had heard about
one girl in particular, whose name was Maddy Kent. The word was that
she was very special: smart, pretty, fun, and (clearly) very popular. I never
actually met her in high school, but I knew who she was, and I'm sure I
wasn't alone among the young men in my neighborhood in wondering if
our paths would ever cross. Then when I was in college on spring break,
I was crashing with my buddy Paul Felsen and some friends in Miami
and saw this beautiful girl at a party. She had an exquisite face and large
brown eyes. It was Maddy Kent, and I briefly talked with her through a
haze of pot smoke, but we didn't exchange phone numbers, and nothing
came of it.

Years later, in 1981, I had just ended a relationship with a beautiful and
soulful woman I had been involved with for about a year (she followed
up with a relationship with some nutty Bay Area entrepreneur named
Steve Jobs). Entering my thirties, I was growing weary of the sugar rush
of new relationships and then the thud of the rush wearing off. Even
though I had loved the free-spiritedness of the "Make love, not war" era,
I was suddenly yearning for something deeper and more committed. This
was a new feeling, and it was worrying: Would I ever 'settle down' with
a wife and maybe even have a family? Would I ever have a soul mate?

During a visit with old friends on the East Coast, one of them said,
"I just heard some interesting news about a Jersey girl you might know.
Maddy Kent from Short Hills. Do you remember her?"

I definitely remembered her. My friend filled me in on some of Maddy's
life: she had had a failed marriage and was supporting herself as a

working actress with gigs on *As the World Turns*. She had recently moved to California because she was being considered for the role of Anthony Geary's new wife on *General Hospital*. I was curious and wanted to learn more, so I decided to track her down and give her a call. Hoping that she would remember meeting me from that party in Miami a decade before, I called LA information and got her phone number.

The next night I was giving a speech in Livermore, California. Because there wasn't much traffic, I arrived at the conference center early. I had some time to fill and noticed a pay phone in the lobby (no cell phones then), so I decided to call Maddy. Back in those days I was never a "cold caller," so I felt a little awkward. But I got up my nerve and called her number.

When she answered the phone, I said, "Hi. Is this Maddy Kent?"

She said, "Yes, who's calling?"

I replied, "This is Ken Dychtwald."

No reaction. Nothing. I then blurted, "'Kenny Dychtwald? We met at Michael Kay's party in Miami in 1970. Do you remember me?"

"Sorry," she said. "I don't remember ever meeting you, and your name doesn't ring any bells."

Feeling pretty embarrassed, I apologized for bothering her. Not making a big impression can be humbling. Making zero impression is downright humiliating. But right before we hung up, for some reason she said, "We probably know some people in common. If you ever want to talk again, give me a call."

I called her again a few days later—and luckily she remembered me this time. We started talking about some of the eccentricities of growing up in New Jersey and of our lives now in California. She told me about her failed marriage and how in her early twenties she had picked herself up and pursued a career in acting, supporting herself every step of the way. I told her about my years in Big Sur and my interest in yoga, holistic health, and the aging of America. I learned that her parents had gone to the same high school as my parents—and me, too—Weequahic High School, and that her aunt's family owned a bakery, Mittleman's, where we regularly shopped when I was growing up. We discovered that we had many similar points of view about music, movies, and style. On the other hand, we had chosen utterly different paths. While I had been howling at the moon with my friends in Big Sur and Berkeley, she had been partying with the movers and shakers at Studio 54. But when each call ended, we both wished for more.

In time, I learned that she was an avid reader, so we exchanged our favorite books. I sent her my five favorite science-fiction books. She sent me historical novels, which we then read and discussed. The way her mind worked, her street smarts, her curiosity, and her sense of humor—all of it captivated me. During that period we never actually saw each other, although we did send each other pictures of ourselves (via the mail, as was the only option back then). She was winding down a relationship, and I was seeing other people, so we didn't try to force anything. For six months we talked regularly on the phone and found ourselves becoming close friends and confidants.

Then one night she told me that she had a meeting coming up in Berkeley, pertaining to a script she was working on. "Maybe we could meet," she offered. I jumped at the chance to see her and was eagerly waiting for her when she arrived at the Oakland airport. As she walked off the plane in her jeans and T-shirt, she was absolutely radiant, beautiful, amazing. That afternoon we walked along the Berkeley pier at sunset, ate at my favorite Italian restaurant (which she thought was only so-so), told stories about our lives and loves that made us both howl with laughter. She canceled her flight home, and over the next couple of days we totally swooned over each other. It was a truly amazing and all-consuming encounter—unlike anything I had ever experienced.

And then she left to go back to LA. We missed each other and began talking every night for hours and started planning our next get-together, which was only a few weeks later. Over those magical months, I fell deeper and deeper in love with her insightfulness, her beauty, her playfulness, her athleticism, her hopes, her dreams, her voice, her eyes, her lips, her touch, her heartbeat—I could go on and on.

During this long-distance phase of our relationship, she asked me to fly back east with her to be part of a yahrzeit memorial ceremony for her grandfather, who had passed away in New Jersey a year before. I imme-diately agreed, knowing it would also give me time to meet her family. The day of the service, we drove to a sprawling Jewish cemetery in Iselin, New Jersey, and found our way to the plot where her grandfather was buried. While waiting for the rabbi to arrive, I said to Maddy, "I don't know why, but I feel a need to stand over there," and I pointed to a spot a few feet away. Although she rolled her eyes at my peculiar request, she said okay and we moved. A moment later I looked down and was absolutely stunned. We stood at the exact spot where my own grandfather and grandmother were buried, just a few feet from Maddy's. Cue the *Twilight Zone* music. Any lingering doubts about the depth of our soulful connection were instantly and irrevocably erased.

We decided we were no longer interested in seeing other people and being apart no longer felt right: we should try living together. After some back-and-forth, we felt that we'd have a better shot at relationship success living in Berkeley than in LA, so Maddy agreed to move in. I quickly learned that in addition to being beautiful, fun, and sexy, Maddy was also smart, opinionated, and strong-willed. Rather than being the yin to my yang, as had often been the case in my previous relationships, Maddy and I stood toe-to-toe when it came to personal strength and power. Once when we were having an argument about something or other, she said, "Look, it's clear that you have some kind of checklist in your mind about who you think your perfect mate should be. I'm definitely *not* that person. But if you put that checklist down, you'll see that I'm much better for you than that." She was right.

Not only was that the most consequential confrontation of my entire life, there was also a radical curiosity lesson for me in the exchange. Sometimes we think that by being mindful, or contemplative, or self-analytical, or smart, we can convince ourselves that we know what's best for us. Just because we can make a list, or imagine a possibility, doesn't mean our own biases and limitations are not be distorting the list making in the first place. We can be wrong. So aside from being even more impressed with Maddy, I had a big aha moment that day. Maybe one of the great advantages of having a partner, a soul mate, is that you get to see the world through another point of view alongside your own. The same is true, in some ways even more so, of having kids—but I'm getting ahead of myself.

With her decision to let go of her LA life and move in with me, one of my "personal growth" zones had to do with money. Maddy had grown up around more middle-class wealth than I had, and as a self-supporting actress previously living in New York, she had been earning more than I ever had. I hadn't the foggiest idea about wealth when I met her. I hadn't ever earned much money. I didn't understand its power, meaning, or usefulness. I wasn't particularly driven by it. However, when she was preparing to give up her LA apartment and move to Berkeley, she playfully asked, "Did you get all this furniture at the flea market? Can we replace it with some of mine?"

"Okay, fine," I said.

There was more: "Is that framed Bruce Springsteen poster on the dining room wall your only piece of art? And how come your silverware doesn't match?"

It was dawning on me that in one's thirties, relationships weren't just about sex, drugs, and rock and roll, they were also about being able to trust each other, being compatible roommates and financial partners. I realized that my hippie-ish disregard for money and my inability to earn it was going to have to change—especially if we ever planned to have children.

Maddy walked away from her acting career, moved in, the Springsteen poster came down, and little by little our lives and perspectives became intertwined. After a year of living, traveling, and even doing some work together, I was convinced that Maddy was my perfect match. Luckily, she was feeling the same about me. She realized that I could be a moody, self-indulgent jerk, but she seemed to be falling in love with me. On a work/vacation at Rancho la Puerta in Mexico, I proposed to her, and she said, "Yes, yes, yes!"

We got married on Thanksgiving 1983—on purpose. We both felt that getting married on a day when everyone was giving thanks made wonderful sense. We had a small, intimate wedding with only our immediate family in our home in Berkeley. Since it had been raining for days before and there were numerous leaks in our ceiling, Maddy and I spent the morning of our wedding on the funky roof, hand-sealing the cracks and leaks with gooey cold tar. On the day of our wedding, we were flat broke: no savings, no investments, no 401(k)s, nothing. Just credit card debt, and lots of it. But we were in love and we believed we could make a life together.

Our wedding service was conducted by two brothers, Nathan and Joseph Siegal, known as the "singing rabbis from Marin." They were kind, thoughtful men, and when they sang, they sounded a lot like Simon and Garfunkel. During the beautiful service, as they played their guitars and sang prayers in Hebrew, the rain stopped and the sun lit up our living room, causing Maddy's face to glow. My mom, dad, brother Alan, and his fiancée, Lynn, were all beaming, as were Maddy's mom, dad, two grandmothers, brother Richard, and his wonderful wife, Linda. The wedding service was touching, heartful, and moving in every way. We both said, "I do!" and then I crushed the glass under the chuppah as is Jewish custom. Then—another Jewish custom—Maddy and I went off for a few minutes to catch our breath and feel the joy. We were newlyweds, and I liked it! We returned to the living room, and everyone was seated for a fabulous feast with toasts, roasts, stories, and celebration. When dessert was being served, a projector and screen was set up. Maddy's parents had prepared pictures and films of Maddy when she was a child, replete with hilarious stories. Then my mom and dad did the same with pictures and films of me growing up.

I loved every minute of our wedding— saying our vows, having my family get to know Maddy, having hers get to know me, and exchanging rings. It was like a fairy tale. Our wedding day was, without a doubt, *the very best day of my life*. It was perhaps why I said to Maddy, as we were cuddled up at a cozy bed-and-breakfast in San Francisco, "I loved marrying you. Want to do this every year?"

It had been a spontaneous idea, and my new wife was puzzled. Unlike driver's licenses, marriages did not have to be renewed. She asked what I was talking about. I said, "Why don't we get remarried every year."

She said, "That's not what people usually do."

I responded, "I don't really care what other people usually do. I love you so much, I want to marry you again and again and again. Why not make our own rules?"

A big smile appeared on Maddy's face. Then on the spur of the moment I added, "Let's make it even more special and interesting. Let's agree that every year we'll get married in a different location with a different kind of ceremony or a different religion. That way the experiences will always be unique, and we'll always be connecting with each other from within a different culture or part of the world."

Maddy replied, "Let's do it! But let's add in one more thing. When we have these rituals, let's be sure to really talk about our relationship— what is working, what we could each do more of or less of, and basically how to keep growing together rather than apart."

"You're on," I said. "I love you."

The next Thanksgiving we got remarried in a Presbyterian ceremony at sunset on the beach in Kona. The following year we got married in Cabo San Lucas, Mexico, by a sexy female judge wearing a see-through blouse (that was entertaining!), with a mariachi band providing the music. Our intent was not to create a lavish or expensive affair but rather to put ourselves in a different part of the world for a few days, renew our vows, and focus on what it took to nurture a lasting relationship.

The next year we got married Baptist on Saint John in the US Virgin Islands. The day of this remarriage not only was Maddy pregnant with our first child, Casey, but we were also having a big fight. Midmorning, we were arguing about how we didn't feel properly paid attention to by each other and how this was a potential deal breaker in our relationship. Then Maddy looked at her watch and said, "Oh shit, we're supposed to be getting married in half an hour. We've got to get it together." And we did, and when we faced each other and said "I do," we forgot what we had been fighting about for the moment. Afterward, rather than fighting, we tried to figure out how we could get along better.

One year we decided to renew our vows on a ski slope in Vail, Colorado. We arrived in town, looked in the yellow pages of the local phone book under "wedding ministers" (this was before the Internet), and saw a listing for the "skiing judge of Vail." We called him up, and he said that if we told him what slope we were going to be on and at what time, he and a photographer would meet us there. The next day, right on time, he skied over to us along with a Bible and a photographer and married us. I gave them their fee of a hundred bucks, and they skied off.

Because our anniversaries were during the Thanksgiving holiday, these marriage renewal getaways were the perfect time to disconnect from work, unpack the preceding year, and prepare for what might be next in our lives. We would both openly reflect on what was working in our relationship and what wasn't. We tried our best to honestly discuss what we wanted to have more of and what we wanted less of. Without having any certain rules or regulations, these remarriages became a sort of a private ritual where, each year, while we were giving thanks (it was Thanksgiving, after all), we would take the time to remember why we were in love with each other, recommit to our relationship, and course correct where needed. I should note that during these years things weren't always going well—or easy—in our lives. We were getting used to being parents, our bills were piling up, we were trying to be business partners as we launched Age Wave, and then Maddy's dad tragically died of mesothelioma at the age of sixty, which we mourned together. A few times, we invited our kids to be a part of the wedding ceremonies. Some years I'd be bothered by something Maddy had or had not done in our relationship. Many years she voiced her concern about my workaholism and my insane travel schedule. While these remarriage ceremonies couldn't erase the difficulties or challenges we were having, they did allow us to clear the air, realign, and reprioritize our love for each other.

One year we decided to go to Moorea, Tahiti, to see what sort of wedding we could conjure up there. As fate would have it, we were staying at a local hotel near a spot where tourists could swim with dolphins. We wondered if one of the dolphins would be willing to marry us. We were told that they were quite smart and might be able to sense what we were trying to accomplish. So we put on our bathing suits and life jackets and jumped into the warm South Pacific, and in a little while one of dolphins began to circle us. It seemed to us that the dolphin sensed something about us as we held hands and bobbed in the water. Eventually it positioned itself in front of us and made a few peculiar sounds. We took this as its confirmation of our love for each other, we had some pictures snapped, and then off it swam.

Another year, when we were struggling financially, we decided to get married at the Chapel of Love in Las Vegas, both because of the novelty and because it was super cheap. The Chapel of Love offered limo service round trip from a local hotel, a minister (who assumed any faith we preferred), a choice of which Elvis song would be playing when we walked down the aisle, a garter belt for Maddy, two engraved champagne glasses, and a videotape of the entire service. For $175, that was a terrific deal!

In advance, I had my secretary call around to see if there was anyplace where I could rent an Elvis outfit, and apparently there were more than a hundred Elvis costumeries in Las Vegas. I chose one that specialized in "Vegas Elvis," as differentiated from the ones that featured "Hound Dog Elvis" or "Jailhouse Rock Elvis." When we arrived at the Chapel of Love, a clerk took our thumbprints and saw to it that we filled out all the legal forms properly. While Maddy was dressed to the nines and looked like Priscilla Presley, but better, I hadn't yet changed into my alter ego Elvis Presley. I said to the clerk, "Is it okay with you if I put my Elvis outfit on?" "No problem," she said. "There's a dressing room over there." She acted as though there was nothing at all unusual about this request. I put on my white one-piece jumpsuit with red trim, replete with a tacky gold medallion around my neck and a matching humongous gold big-buckle belt. With Maddy's help, I greased back my hair, and with her eyeliner, she drew big muttonchop sideburns on me. I looked like a total idiot.

As we were waiting for our minister to begin our ceremony, I said to the clerk who was checking out my sideburns, "Is this crazy or what?"

Without hesitating, she said, "Not at all. I see lots of grooms dressed as Elvis."

I followed up: "How weird is it that you have a couple that's getting married for their fifteenth time?"

She said, "It's not that weird."

So I asked, "Okay then, what qualifies as weird here in the Las Vegas Chapel of Love?"

She thought about it for a moment and said, "Well, around once a month, I'll be filling out forms with a couple and the about-to-be husband turns to the about-to-be wife and asks her, 'What's your name?'"

Hey, viva Las Vegas!

After our silly/wonderful Chapel of Love wedding, Maddy and I spent the evening at the casino at the Mirage Hotel, where we were staying. Just for fun, I thought I'd leave my Elvis outfit on. I was a hit, a big hit. Everywhere I went, as far as I could see, there were thumbs-ups and cheers for me. I learned that in Las Vegas (maybe everywhere, for all I know), it doesn't matter who you are or what you look like: you can be white, black, female, male, gay, straight, old, young, or one-legged, it doesn't matter. If you're dressed as Elvis, everyone will respect and love you. All I've got to say is "Thank you very much."

While I don't think I can claim to be an expert on relationships, from my marriage to Maddy and from the remarriage rituals we have practiced, I'm certain that it's essential to not allow your relationships to go on automatic pilot—ever. It's essential to continually explore each other more deeply, to deal with life's celebrations and shit storms as a team, and to always give radical curiosity a seat at your table. *Breathe, learn, teach, repeat!*

A METEORIC RISE

Twenty years from now you will be more disappointed by the things that you didn't do than by the ones you did do. —Mark Twain

On some days I am deeply immersed in simply "be-ing." At such times my mind is calm and deep, and I am at peace with who I am. I have great respect for—and feel in harmony with—the underlying meaning of the Tao.

On other days, I am deeply immersed in simply "do-ing." At such times my mind is energized toward self-improvement and I am attempting to add value to my personal stock. I have great affinity for—and feel in harmony with—the underlying meaning of the Dow.

Even then, still relatively young and inexperienced, I was learning that part of radical curiosity was seeing both sides of a perspective or way of being. Finding balance would be the trick, the challenge, and almost my undoing.

*

In 1982 I was a hippie-ish, holistic, body-minding, fascinated-by-old-people guy. However, because of the success of our SAGE Project, which had been receiving attention worldwide, I was invited to join a future-envisioning study group being put together by the Office of Technology Assessment, the think tank of the United States Congress. This particular investigation was to comprise twenty experts from every aspect of the aging field. I was, without question, the runt of the litter. The team included such luminaries as Dr. Robert Butler, founding director of the National Institute on Aging; Maggie Kuhn, head of the Gray Panthers; Dr. Caleb "Tuck" Finch, the country's leading expert in biogerontology; and Drs. Robert Binstock and Bernice Neugarten, the nation's experts on social gerontology. Over a two-year period we flew to Washington and collectively examined not the elderly or even the aging but aging demographics and their imminent impact on our society, families, communities, politics, the workforce, healthcare, economics, and even business.

The focus of our discussions, debates, and the research we reviewed was how America would be altered in the twenty-first century as the result of flattening birthrate, increasing longevity, and the aging of the massive baby boom generation. To be honest, I hadn't thought much about these things before, but the ideas we were to be investigating energized my curiosity. Initially I thought aging was something the elderly did, and a few years later I thought I was a clever fellow by proclaiming, "Hey, we all age; aging is a lifelong process. There's the 'aged' and there's 'aging.' Consider that!" But the idea that somehow all civilizations and cultures were grounded in their demography, which had been stable for thousands of years but now was being disrupted in ways that would shift the center of gravity from the young to the old—that was big. That was new. That was uncharted territory. It intrigued me in every possible way.

What happens to a world that has been principally composed of young people when it's soon going to be principally composed of middle-aged and older people? My mind reeled. What would happen to our automobiles, which were currently designed around the form and fit of twenty- two-year-old men? What would happen to our medical system, which wasn't really designed and organized—in science or service—for chronic degenerative diseases? What about the size of the typeface in our books, magazines, and newspapers—won't it all be too small for older eyes? And what about the time it took for the traffic lights to change—geared to the way young people zip along when they're crossing the street? What happens when you've got tens of millions of older people? What happens to the family? Instead of being focused on children, will we become increasingly focused on parents and grandparents?

As I wondered about all of this, I was coming out of a decade spent in the not-for-profit sector. Like nearly all my New Age friends, I thought capitalism was driven by bad people trying to make other people buy stuff they didn't need. I didn't understand business at all. I never went to business school; I had never even taken a business course. None of my friends were businesspeople. They were all social scientists, yoga teachers, New Age philosophers, or whirling dervishes. For those of us working in the gerontology and human potential fields, capitalism was simply out of bounds. I remember one colleague saying to me, "You lie down with dogs, you wake up with fleas." I took note.

However, I was becoming increasingly frustrated by how hard it was to really innovate from within the not-for-profit sector, and how there were *always* funding challenges.

The massive aging and longevity-related changes I saw coming seemed so obvious to me, and I was perplexed as to why so few people were paying them proper attention—and instead were too often viewing them as business as usual. With the future aging of our entire population, it wasn't just senior centers, nursing homes, and grab bars in bathrooms we'd need to be thinking about. We'd need to redesign cars, food, furniture, media, medicine, pharmaceuticals, education, housing, technology, and transportation systems. I wondered if it was even possible to motivate the for-profit sector to make the products and services that tomorrow's older people were going to need.

I began contemplating life in the for-profit sector. Maybe I was bullshitting myself, but here was my rationale: we were a democratic, capitalistic society. We have a left brain and a right brain, and when they're in sync, everything works better. On one hand, we're about life, liberty, and the pursuit of happiness. On the other, we're about a continually innovating marketplace. I did a little bit of homework on the roots of modern capitalism to see if I had any kindred spirits there. I learned there were some great companies that had begun with a desire to do good while doing well.

For example, in the 1830s, William Procter and James Gamble—who had originally joined forces as candlemakers—were troubled by the amount of dirt and grime people lived with. They believed filth was akin to ungodliness. The flip of that is cleanliness is next to godliness. They imagined that if the people of America had soap, they could rid themselves of filth and be closer to God. Procter & Gamble was begun, not with the mission of selling toothpaste or dishwashing detergent, but with the idea of making soap, Ivory soap, so that cleanliness was available to everyone. Their goal was to allow a filthy country to become clean. I thought, That's kind of cool.

Another of my favorite examples of conscious capitalism emerged in the 1880s. Entrepreneur George Eastman believed that a camera, which was a novel technological breakthrough, shouldn't only be in the hands of professionals. He felt that taking pictures should be the art of the common man, so he gave cameras away during the first years of his company. He thought everybody should be a photographer; everyone should be an artist. A century before Steve Jobs made the same points, George Eastman was a philanthropist capitalist with a desire to make technology available to all. I thought, That's kind of cool, too.

Another example—and there were many—was Coca-Cola. Originally, in the 1880s, Coca-Cola was made with cocaine, which was legal and considered a miracle medicine. The founders believed that their medical drink was the elixir of vitality and immortality, and they wanted to make it available to everyone. Whoever drank Coca-Cola would think better, run faster, have more energy, and feel like they weren't getting old. Of course, cocaine later became an illegal substance and the drink was reformulated with sugar and caffeine.

So, I thought to myself, maybe capitalism, like so many things in life—including people—has two sides. There's the capitalism where people are really trying to meet people's needs—at a fair price—and help them live comfortably, healthfully, and happily. But there's also the other, crappier version of capitalism driven by greed and self-interest, aimed at selling people things they don't really need at an unfair price and far too often sacrificing the health or well-being of communities and the environment in the process. I wanted to be on the good side of that equation. After countless late-night discussions, Maddy and I agreed to give it a try. We thought, Let's create a consulting and communications company together and make an attempt at being capitalists for the social good. We were hoping to create a more positive image of aging in America. Our intention was not to get rich. We simply wanted to be able to pay our bills, and just as important, we wanted the freedom to say and do what we wished. And so in 1983, Dychtwald & Associates was born.

In the beginning in the early 1980's, it was just the two of us working out of our house, with administrative support provided by a resourceful South African woman named Nesta Lowenstein, who was also our housecleaner and dog walker. Our plan was that (maybe) I could make more money as a communicator—a speaker—than in some sort of normal job. And maybe Maddy could help craft and produce our presentations. We had looked around and seen that there were some people, mostly in the business world, who gave toastmaster speeches or inspirational talks. They were getting paid around $500 to $1,000 a day or even more. Given my particular perspective, we bet I could do that too. I saw myself as a Paul Revere–like proselytizer—spreading the word, "The aging are coming," and getting paid for it.

I gave talks at the local UC Berkeley Extension program, at the Y, and at various other popular gathering spots in the Bay Area. They didn't always go well. Once I was invited to give a talk called "Realizing Your Potential" for the Singles Club at the San Francisco Y. I arrived looking sharp in my rainbow-painted T-shirt and my yoga pants. I proceeded to sit in the lotus position on top of a table in the front of the room as I had seen the guru Ram Dass do recently. Well, it might have worked for him, but it didn't exactly catch fire with my crowd. They began heckling me—asking why I was acting like such a New Age asshole and why didn't I sit normally in a proper seat? One man asked me if I thought I was going to charm some snakes with my mystical getup. I kept my cool and attempted to explain higher consciousness to these haters, but when I started chanting, they left en masse, howling with laughter at what a jerk they thought I was.

I didn't give up. Instead, I became even more curious about how to become an effective communicator. This wasn't easy, as so much about how we communicate is tied to our ego. To do it well, we need to be open to learning and willing to make changes in ourselves.

I started taking workshops on public speaking, storytelling, and improvisational theater. I wanted to learn how to better connect with my audiences and also build some confidence. I identified individuals who were considered great orators—like John F. Kennedy and Martin Luther King Jr.—and watched their great speeches over and over. I joined the National Speakers Association and watched the most successful speakers, such as Nido Qubein and Fred Pryor, mesmerize a room. In time, I felt I had two solid speeches, one called "The Keys to a High-Performance Lifestyle" and the other "Toward a New Image of Aging in America," both of which were finding interested audiences. As it is with public speaking, the more you do, the more you'll do. And if you're willing to course correct with feedback, the better you'll get. Although you may think you're just talking to one group, somebody in the room is on the board of something and someone else hosts some sort of conference each year. One thing leads to another. Most important, I discovered that I loved telling stories. I still do. In fact, while I understand that most people are frightened of being asked to speak in public, I have become frightened of *not* being askedto speak in public!

It's exhilarating to have the opportunity to impact people's thinking about their lives, the future, and the new challenges and opportunities that are emerging. It's an opportunity to change the course of history. And it's a craft where there's always room for improvement—for decades I have practiced and sought out coaches to help me up my game. It's also a fantastic way to meet lots of interesting people. When you're on the speaking circuit, as I have been for four decades, you get to meet famous athletes, generals, celebrities, professors, and even presidents. And last— you can get paid, handsomely, if you do a great job.

Finally, I was starting to make a little bit of money. Maddy and I decided we would rename the company, as Dychtwald & Associates didn't convey much. As we discussed it, we perceived this whole transformation going on as a sociologic wave. First I called it an "age tsunami." Nobody understood that. Then I'd tell people, "You know, it's like a big wave, an *age wave*." Once we landed on that phrase, it stuck—like its destiny was to always be there.

Maddy and I filed the papers and officially started Age Wave in 1986 with the wise and enthusiastic counsel of our mentors Dr. James Bernstein, physician and entrepreneur extraordinaire; Fred Rubenstein, sales machine; and Bob Huret, finance master. I met these talented men through talks I was giving, and I guess they were attracted to the business potential of the opportunities I was considering. We negotiated agreements through which they'd help guide me in exchange for some founders' equity.

Back then, as an enthusiastic but largely naïve entrepreneur, I knew that I didn't want to create just any kind of company working on any kind of project. I had my ideals and related hopes for the focus of our work. I wanted Age Wave to be steadfastly committed to the following goals:

1. liberating the consumer marketplace from its ageist, youth-obsessed orientation in order to increase the comfort, security, engagement, and well-being of older adults;

2. working to avert a new era of mass elder poverty;

3. preparing our healthcare system for the chronic health challenges of tens of millions of older adults and their caregiving families;

4. turbocharging the frontiers of global science to beat Alzheimer's before it beats us; and

5. helping to envision a new purpose for older adults.

As our work intensified, other aspects of my life were changing too. Without question, the most cosmic experience I ever had was in the winter of 1986. On that day, as Maddy's gynecologist Dr. Risa Kagan placed an ultrasound probe on Maddy's abdomen, we heard a heartbeat—steady and quick. It was the sound of the new human being Maddy and I had created together by our joining in love. It was the sound of a life that Maddy was growing in her womb. It was the sound of a miracle, more astonishing than any new client, breakthrough idea, or well-written book. It was the sound of our daughter (and first child) Casey's heartbeat. Her little heartbeat rocked my soul.

I felt humbled by both the primal and otherworldly process of human procreation and fatherhood itself. I immediately felt responsible for our daughter's precious and vulnerable being. And I felt concerned for the future—bounded no longer by my time horizon but by hers.

And then three years later Zak arrived. Being a father to a son has been a ride unlike any other. With each step he has taken and mountain he has climbed, my heart has swelled with both terror and pride, in a way that I only partially comprehend—but it has connected me to manhood in so many profound ways.

And believe it or not, during all of this, Maddy and I kept getting married. The year we got married Baptist on Saint John, in the US Virgin Islands, Maddy was pregnant with Casey. We were also having a big fight. Midmorning, we were arguing about how we didn't feel properly paid attention to by each other and how this was a potential deal breaker in our relationship. Then Maddy looked at her watch and said, "Oh shit, we're supposed to be getting married in half an hour. We've got to get it together." And we did, and when we faced each other and said, "I do," we forgot what we had been fighting about for the moment. Then afterwards, rather than fighting, we tried to figure out how we could get along better.

One year we decided to renew our vows on a ski slope in Vail, Colorado. We arrived in town, looked in the yellow pages of the local phone book under "wedding ministers" (this was before the internet) and saw a listing for the "skiing judge of Vail." We called him up and he said that if we told him what slope we were going to be on and at what time, he and a photographer would meet us there. The next day, right on time, he skied over to us along with a bible and a photographer and married us. I gave them their fee of a hundred bucks, and they skied off.

Because our anniversaries were during the Thanksgiving holiday, these marriage renewal getaways were the perfect time to disconnect from work, unpack the preceding year, and prepare for what might be next in our lives. We would both openly reflect on what was working in our relationship and what wasn't. We tried our best to honestly discuss what we wanted to have more of and what we wanted less of. Without having any certain rules or regulations, these remarriages became a sort of a private ritual where, each year, while we were giving thanks (it was Thanksgiving, after all), we would take the time to remember why we were in love with each other and recommit to our relationship and course correct where needed. I should note that during these years, things weren't always going well—or easy—in our lives. We were getting used to being parents, our bills were piling up, we were trying to be business partners as together we launched Age Wave, and then Maddy's dad died. He had developed mesothelioma—a cruel cancer, probably due to his involvement in the family's dry-cleaning business—and died within months of being diagnosed. Some years, I'd be bothered by something Maddy had or had not done in our relationship. Many years, she voiced her concern about my workaholism and my insane travel schedule. While these remarriage ceremonies couldn't erase the difficulties or challenges we were having, they did allow us to clear the air, re-align, and reprioritize our love for each other.

WHEN SALLY MET RAY
A LOVE STORY

About a year after my father-in-law Stan's somewhat sudden death of mesothelioma, I was sitting in my office when I received a phone call from my mother-in-law, Sally, who was at home in LA. A woman who had been with only one man for more than forty years, she found herself suddenly a widow at sixty. While Stan's death was deeply painful for all of us, for her it was devastating. She felt that she had been cast adrift.

That day she asked me if I could fly down as soon as possible to have a private talk with her. She sounded anxious, and that worried me, even more so when she requested that Maddy and our daughter, Casey, not come. Sensing my rising alarm, she said, "Nothing bad, Ken, but I need to talk with you right away." So I flew to LA the very next day and met her at 6:00 PM in the designated restaurant. I was very uptight because I imagined she was going to share some very bad news.

I saw Sally waiting for me at a quiet booth in the corner. When she saw me, she got up and gave me a great big hug. She said, "Thanks so much for coming, Kenny. Please sit down."

"Okay, but what's wrong?" I asked impatiently.

She responded, "Have a glass of wine." An open bottle of wine sat on the table.

I said, "No thanks, I'm not going to drink any wine. What do you need to talk to me about?"

Sally repeated, "Have a glass of wine."

I said, "Sally, what's going on?"

She took a long sip of her wine and a deep breath and said, "I'd like to talk to you about sex."

I poured myself a glass of wine. "What do you mean, you want to talk to me about sex?"

She nervously explained, "Well, you know, I'm sixty-one years old. I'm an attractive woman. And men are starting to ask me out. I may be alive thirty or forty more years, and I'll probably find myself dating at some point, and I'll be honest with you, I've never dated. I've never been with a man other than Stan, and I missed the whole sexual revolution. I'd like for you to fill me in."

I downed my glass of wine and asked, "Oh, you mean you want to know the trends and the dating patterns and—"

She cut me off. "No, I want to know the real stuff. How many times does a guy expect you to date him before you put out, and in whose apartment? His or mine? And who's on top? Who's on bottom?"

I called the waiter over and asked, "Can I have a glass of vodka, please?"

But part of me was thinking, Hey, where does a sixty-one-year-old woman go to talk about sexuality? There are not a lot of books, movies, or TV specials to provide guidance. We think if people want to have sex when they're old, they're dirty old men or silly old ladies. I respected that Sally felt comfortable enough with me to ask. So we both jumped in and talked about her potential sex life, with lots of spicy questions and, hopefully, some useful answers. After dinner, I took a taxi back to the airport and flew home thinking, Did that just happen? Neither Sally nor I ever said a word about that discussion again.

A few months later Sally did indeed begin dating several different men, and I couldn't help but wonder if my advice was proving to be of any use.

Then one day Sally called our home and asked if Maddy and I could both be on the phone. We put her on speakerphone, and Sally said, "I'm in love."

"What?" Maddy and I both responded.

"Yes, that's right, I'm in love."

In that instant I got to watch Maddy—who was, and still is, a very hip, contemporary woman—become a mother to her mother. She immediately told her mom, "You don't know what love is. What do you think you're doing? You can't be in love, you're just on a rebound from Dad's death."

"No, you're wrong," Sally said. "I'm really in love—maybe more than I've ever been before."

I asked, "Gee, when'd you meet the guy?"

To which she responded, "Two days ago. And I'd like for you to come meet Ray the next time you're in Southern California—but come to visit soon, because he's really great and we're so happy."

"Where does he live?" Maddy asked.

"Here," Sally said.

"You mean 'here' as in Calabasas?"

"No," she told us. "He lives here in my home with me. Isn't that great?"

A two-day romance culminating in a move-in? My mother-in-law was a very straight, perky, buttoned-up woman, and we immediately thought she'd gone a little crazy. And who was this Ray guy? He must be one of those con artists you hear about from time to time who prey on older women. After we gathered our wits, we reached out to Maddy's brother, Richard, who was a lawyer. He and his wife, Linda, were just hanging up from a similar call. Richard was already setting in motion a criminal-record search of Sally's new friend/roommate Ray. We were all alarmed, believing that in some way Sally was being bamboozled. There was no other explanation.

But she wasn't, and there was. You know what happened? She had fallen in love. And not only that, she had fallen in love with a truly great guy, a loving and caring man whose first wife had passed away a few years earlier. The following year we celebrated their love affair with a glorious wedding at our home, attended by their friends, their adult children and children-in-law (thirteen), and their grandchildren (lots). At their ages, they didn't get married to have kids. They did not get married to pursue their careers. They got married to enjoy each other. And they did—with both of them feeling that in their second time around they had found the true love of their lives.

It was a sad day in 2016 when Sally passed away with her dear soul mate, Ray, crying his eyes out by her side. Theirs was a true love story.

AGE WAVE'S EXHILARATING SUCCESSES

If you don't build your dream, someone else will hire you to help them build theirs.
—Dhirubhai Ambani

Things at Age Wave started happening at hyperspeed. Our company's initial goal was to "influence the influencers." We reached out to several speakers' bureaus, who began promoting me as both a futurist and a so-called expert on consumer trends. Early on, I remember being contacted by an organization called Institutional Investor, which put on big corporate meetings. They heard I was talking about the aging of America and thought it was an interesting topic. I had written a few books by then, which added to my nascent credibility, so they asked me to come speak at their annual meeting. It went well, and numerous people asked for my business card.

Several weeks later I received a call from a man named Fred Meyer. I had no clue who he was, but when I called him back, he said, "Hi, I heard you speak at the recent Institutional Investor conference. I'm the chief financial officer at CBS Television, and I told Mr. Tisch about your talk and he would really like for you to come speak to our senior executives."

I said, "That's great. I'd love to do it." We set a date and I made up a number. I said, "That'll cost ten thousand dollars."

He said, "No problem." He went on to say that Mr. Tisch would like me to talk with them about this, and Mr. Tisch would like me to talk about that, and he wants me to cover this and that. Right before the end of the call, I remember saying to him, "If you don't mind my asking, who's this Mr. Tisch you're talking about?"

He said, "It's Larry Tisch. He's a wealthy investor and the chairman of our company." As there was no Internet or Google and I was a novice in the business world, how could I have known? He could have been the local butcher for all I knew. From that point on, I've made it my personal practice to learn everything I could about any individual or organization I'm invited to do business with, both so that I can be more effective and as a show of respect.

In 1988 I got very involved with CBS and their team of professionals, who asked if I could help them figure out how to influence the advertising community. CBS was known at the time as the "Tiffany Network" because of the high quality and style of their programming. However, they had older viewers, and advertisers were paying a lot less for those eyeballs than for young viewers watching other networks. As it turned out, *Time* magazine had the same demographic dynamic. They joined forces and explained to me that they'd like to get the advertising community to understand that the new versions of fifty- and sixty- and seventy-year-olds weren't over the hill but rather still had a lot of middlescence in them, and they were buying all sorts of things, from cars to toothpaste. They asked if Age Wave could envision and craft a four-hour presentation about the maturing marketplace that I'd deliver solo to their top two thousand advertisers in New York, Chicago, and Detroit. I asked why they'd hire me to do this and not Dan Rather or some Harvard professor, and they said, "You have a unique blend of substance and showmanship."

Maddy had been trying to get me to make my presentations more multimedia. She believed that the more senses you could engage, the better. With her help and multimedia production skills, I was stepping up my use of photos and movie clips to help make that happen. Normally for a keynote speech I used around a hundred slides, loaded into a slide carousel, and a few video clips played off a recorder. For this CBS/*Time* assignment, I wanted to push myself and my growing team beyond anything anyone had tried before. We produced a presentation supported by twelve hundred slides and video clips projected from sixteen coordinated projectors. We wanted it to both educate and dazzle.

Around this time, in addition to Bernstein, Rubenstein, and Huret, a few people of power and substance wanted to become involved with Age Wave as board members, advisors, or agents. I welcomed them, as I had so much to learn about everything from accounting and HR to deal negotiating and client management. Some of them turned out to be pleasant, others were ultimately quite unpleasant, but I naïvely welcomed them all and then struggled to keep the good ones and discharge the rest.

While the work on that project was under way, I was growing increasingly troubled by the lack of knowledge about how to medically care for older people. My best buddy at Age Wave was Dr. Bruce Clark, who was trained in public health and was also a master of shenanigans. I always loved working on projects with him because he was massively capable, ingenious, big-hearted, and just plain funny—in the longstanding tradition of the wise-guy school.

Bruce and I imagined creating an educational video curriculum that would focus on geriatric medicine and nursing. At the time there was very little multimedia continuing education: it was a publish-or-perish world. But video learning was on the rise, and there were many top experts eager to get involved. We got connected to the Hospital Satellite Network and their producer, Neil Steinberg, who is still my close friend and producer nearly forty years later. Together we decided to create a twenty-part series that we were going to call *Caring for an Aging Society*. It would be the first geriatric medical and nursing educational curriculum ever produced. We asked Dr. Robert Butler, the Pulitzer Prize–winning geriatrician who served as the founding director of the National Institute on Aging, to be the senior advisor to the entire project. He enthusiastically said yes. Creating and producing a geriatric medical and nursing curriculum was a total stretch for me, but with my human potential mind-set, I thought that if we were determined and found some good mentors, we could do anything. After all, I thought, I did teach myself how to play guitar, do headstands, and write a book. Producing medical educational curricula—maybe it will be a piece of cake. And now that I had learned a bit more about sales, I was ready to try new things, and my growing team was game to try anything.

My advisors suggested I try to find a sponsor for it, maybe a pharmaceutical company that regularly sponsored patient and physician educational materials. They coached me on the idea of selling based on value. What was something like this worth to the sponsor? How could it add to their business image or strengthen their brand? We concluded that since it would cost around $700,000 to produce these programs, we should charge $1 million so that there would be a profit to be shared between Age Wave and the Hospital Satellite Network (HSN). So HSN's chief operating officer, Michael Farmer, and I flew to Kansas to meet with the senior management of Marion Laboratories, a company that I had given some speeches to and whose leaders I liked. The meeting was going really well. They said they loved the idea and they would really like to sponsor the programs. When they asked how much we'd charge them for the whole series, I took a deep breath, and getting a little carried away with the situation, I doubled the number and said, "Two million dollars." They said, "Great, no problem." So we got into the television production business, produced that series, and began reeducating the medical system, one doctor at a time, one nurse at a time, one hospital at a time.

Meanwhile, CBS Television and *Time* magazine were so pleased with their advertisers' reactions to the three large-scale presentations I had developed and presented for them, they circled back to me with another request. They said, "The reaction to your conferences was unlike anything we've ever experienced with our usually set-in-their-ways advertisers. We'd like to hire you to give one of your 'Marketplace 2000' presentations to each of our ten top clients." These happened to be the ten biggest marketers in the country, including Johnson & Johnson, General Motors, Chrysler, Ford, Procter & Gamble, Pepsi, Coca-Cola, and Warner Lambert. I thought about it for about one tenth of a second and said, "Yes, of course!"

To create and produce ten customized presentations, Age Wave hired consumer researchers and multimedia producers. Before long, we had leased an office and gone from Maddy and me and a couple of advisors around our living room table to about twenty-five people—researchers, writers, trainers, business developers, and admins—working for Age Wave. We were on fire. I put out my eighth book, *Age Wave*, in 1989, at the age of thirty-nine, and it really exploded. For some reason the timing was great. I landed on the covers of *Inc.* magazine, *On Wall Street*, *Continental Airlines Magazine*, and *Training & Development Journal* (American Society for Training and Development) and appeared on TV shows from *The Oprah Winfrey Show* and *Good Morning America* to *60 Minutes*. That led to even more opportunities.

During this period, we embarked on one of our most ambitious initiatives. While working on the *Caring for an Aging Society* series geared to clinicians of all stripes, we realized that healthcare systems were mostly asleep at the wheel when it came to developing the right skills, services, and programs to better meet the needs of their aging communities. We partnered with the brilliant healthcare visionary and lawyer Rick Carlson, author of *The End of Medicine*, and speculated that in the future, doctors, hospitals, and insurers were going to need to work more closely together. Because numerous HMOs had approached us about helping them do exactly that, we wondered if we might create a consortium of interested organizations nationwide. We would focus on three areas: (1) aging-readiness organizational strategy, (2) basic geriatric medical training, and (3) patient wellness education. We mentioned this idea to Searle and Merck, both clients of ours. Searle, a smallish company, was indecisive, but Merck was a powerhouse and they indicated they'd be willing to sponsor the whole thing if we could get at least five HMOs to participate and ensure that each HMO's key leadership—including the CEO, CFO, and medical director—participated in the events and activities we'd be producing. They agreed to pay us an attractive annual fee for each participating organization, as long as members of their senior management could also participate, at arm's length, in all the programs. We invited fifty-five HMOs to join us, hoping for five positive responses, and to our astonishment, fifty-four signed up. (It would have been fifty-five, but one of the HMOs was acquired by another during the entrance period.) Under Bruce Clark and Rick Carlson's leadership and with involvement of many of the country's leading experts such as Drs. Bob Butler, Jack Rowe, John Farquhar, and May Wykle, Age Wave's growing team masterminded the summits, conferences, training programs, and wellness resources—including a custom monthly newsletter for each member—that helped transform healthcare systems in almost every part of the country. Nearly 75 percent of all Medicare HMO members nationally were covered by these fifty-four leading organizations, including Blue Cross/Blue Shield, Henry Ford Health System, PacifiCare, United Healthcare, Group Health Cooperative of Puget Sound, Harvard Pilgrim, Cigna, Humana, and Health Net.

When we were sending out letters to invite organizations to participate, I was traveling, and so I dictated the outgoing note to my assistant, Betty Cormier. For some reason, when I said we were calling our project the "Alliance for Health and Aging," she misheard me and instead invited everyone to join the Alliance for Healthy Aging—and while you might find this hard to believe, the new phrase "healthy aging" was inadvertently born, thanks to Betty, in 1990. Over the next several years, as our initiative rolled out, the phrase and our ideas were transported at lightning speed through hospitals, insurers, doctors' offices, and community programs nationwide. These days everyone refers to healthy aging, but it's worth noting that at first, many curmudgeons in both the aging and health fields—particularly academics—protested this phrase, believing that talking about healthy aging would create false hope. We pushed back and insisted that you could be both old and healthy. We completely agreed with Stanford's Dr. Jim Fries's belief in the need for the "compression of morbidity," and through our expanding work we were attempting to introduce a more positive approach to aging. It sure caught on.

Note: Remember my notions about conscious capitalism and how corporations could be high-minded and kindhearted? That proved to be naïve.

Just like some people are kind and supportive and others aren't, so it is with companies. For example, when we established the Alliance for Healthy Aging, all the legal documents clearly stated that this enterprise was conceived and owned by Age Wave. Merck was paying for the right to be the sponsor. The initial sponsorship term was three years. If they wished to continue beyond that term, we'd welcome it and they would have the right do so. It was agreed that they would need to let us know six months prior to the end of the third year. This notice period was critical, because if they were going to bow out, we needed the time to find a replacement sponsor so that all the resources, courses, and conferences as well as all of the participant organizations' rollouts could continue uninterrupted. When the six-month notice date arrived, there was no word from Merck. We sent an enquiring note and were told, "There are no problems, you'll hear back from us soon." A month went by with no word, and then two, and then three—notwithstanding the stream of calls and notes that we and our lawyers were sending to them. With only sixty days before their sponsorship contract was due to end, Merck assured us that we should relax, as everything was going to be okay. The dozen or so Age Wave employees who were staffing this project started getting very nervous, as did I. Was this project, which was going so well, about to blow up? That seemed inconceivable to us, as we trusted Merck's integrity.

Finally, one week before the end of the contracted term and four weeks before the annual Alliance conference with all participating organizations, we received a note from Merck's lawyers informing us that our services were no longer needed and that we were being removed from the "Merck Alliance for Healthy Aging." After ditching us, they intended to continue operating with all our fifty-four clients. They were outright stealing our idea, our program, and our clients.

After we caught our breath, we immediately had our lawyers send them a formal note explaining that what they were proposing was not acceptable or legal. They responded the very next day by lodging a massive lawsuit against Age Wave and me, which was intended to completely shut down our company and bankrupt my family. This was a moment when my Newark background superseded my Esalen point of view. When I was growing up, there were always mean-spirited bullies on the playground and in the neighborhood, ready to beat you up or humiliate you for their own sick gratification. When I was young my dad taught me to never give in to bullies; if you do, they won't stop. So here I was face-to-face with a corporate bully that was every bit as much of an asshole as some of the guys in the neighborhoods of Newark. I had my family, my company, my staff, my honor to defend. And I did.

I immediately called Dick DeSchutter, the chairman/CEO of Searle, and told him exactly what was going on and that we were now shopping for a new sponsor. Two days later, at his request, Rick Carlson and I had a private meeting at O'Hare Airport with Tim Heady, Searle's head of client relations. We swiftly hashed out a win-win agreement. The very next day we notified Merck that they were in breach of our agreement and we were requiring that they "cease and desist" any involvement with *our* Alliance for Healthy Aging. We also told them that their lawsuit had no merit and they could shove it up their asses.

For the record, this was not the only time that a Fortune 500 company tried to bully Age Wave. When this kind of thing happens, it can be painful, even lethal. While there's lots of media attention given to the romance of entrepreneurialism, there's barely ever a mention of the ongoing abuse that small companies often receive when attempting to engage with big ones. While most of the people we have done business with over the years have been decent and honorable, there have been a few bad apples. I also want to say that it's not just corporations who misbehave. Equal time should be given to what it's like to deal with folks in the nonprofit and government sectors. There, too, one can sometimes find dishonest and dishonorable actors.

A lot of my New Age friends believe that key lessons about life will usually be learned through personal reflection. I generally agree, yet I learned so many amazing things from the crucible of business innovation. While some capitalists are greedy knuckleheads, other are ingenious problem solvers. For example, one of our clients during that period was General Motors, who reached out to us because they were hoping to be more successful at selling cars to older women. Specifically, they were hoping to learn how to better engage with America's fourteen million single older women—many of whom had never bought a car, because in that era their husbands had been the car buyers. Under the leadership of GM's head of advertising, Phil Guarascio (who at that time controlled the biggest corporate media spending budget in America), and Age Wave's Leda Sanford, we dreamed up a magazine, which we named *Get Up & Go*, that would be direct-mailed to one million single women age fifty-plus per month. In addition to fun, inspirational, and helpful editorial content, it also contained special promotions for Buick automobiles. The folks at GM told us that the average older woman bought a new car every six years. Since this was a pre-Internet era, we purchased names and addresses from the Department of Motor Vehicles of women over fifty whose cars were five and a half years old. Over the coming months, millions of magazines were sent to these women's homes, but in terms of the initial sales impact, the strategy was a total flop. Why? After doing some more homework, we learned that around half of these women liked the look and feel of a new car and were inclined to buy one every three years. The other half of these women preferred to drive their cars until they could barely function and were inclined to buy a new car every nine years. No one bought a car at six years—and averaging out the three and nine was worthless. We immediately directed the next issues of our magazine to single women over fifty whose cars were either two and a half or eight and a half years old. The sales impact was explosive—and I learned a critical life lesson: averaging anything doesn't always lead to impact— whether its people's social behavior, medical results, sexual preferences, or car-buying schedule.

In the mid-nineties I found I had a knack for imagining what products and services older consumers might need and want. This was curious to me and a lot of fun, as a few years before I had been a bodymind psychologist, then a public gerontologist/speaker/writer. Our business started morphing. Over the next several years, Age Wave's team of professional advisors was brought in to work with many companies and nonprofits that were becoming fascinated by the impact of longevity and changing demographics on their marketplace. For example, Johnson & Johnson's tag line then was "Babies are our business... our only business." We managed a big briefing for their leadership about the age wave. Their chairman at the time, Ralph Larsen, reflected that with the age wave coming, they'd be wise to widen their scope to better meet people's needs at every stage of life. In response, over the next two years, Age Wave put together a team of physicians, biochemists, pharmacists, marketers, and advertisers. We went through every single product in all the Johnson & Johnson companies to show them how to reposition each and every aspect of themselves and/or reformulate their products to be more respectful and more beneficial to older people. Then we did an even deeper dive with one of the Johnson & Johnson companies, McNeil, based in Pennsylvania. They asked what they might do differently, specifically with their highly successful Tylenol product. We said, "Well, you're marketing Tylenol for toothaches and menstrual cramps. That makes good sense. However, since there are more than forty million people in this country with chronic pain, mostly arthritic pain, why not also market it to them? And most of them are over fifty years old."

They said, "While we know that acetaminophen is an effective analgesic, it doesn't have an anti-inflammatory agent in it." We pointed out that the popular anti-inflammatory ibuprofen products, which then were Advil and Motrin, had an unpleasant side effect for many older people—they often upset the gastrointestinal system. Why not develop a version of pain-suppressing Tylenol that would be extended release? And because people with arthritis often have trouble with childproof containers, we proposed that they create a container that would be easy to open for this new product, which would be named Tylenol Arthritis. Within about a year, Tylenol Arthritis became a billion-dollar product and the container was winning design awards and turbocharging the emerging field of universal design.

Our entire team was stoked. Nearly everything we pursued led to either a new product or a new marketing strategy. We were definitely having an impact, and it felt great.

Then we got a call from Chrysler Motors saying, "Mr. Iacocca has taken notice of your ideas about the aging of the population. It's the chairman's job to look to the future. We'd like to send our jet to Oakland Airport and have Dr. Dychtwald come out to talk with Mr. Iacocca about how you could help us envision the future of automobiles."

"When?" I asked.

"Tomorrow," they said. This one rattled me, as Lee Iacocca was a very charismatic, prominent figure. He was already a legend for bringing the Mustang to America, as well as transforming Ford. Now he was taking on his next challenge—rebuilding Chrysler after a massive government bailout—and I wanted to be a part of it. The next day I flew out to Detroit, and after I was escorted into his huge office, Iacocca said to me, "Dykman"—he never got my name right— "these baby boomers, I'm really interested in them. And I'm interested in their parents, too. I'd like to know everything you know about changes in demography and what people think and feel at different stages in their life."

I said, "I'll tell you what, I'll make a deal with you. I'll try my best to do that, but would you be willing to teach me what you know about business—and especially deal making? What it's like working with unions and manufacturers, dealing with shareholders and the media?"

He said, "All right, Dykman, let's do that. You'll come out on the road with me a lot this next year."

Within a few months, I found myself perched alongside Iacocca, his senior managers, and his entourage at numerous press meetings. He was a Detroit, old-school, punch-you-in-the-face kind of guy. For me, it was like being in the Rat Pack. On one of those days I was sitting with him in the greenroom at the Bonaventure Hotel in LA as he was preparing for what turned out to be a big and ornery press conference, during which he totally went off about how the US government was not protecting its automakers from Japanese government–subsidized cars like the new Lexus. To kill time, Iacocca said to me, "These baby boomers are having kids, and they're going to need station wagons, right?"

"Yes," I said, "but I don't think they're going to want station wagons because that's what their mommies had." I explained that the boomers had repeatedly diverted from their parents' choices—like when they bought cars made in Japan and Germany, contributing to the hole that Chrysler, GM, and Ford were still digging out of.

He said, "When I was at Ford, we created a sports utility type vehicle— a minivan—that we're now working to make popular here at Chrysler." Several months later he asked my opinion as to whether I thought Jeeps would be popular with boomers, who were beginning to buy more than one car for their family's different needs.

I told him yes. Many boomers fancied themselves as "off-road" kind of people, and I believed that minivans and Jeeps were both in line with boomer's needs and appetites.

In the coming years, Iacocca's minivans became a mind-boggling success as they pushed most station wagons into the past. I bought one myself. And I currently drive a Jeep Wrangler. Although I was his advisor, he was a potent mentor to me, particularly as I watched him repeatedly investigate what he thought would work and then didn't let anything get in his way. Perhaps even more interesting was all that I was learn-ing from Iacocca. As I stepped into his world, my newfound curiosity about automobile manufacturing, dealing with unions, motivating deal-erships, envisioning the future of transportation, and squaring off with the media surged. And Iacocca seemed to get a kick out of tutoring me on all of it.

Then we got a call from the office of Lou Gerstner, President of American Express. He was a former McKinsey superstar and massively smart. American Express was a unique business conglomerate: a global travel business, a worldwide charge card platform with ties to tens of thousands of retailers, and with IDS insurance, a powerhouse financial-services company. American Express's consumer client base was both wealthier and older than the average credit card user—and their business network included just about everything. Watching him handle his people, new market opportunities, and his shareholders with both honesty and strength, I came to see him as one of the most thoughtful and high-minded business warriors of the modern era—truly a starter on the CEO all-star team. He told me, "I believe that in the future, the biggest changes are going to be driven by information technology and demography. Would you be willing to be my tutor on our changing demography? Maybe we could meet every month or two and discuss both the aging of the world and any other issues you or I find interesting."

I said, "I'd be honored, but only if you agree to help me understand business strategy and how you lead."

We were now a little Age Wave army of talented and dedicated people seeking to change the world. For American Express we tried to formulate a deeper understanding of how the aging of the population was going to impact travel and the charge card business and also financial services. Gerstner was particularly interested in what motivated older consumers to travel, spend, and save. At one point in our discussions he asked for my opinion as to what TV commercials did the best job of portraying men and women over fifty. That was easy. In the mid-1990s there were only three commercials on television that had anyone over fifty in them: Mr. Whipple (Charmin toilet paper), Mrs. Olsen (Folgers coffee), and, hot off his role in *Cocoon*, Wilford Brimley (Quaker Oats). Of those three, only Quaker showed much respect for the older protagonist in the ad.

As we were completing this project, Lou Gerstner got recruited to become the chairman of RJR Nabisco following what was then the biggest leveraged buyout in US history, chronicled in the book *Barbarians at the Gate*. Gerstner brought me into his very first offsite retreat with his new management team. I asked what he wanted me to talk about—the age wave, boomers, old people, what? He said, "Talk about whatever you want. I just want them to see what someone's mind is like when they're not all worried about making their boss happy." I thought that was a very cool, bold request. After my presentation on "How the Age Wave Would Transform the Food, Snack, and Beverage Industry," to his senior managers, he invited me to address a large group of employees at RJR Nabisco's corporate headquarters in New Jersey. While there, he said to me in front of his people, "Let's see if we can together come up with a cookie product for everyone, but particularly appealing for people over fifty who are growing concerned about heart health and weight management."

We assembled a team of nutrition scientists, geriatricians, and food creators and investigated the idea that as people grow older, they still love the taste of cookies but have concerns about how unhealthy cookies can be. Most had too much lard, sugar, and refined carbohydrates, with no nutritional benefits whatsoever. We hypothesized that if you could reduce the negative ingredients and even slightly enrich the positive, maybe you'd have an almost-healthy cookie product. This collaboration led to the invention of SnackWell's, which the following year unseated Oreo to become the number one best-selling cookie in America.

But then Lou called me into his office with an uncomfortable request. "Now I've got something special I want you to do."

I said, "Okay, what's that?"

He said, "I'd like you to go to Winston-Salem to give a speech to one of our companies, the RJR Reynolds tobacco company."

"No way," I said. "I'm not doing that."

"Why not?" he asked. "I'll pay you your full speaking fee."

I told him, "Because I think what goes on in that industry is deadly, it's foul, it should not exist."

He said, "You tell them that. They need to hear this from a well-informed and influential person who has strong feelings about the harm of cigarettes."

This was a prickly decision for me. I have steadfastly drawn a line in all my work to only engage with people, companies and organizations whose morality and approach to market I align with and respect. To all the rest, I have repeatedly said, "No thanks."

In nearly all work, there are moral dimensions to decisions regarding who to help and who to refuse. Within the ecosystem of capitalism, some companies make products that are bad for people, or they market and advertise in ways that are disrespectful to people, or they behave toward their employees or communities in ways that are reprehensible. It's not just companies. There are countless nonprofits and government groups whose mission or purpose I don't align with and have chosen to not work with. And there are confusing crossbreeds: the capitalistic for-profit company that helps make people's lives far better and the nonprofit that rips people off.

My whole life has been oriented toward lifelong health and well-being, and I knew for certain that cigarettes were a key contributor to cancer and heart disease and incredible amounts of costly suffering.

I thought about Gerstner's request long and hard and discussed it with Maddy at length. We decided that I would indeed take the assignment and tell them my truth, unfiltered. So I flew to Winston-Salem, and the morning of my presentation there were crowds of people milling around outside the conference center and wearing little buttons that proclaimed, I'M A SMOKER AND PROUD OF IT. It was a very professional, corporate-seeming group, and nearly everyone, from the company's medical director to the secretaries to the CEO, was smoking a cigarette when they came over to meet me.

By the time I was introduced and took the stage in the auditorium, more than a thousand people had filled the room. I noticed that every seat had an ashtray built into it. For the next hour, while I was lecturing to them about health and the deadly evils of their product, *all* of the attendees smoked their way through my entire talk. I'd never encountered anything like that before—it was insane. I told them, "I'm a wellness guy, I'm a health guy, that's who I am. I see what happens to older people who have smoked cigarettes. What you guys do is murderous. You ought to be outlawed, and you ought to be ashamed of yourselves, causing so much misery in so many lives."

Back then, we used slide projectors to project an image on a big screen on the stage behind me. But as I was talking, big clouds of smoke were billowing up from the audience and distorting the images that we were all looking at. At the end of my presentation I received a respectful ovation from the entire crowd. Maybe they were applauding because I was done, or maybe because they respected my nerve, or maybe because they knew that Chairman Gerstner had sent me. Who knows?

After my session I attended a private lunch in the company's executive dining room with RJ Reynolds's president, executive vice president, and all the senior vice presidents. I had just basically reamed out their company and the whole industry. So now we were sitting at lunch and again they were smoking. I asked, "Are you guys okay with what just happened?"

"Absolutely," they responded.

I probed. "How do you reconcile what you do?"

The president explained to me, "Ken, I see you're pretty suntanned."

I said, "Yes, I am."

"You realize that being out in the sun causes skin cancer?"

I said, "Yes, I know that."

"But you do it anyhow, don't you?"

I said, "Yes I do."

He continued. "Likewise, smoking is legal. It's a legal choice. We're not telling people they must do it. There's no law that says you must be a smoker, but as long as it's legal, people can choose to smoke, even if they know it could do them harm. And if they do, we sure hope they smoke *our* cigarettes."

He then asked me if I'd be open to becoming a paid ongoing consultant to them and help with their marketing and communications."

I said, "No way. Not under any conditions." I finished my lunch, said good-bye, was driven to the airport, and began my journey home.

For the record, I and the Age Wave team have had many opportunities that we have turned down. I have always felt that at the end of the day, I'd have to look myself in the mirror and decide whether I had held true to my core values and principles.

There were many other moments in Age Wave's history when I just couldn't jive with what clients were asking of us and we walked away from the opportunities. For example, in the mid-1990s I got the idea that I might be able to launch a competitor organization to AARP. With millions of boomers passing fifty, it was pretty clear that they felt that AARP was far too fuddy-duddy for them, but they liked the idea of a joining a club that could negotiate great deals for them and publicly advocate on behalf of issues and policies of importance to them.

With the help of a terrific team of Bain consultants, our Age Wave team pieced together a fantastic business plan that would be offering a better operating system for people's busy lives while simultaneously creating a world-class marketing ecosystem with a potentially high market value. We were going to call it Millennium, and it was going to have a cool website and magazine, a travel service, connections to the financial industry through which preferred arrangements on pensions, loans, health, life and property insurance, and LTC policies would be offered. It would offer discounts at many desirable retailers and also be a meeting ground for folks in this new chapter of their lives to engage with other kindred spirits.

I was going to be the public spokesperson, the chairman, and the CEO. Because the idea was so captivating and the two-hundred-page business plan was so compelling, we raised $50 million in capital relatively easily from high-quality firms that would also be provider partners. Everything was going great until I received a joint letter from the legal departments of my three investors/partner companies, saying essentially, "Going forward, should you wish to make any comments about the state of America, or any major consumer or public policy issues, you'll need to have them cleared by our compliance departments first." Basically, they were saying, "Ken Dychtwald, if you take our money, you are no longer free to speak your mind."

Whoa! I hadn't bargained for their intention to put me on a leash—no matter what the potential financial upside. Over the coming days, Maddy and I had many deep discussions about this predicament and decided that I wouldn't be very happy with a muzzle on. So, disappointed, I said, "No thanks, I'm not interested in spending the rest of my life being controlled by your legal departments. Thank you for your interest, but we're done."

I had tried to create something that I believed in, but it didn't work out. I was taking so many risks and interacting with so many new ideas and trying so many things, while some initiatives took off, others floundered or crashed altogether. Life goes on. My life went on.

Over the next few years, because Age Wave and I were being featured a lot in the media as experts on the hopes, dreams, wants, and needs of a new generation of older adults, the calls from prospective clients kept coming. After I appeared a few times on *Good Morning America*, the Wyeth Vitamin Company called and asked, "Would you come and look at what you think the future of vitamins is going to be?" I had been fascinated by the Cycle dog food line, wherein someone clever had come up with the idea that you should formulate dog food based on the weight and age of a dog: a two-month-old Schnauzer probably doesn't need the same nutrients as a fourteen-year-old German shepherd.

After a thoughtful period of research about the nutrient and supplement needs of older bodies, our team said to the scientists at Wyeth, "Maybe you ought to use the Cycle model with vitamins. Maybe you ought to come up with a line of vitamins that's formulated for older bodies—to help them be healthier, more vital, more potent, more resilient." In a way it would be like a modern version of Geritol, but that product was clearly fuddy-duddy, so we suggested calling it Centrum Silver.

In fact, the success of that product proved the points that we had been making for a long time: an aging population was emerging; one that demanded respect and took its health seriously.

AGE WAVE'S ATTEMPTED TRANSFORMATION

*There are no secrets to success. It is the result of preparation,
hard work, and learning from failure.* —Colin Powell

I was on a roll. Age Wave was on a roll. We had gone from Maddy and me and a few advisors to nearly one hundred people. Our team was very talented, and we were excited that we were putting good ideas to work and bringing out products and services that could help older adults be more mobile, secure, informed, included, and respected. Our clients ranged from the Hearing Industries Association to the Magazine Publishers Association to the International Spa Association to more than fifty health insurance companies.

During those years, like many other women of her cohort, when Maddy was being an attentive mom she was stressing out over the impact on her professional identity. When she was hard at work at the office or on the road giving speeches, she was stressed out about being away from the kids. Maddy decided that she would try to create a more balanced work-life arrangement and became a flextime worker for Age Wave. While being a nearly full-time mom, busy shuttling the kids to swim team and public speaking practice, she hammered out her first book, *Cycles: How We'll Live, Work and Buy*, which won the Book of the Year award from the American Association of Community Colleges. As a successful entrepreneur, writer, public speaker—and as our kids would say, "badass mom"—Maddy has been a role model to legions of young women. At the same time, like many men of my cohort, I was trying my best to be a dad deeply involved in the lives of my children. I loved them and loved being there for them in any way I could. But our overhead had multiplied, and a bit like my dad before me, I needed to make sure the bills were all paid and that Age Wave continued to flourish. So I pressed on with the business while trying always to remain involved in the lives of my kids. I tried to never be on the road longer than three to four days and always kept my schedule clear for birthdays, family gatherings, and special school events.

Juggling the pieces of my life wasn't easy, but I didn't want to be an uninvolved father like my dad had been. I wanted to be deeply connected to Casey and Zak at every step in their lives. I still do, and I still am.

But then people started asking, "If you were involved in the development of that car or that vitamin..." "If it was your idea that led to that product..." "Do you own a piece of that?" "Centrum Silver is a billion-dollar product now. Do you own any of that?" The answer across the board was "No, we don't. We were paid respectable consulting fees, but we received no ownership participation." My response was met with furrowed brows. Some folks even said, "If you leveraged your knowledge and time better, you could work less, have more time with your family, impact more people, and make more money." Lots of investor-type business-people told me their own version of the Harland Sanders success story. He famously said, "If you'd like to franchise my special recipe for Kentucky fried chicken, just give me a nickel for every piece of chicken you sell."

This all made me curious. Maybe I wasn't doing things the smartest way? Why were we giving our ideas away for a mere consulting fee? Why didn't we raise capital and create our own businesses?

That piece of curiosity almost killed this cat.

AGE WAVE, THE BUSINESS INCUBATOR
GOOD IDEA, BAD TIMING

Observe due measure, for right timing is in all things the most important factor.
—Hesiod

In 1995, the year Microsoft launched Internet Explorer and Sony its first iteration of PlayStation, and when Maddy and I were forty-five, Casey was eight, and Zak was five, Age Wave made a hard-right turn and changed itself from a fee-for-service public speaking and consulting firm to a venture-capital-based business-development incubator. I became a beginner again and started asking accountants, entrepreneurs, investors, professors, and friends, "How do you make your own products or businesses?" I was told, "First you need to target an unmet market need. Then you need a terrific business idea and thoughtful business plan with aspirational but achievable financial projections. You'll need a first-rate leadership team at the helm, and you'll need rounds of capital to fuel your growth." I thought, that sounds doable.

In our new corporate brochure, we shared that Age Wave was transforming from a caterpillar to an assortment of butterflies. Structurally, we took Age Wave, Inc. and turned it into an LLC. The first company we spun off was called Age Wave Communications. Why? At that time, we had noticed that local senior magazines were popping up across the country and appealing to advertisers such as HMOs, banks, and grocery/drug stores that were trying to reach people over fifty. There was one in Sacramento, three in LA, two in San Diego, one in San Antonio, one in Portland, one in Saint Louis, two in Miami, and four in New York. All of them had lots of local advertisers and were writing very similar articles. Why not roll them up and thereby have a national media platform that could attract both local and national advertisers, using common national editorial content blended with timely local content? (I hadn't even known what a roll-up was the year before.)

I raised around $10 million to do this, and then Paul Robershotte, the senior partner at Bain who had overseen the writing of the business plan for this company, was so taken by what we were about to do that he jumped ship from Bain to become president and CEO of Age Wave Communications. Paul was former military—Army Corps of Engineers— and a Harvard graduate with one graduate degree from MIT and another from Harvard. He was smart, conscientious, solid. Under his leadership, we began buying and rolling up senior newspapers and magazines all over the country. In each case, we changed the name from *Senior this* and *Senior that* to *Get Up & Go,* and we were on a tear. With the roll-ups came employees and offices in San Diego, Saint Louis, Portland, Denver, New York, Miami, and many more cities. Suddenly we were becoming the second-most-read fifty-plus-oriented media platform behind AARP's *Modern Maturity.* Just like in the movies, we put a floor-to-ceiling map on the wall of our conference room and every time we'd acquire another magazine in a different part of the country, we'd put a little flag on the map.

We also rolled up retirement-expo businesses. There were different companies putting on multiday retirement expos in different parts of the country, and we decided to merge them with our magazine platform. We got both local advertisers and some big brand-name national advertisers. The expos began attracting tens of thousands of older men and women. Maybe it was the great seminars that were offered, or the hundreds of sponsored booths with lots of free samples. Or maybe it was because we got Richard Simmons to speak at many of them—he was absolutely loved by the attendees. Within Age Wave Communications, we were now in the publishing and expo businesses.

Then we asked ourselves, What about retail stores? We'd learned a lot from our consulting projects with Kmart, Eckerd Drugs, Lucky Stores, and Kroger Stores. We thought, There's got to be an Age Wave retail play. Out of left field, the number two executive at Kmart, a young, hard-driving man named Kevin Browett, reached out to us and said, "If you guys ever want to make a business creating a national chain of home health and self-care stores, I'm your man to head it up." He quit Kmart, and we ambitiously started a company called MedMax. It was going to be a national chain of 20,000-square-foot stores, and its focus was going to be wellness, mobility, pharmacy, nutrition, supplements, homeopathy, healthy apparel, and aids to daily living. It was going to be the first "big box" health store in the world.

We headquartered MedMax in Detroit, where Kevin lived, and he swiftly recruited a talented management team. Because it takes a lot of capital to lease and build out retail stores, Browett and I were out raising tens of millions of dollars. He envisioned a magnificent health-oriented retail environment and then built one in Detroit, then another in the greater Detroit area, then one in Philadelphia, then another in a different part of Pennsylvania, and so on, until we had ten megastores. The idea behind MedMax and the speed with which we were growing created quite a stir in the retail world. It started landing on covers of retail magazines. For example, the headline of the October issue of *Crain's Detroit Business* proclaimed: MEDMAX INC. GETS PARTNER, PLANS TO ADD 15 SUPERSTORES."

Around the same time, some of our clients were bemoaning their advertising agencies' poor understanding of men and women over fifty. So we said, "Let's build a fifty-plus-oriented marketing and advertising company and call it Age Wave Impact." In our executive search, our CEO, Bart Penfold, found a terrific guy named Bill Burkart, who said he would be willing to leave his position running a big database marketing company in Illinois and relocate his family to the Bay Area. We raised tens of millions of dollars in capital and swiftly hired more than a hundred people. We had our own creative team, art directors, writers, and salespeople and took over nearly an entire floor of our modern office building in Emeryville, with a satellite office in New York and a branch office in Tokyo. To round out its offerings we then acquired a full-service call center in Louisville, Kentucky.

Then we said, "What about the food industry? It's totally youth-and young-family-focused. There's got to be a fifty-plus-oriented breakthrough opportunity in that sector." We envisioned a line of natural, organic, delicious meals that would be clinically proven to make you healthier if you had diabetes or heart disease. The chief operating officer of Kellogg, Jonathan Wilson, quit to become our CEO. Eric Bjerkholt, the head of healthcare investment banking at JP Morgan, quit to become our chief financial officer, and John Hale, who ran operations for Frito-Lay, quit to become our head of operations. We raised tens of millions of dollars and created a company called Life Source Nutrition. It was delicious, organic, health-promoting "real" food with no artificial preservatives, delivered directly to people's homes. In partnership with the SCAN health system, a pioneering social HMO in Southern California, we even ran clinical trials that proved that our foods actually improved health. This was long before home delivery of meals became a thing and long before "food as medicine" became the hottest trend in wellness.

There's one more venture. I had become a pro bono strategic advisor to the Alzheimer's Association, and it was painfully obvious that there were scientists in different parts of the world doing very interesting things, but they were not well connected to quickly optimize their collective work. In response, we created a company named Tithon—after the Greek warrior Tithonus, who was granted immortality but not lifelong health. One of Age Wave's co-founders and board members was Dr. Jim Bernstein, a Harvard-trained physician, entrepreneur, cellist, and painter. He left his other work responsibilities to head up Tithon along with Dr. Zaven Khatchiturian, head of Alzheimer's research for the National Institute on Aging. The idea was that we were going to secure the intellectual property to anything and everything important that had to do with diseases of the aging brain. We'd have a virtual intellectual-property company and thereby speed up all the progress toward beating Alzheimer's, Parkinson's, and dementia.

Obviously, to make all these things happen, we needed capital—lots of it, round after round. Along with the CEOs of each of our five different companies, I went out to various investment groups and strategic investors and all together we raised about $100 million. Some of the money went to our holding company, which had a piece of all the different subsidiaries, but most of those funds went to one of the individual companies. In addition to Age Wave LLC, we had launched five different companies within three years. We went from about 150 people to more than 1,000. Our floor-to-ceiling map now showed offices and branches and businesses all over the country (and Japan). During this period, I continued to try my best to be a loving husband and involved dad. I was zooming back and forth between board meetings and swim meets, store openings and birthday parties. I was reviewing business plans and homework assignments. It was exhilarating—but it was exhausting, too.

And I was so caught up in the thrill of "growth" that I didn't see the really dark clouds that were starting to gather.

MY TWO FAVORITE TEACHERS

Children are our most valuable resource. —Herbert Hoover

Although there is much I have learned from my parents, Maddy, the elders in the SAGE Project, and various gurus and wise souls, my two absolutely favorite teachers are my kids, Casey and Zak. When they were little, I couldn't get enough of watching them play with their friends, learn, eat, laugh and to my delight and surprise, while they were sleeping peacefully I learned how much love a parent could feel for his children. I have particularly enjoyed comparing their youthful experience of life to mine and learning from their experiences.

For example, after Zak was born in 1990, I thought it would be a good idea if three-and-a-half-year-old Casey and I had some sort of special activity she and I could enjoy together. We decided to build a vegetable garden. First we cleared an area beside our home for planting. Then we turned and fertilized the soil and allowed it to settle. Finally, after days of preparation, Casey and I donned our overalls, armed ourselves with shiny gardening equipment, and marched off to plant our magical new garden.

We carefully dug small holes in nearly straight lines into which we dropped seeds—lettuce, tomato, squash, spinach, cucumber, and pepper. When we finished planting, I took a few more minutes to clean up and then walked into the house for a shower and a nap. I woke up around four in the afternoon, and Maddy asked me if I knew what Casey was up to. I said I hadn't seen her since we finished planting the vegetable garden early that afternoon. We looked out our bedroom window and saw her sitting quite still on a tree stump in the middle of the dirt area we had just planted.

Feeling touched that she was so entranced by our gardening efforts, I went to the garden to join her. I asked her what she was up to. She replied, "What do you think I'm doing? I'm waiting for the vegetables to come up. I want to eat them for dinner." Note: Although she's now thirty-three,

Casey still leans in this same direction with her expectations about nearly everything, from boyfriends to work tasks. Through her unbridled enthusiasm for everything she explores, Casey consistently reminds me that radical curiosity is often accompanied by a sense of urgency—like an itch that absolutely demands to be scratched, *now*.

When Casey left home to study communications at USC's Annenberg School, her encounters with entrepreneurs and LA creatives served as a continual hookup for me to have a finger on the pulse of Tomorrowland. I simply couldn't get enough of her views and crazy stories about the modern iteration of sex, drugs, and rock and roll in the LA scene. Then, when she became global head of productions for the Creators Project, a partnership between Intel and Vice Media, I sponged up her and her friends' insights about the emerging intersection of technology, media, and fashion and how young people in Brazil, South Korea, China, France, and the United States viewed life differently.

More recently, when she took a break from working to get her master's degree in global communications from the London School of Economics, she became my tutor on the new frontiers of digital communications, with social media swiftly replacing traditional communications and advertising. We have had countless discussions about millennials' tragic addiction to the new digital domains—with the fear of mission out, usually referred to as FOMO driving their lives—but also about how these young "digital natives" think, feel, and reason differently than "digital immigrants" like me. On a pop-culture level, Casey continually schools me on the genius, madness, and popularity of such music stars folks as Childish Gambino, Billie and Finneas Eilish, Megan Thee Stallion, Cardi B, and Kanye West. Without Casey's tutelage, I'd be missing out on a big chunk of modern life.

On a deeper level, from Casey I have learned how to be a father to a powerful, complicated young woman who demands that I be authentic and growing all the time. She'll accept nothing less from me—and I love her so much for that.

And then there's. I truly can't imagine going through this life without including the crazy mix of curiosities and learnings I've encountered with Zak. And more than with anyone else, Zak and I have been "menterns" when it comes to providing hard-core feedback and life coaching for each other. But we've had to learn how to do that. It wasn't anywhere in the user's manual. For example, when he was around twelve years old, he was trying out for a community basketball team that lots of the neighborhood kids were hoping to make. I had gone to watch a few of the tryouts, and it sure seemed to me that Zak was goofing around a lot and not playing as well or trying as hard as many of the other kids. I was not impressed with his commitment or effort.

After the try-outs ran their course, Zak was eagerly awaiting a call from the coach to let him know if he had made the cut or not. When Coach Williams called to tell him that he had, indeed, made the team. Zak was elated and I was surprised. He wanted to know what I thought about that. I asked him, "Do you want the touchy-feely version of my reaction, or the man-to-man version?"

Hesitantly, he said, "Give it to me man-to-man."

So I told him, "I honestly don't think you deserve to be on the team. You didn't work hard enough, and it doesn't seem right or fair to me." I then asked him what he thought about my reaction.

He said, "I should have asked for the touchy-feely version."

Years later, when I asked grown-up Zak to read through an early draft of this sort-of-memoir and provide any and all feedback, he called and asked if I was ready to hear his observations—as a son, a guy who had studied literature at Columbia and is himself a respected author, I told him, yes, I was eager to hear his feedback. Then he asked me, "Do you think you can handle the man-to-man version, or would you prefer to hear the touchy-feely version?"

I swallowed hard and told him, "Man-to-man."

He did not hold back when he proceeded to constructively blowtorch nearly every aspect of this book. I needed around a month to regain my wits, but I then rewrote much of the book, based on Zak's insights and suggestions.

When he was in high school, each year we took one-on-one vacations— to do something he wanted to do. (I did the same with Casey, and Maddy took one-on-ones with each of the kids too. If you have kids and you're curious about them and want them to open up to you, I totally recommend this approach.) On one of those grand adventures, Zak and I joined a group that was rafting down the Colorado River in the Grand Canyon. One night as we lay on our sleeping bags and stared up at the billions of stars in which our own galaxy was swirling, we shared our deepest views about life, death, God, and transcendence. Some folks have workout or golf partners; in Zak I have found a fantastic radical curiosity partner.

However, I need to also admit that because I'm his dad, as he has grown up his decisions haven't always been easy for me to take. For example, after he graduated from Columbia, he announced to Maddy and me that since the future was going to have a lot to do with China, he was going to move there and try to figure it out. We were rattled by this pronouncement and terrified that we were about to lose our boy to Communist China. We reminded him that he didn't speak the language, he didn't know anyone there, and he didn't have any money. He told us that these were all things he was prepared to handle—and he did. Over the next seven years, while he was initially sleeping on the floor in tenements with no heat or hot water, then traveling thousands of miles of countryside on trains while attempting to pierce the wall between East and West, Maddy and I were in a continual state of anxiety. Following his early struggles in China, Zak went on to thrive there. What emerged from those years was a Mandarin-fluent, self-confident expert on Young China, which is also the name of the book he wrote, which received incredible reviews and has already made a global impact.

During the past few years, as the mash-up between East and West has intensified, Zak has shared his thoughts with interested leaders, companies, and governments on five continents. I am continually learning from him about the mind and heart of the new China that is emerging on the world stage. And because of his multirooted identity, he forces me to try harder to assume different and sometimes differing perspectives when considering any geopolitical issue—especially America's recent screw-ups, and more generally America's place—on the world stage.

On a deeper level, from Zak I am learning how to be a father to a powerful, driven young man who demands that I not be self-delusional and that I try my best to be open-minded all the time. And as he and his girlfriend, Fey Fey, don't wish to settle down, I am also being forced to learn how to both love and let go—maybe the most difficult part of parenthood I have encountered yet.

Why do I say that Casey and Zak are my favorite teachers? Because they are both so curious, so intent on making something of themselves, and because they live such adventuresome lives. I've also learned so much about myself from the intense disagreements and fights I've had with both of my kids. Casey has been attracted to some very edgy people, places, and substances, which has taken Maddy and me to our wits' end—and a few times to the police department. Zak likes to position himself on the edge of comfort, sanity, and legality—which has also taken Maddy and me to our therapist and to the police department more than once. But because of our family's commitment to stick together and have one another's backs, we're better together than apart (even if we're thousands of miles away). And thanks to our emotional proximity, through their eyes, minds, and hearts, I get to savor their millennial mind-sets, stay at least somewhat current with popular tech, language, and angst, and learn about subjects from Tibetan Buddhism to why Charli D'Amelio is the most popular influencer on TikTok.

Our kids have also played roles in several of our remarriages. For example, in 2000, after years of getting married in different religions and different places, I was in a funk and we decided to try a different approach. We asked our kids to do it. Casey and Zak were thirteen and ten, and they got to work conjuring up vows. We all flew down to Zihuatanejo, Mexico, and our kids prepared thoughtful speeches and prayers they had written especially for us. That one was especially powerful, as our marriage had led to the birth of these colorful kids and now they were standing in front of us telling us how to be better mates. And they didn't pull any punches. If you have children, I totally recommend having your child or children marry or remarry you—and be ready for some sage advice.

Then, a few years ago, we had a doozy of a wedding in which Casey and Zak played a role. After hearing for decades about the splendor of African safaris, because of work we were doing in the travel industry we were invited to take a hosted family safari in Kenya. The experience was otherworldly. Here we were on the Masai Mara surrounded by hundreds of giraffes, thousands of zebras, mighty lions napping not far from baby rhinos nursing, and herds of elephants in the distance. We were witness to natural collaboration and simple coexistence, with every animal and plant sharing land and light and water and resources. Everything was interconnected in a very precise way—an ecosystem teeming with life.

Knowing that Maddy and I were hoping to get remarried there in a local ceremony of some sort, our guide and a Masai tracker surprised us by driving the four of us out to a primitive Masai village. We got out of our Jeep, and four male elders appeared in native attire to welcome us. They were tall, very black, and had their ears carved so that they hung to their shoulders. And they were all missing their two front teeth, as was the custom in their tribe. Before we even knew what was happening, they covered us in traditional garb. Maddy was given a crown, and I was given a warrior's staff and an animal-skin robe. Then the entire village of around a hundred beautiful and traditionally clad Masai men, women, and children converged on us with everyone singing and hopping, and the wedding dance began on a field covered in cow dung. Our kids couldn't stop cracking up. We all loved that crazy and fantastic wedding.

PART IV

BEING IN THE ROOM
WHERE IT'S HAPPENING

What is power and how do you gain it?

·

For that matter, what is success, and do its ingredients shift as we age?

·

Do powerful people see and do things differently?

·

Who are their role models?

·

Who are your role models—and why?

·

How does influence work? Is there a secret "deep state"
cabal running the world?

·

Are Presidents the same as the rest of us, or different?

INTENTION, WILL, AND DRIVE
A LESSON FROM THE TERMINATOR

It had long since come to my attention that people of accomplishment rarely sat back and let things happen to them. They went out and happened to things.
—Leonardo da Vinci

After *Bodymind* was published and the SAGE Project had gained some recognition, in 1977 I was invited to speak at a conference at Harvard, titled something like "The Future of the Mind and Body." At that point, the whole holistic thing was way out at the farthest fringe of both psychology and medicine, so it was quite surprising that such a subject had made its way to Cambridge, Massachusetts. At that moment in my life, I found that one of the benefits of achieving some acclaim was that I got to meet all sorts of interesting people. Whether it was college-sponsored events, private CEO gatherings, or even the top-of-the-power-food-chain World Economic Forum in Davos, Switzerland, there are most definitely orbits and ecosystems where the world's powerful, influential, and often wealthy individuals learn, teach, and wonder. Some of the folks I've met and befriended have been other authors, a few were famous scientists and philosophers, and I've met a football team full of retired generals and political leaders. However, I never did discover a secret cabal with mysterious handshakes, and nefarious deep-state plots.

As the date for the Harvard conference grew near, I received an invitation to join an intimate, preconference dinner at the home of David and Rose Thorne. They were close friends of Peggy Taylor, the publisher of *New Age Journal*. Peggy and her boyfriend, Rick Ingrasci—a thoughtful New Age physician (one of the first)—hosted the dinner with the Thornes, what today would be called a salon.

I flew from San Francisco to Boston a day early to be a part of what I was hoping would be a fun dinner party and a historic conference. The guests at dinner were a most unusual cast of characters. Michael Murphy, the legendary founder of Esalen, was there with his fascinating wife and partner, Dulce. During that period, they were deeply involved in the study of extraordinary mental and physical powers in both the United States and the Soviet Union. Olga Worrall, a mysterious elderly psychic from Eastern Europe, was present. And I was delighted to meet Dr. Itzhak Bentov, the quantum physicist who had just written the book *Stalking the Wild Pendulum*, about the relationship between physics and consciousness. I didn't know what David and Rose Thorne did. It would have been a lot easier had Google been available back then! (As I write this, I just Googled them, and it turns out that David Thorne roomed with John Kerry at Yale, served in the navy during the Vietnam War, and went on to become a successful businessman and diplomat serving for a while as the US ambassador to Italy.)

Dinner began, and various otherworldly discussions started to swirl. It was turning into a wonderful gathering. Then, with a smile, David announced that a special guest was going to be showing up after dinner to join the discussion about mind and body, but he wouldn't tell us who it was. "It will be a surprise we hope you'll all enjoy," Rose added.

Around nine o'clock, as we were finishing a delicious dinner and enjoying the lively discussions, the doorbell rang. David and Rose got up to open the door, and who was standing there but Arnold Schwarzenegger. Dressed in slacks and a short-sleeve button-down shirt, with muscles a-bulging, he was big, and beaming ear to ear.

Pumping Iron had recently been released and received so much attention that everyone at the dinner party had seen it and knew who Schwarzenegger was. *Pumping Iron* was an extremely well-crafted documentary about a young, charismatic bodybuilder, big dreamer, and smooth talker—albeit with a thick Austrian accent. With this movie, the odd world of bodybuilding was brought out of the shadows. Back then, it was generally believed that bodybuilders were all weird and/or dumb. You might be thinking about how you feel about Arnold Schwarzenegger <u>today</u> and his more recent fall from grace. Forget that for a few minutes, please, and allow me to tell you this story about Arnold <u>then</u>. This was a long time ago. In *Pumping Iron*, we learned that Arnold had come over from Austria with nothing but his body and his will, and through hard work, drive, discipline, and focus, he had sculpted his body to perfection. And then he messed with everybody's heads in the highly competitive Mr. Universe competition—and won.

And there he was in the flesh, introducing himself to each of us with his smirky smile and his barely intelligible English. The Thornes then said, "Why don't we go to the living room and have dessert? We're going to turn on a tape recorder, and let's just see what comes of our group's discussion." As we all relocated to comfy couches in the living room, Arnold jumped right into the discussion. It was immediately obvious to all of us that he was exceptionally smart, mischievous, and charming to the max.

Over the next several hours Arnold and I became intensely involved in a head-on discussion about the relationship between the mind and body. (This discussion was recorded and transcribed and published as the cover story, titled "Powers of Mind," in the January 1978 issue of *New Age Journal*.) Of course, I did not have any of the fame or chops that Arnold had—not even a fraction. But I was doing everything I could to try to understand the Eastern and Western approaches to consciousness and the body. And besides, I was an author about to speak at Harvard, so what the hell.

Maybe I was going out on a limb, but I pressed him with all sorts of questions that had been swirling in my head for years. "Does form follow function, or the other way around?" "Can you alter your body through visualization?" "Is your mind fully embodied?" "Is there 'mind' that goes beyond 'body'?"

Schwarzenegger explained that bodybuilding wasn't just about lifting weights. It was about seeing and envisioning what you wanted those muscles to be and then doing the work to get them there. He said it was far more sculpting than weight-lifting. His notion of working out was "about grace, flow, and the integration of consciousness," which had allowed him to drop to deeper and deeper levels inside himself.

Schwarzenegger told us that the mind focused and sculpted becomes the body. He explained how he first envisioned what he intended and then did the hard work to bring it about. He reflected on his life: "When I was very young, I visualized myself being there already—having achieved the goal already. Mentally I never had any doubt in my mind that I would not make it. I always saw myself as kind of the finished product—out there—and it was just a matter of following through physically. It makes it so easy, because then when you work out four hours a day, you don't question yourself. What am I doing here? It's just, Oh yeah, that's why I'm there four hours, to get a step closer."

I asked him, "How can anybody spend four hours a day lifting weights in a gymnasium and not get bored?"

He laughed. "Well, how can anybody spend eight hours a day in an office and not get bored? It would drive me crazy."

I pressed him further. "Is feeling good just pleasure from having done the activity, or do you think there is actually something physiological that happens in the body from lifting?"

He responded, "Yes, bodybuilding does relieve a lot of stress, and I think there's a lot of pleasure in that. Also, you begin to realize you have an enormous command over your body. Just imagine, you get so you can move each individual muscle. I think you gain a lot of self-confidence by having so much command over yourself, over your body, and that, again, is a reflection of your mind and it carries over a kind of confidence into a lot of other areas of your life, so it has enormous value."

I thought of *Pumping Iron* again. I'd always had the image of weight lifters being muscle-bound. But in the film, while some of the competitors were very awkward, some—such as Arnold—had a sense of grace and ease, a sense of comfort in their bodies that changed my perception of his world.

He smiled and said, "For me, it's like dance; dancers are really the most beautiful people to watch. I watched Nureyev last Saturday. I'm absolutely fascinated by the fact that the guy is really a relatively small, skinny guy, but when he walks and moves, you feel that power is walking and moving. When he talks, his head is up and proud. And when he dances, well, I'm always very impressed with him. He is one of my most influential role models."

I asked him if he felt there were any limits to what the mind could do with the body. He said, "The mind is the limit. We know now that it's not the body. As long as the mind can envision the fact that you can do something, you can do it—as long as you really believe one hundred percent."

I was curious about this. "If it is the mind that keeps people from going any further, what, then, keeps the mind from going any further? What keeps us from having larger images? What keeps us from expanding ourselves?"

Schwarzenegger responded, "I think most people only think of getting through everyday life, and they fall into a pattern. But if you could make them aware that there is the possibility of raising this level and going beyond it, maybe they would try to go a step beyond where they are now."

As the night unfolded, our group discussion continued to wind its way through Eastern religion, Hindu philosophy, spiritual practices, mysticism, and supernatural sports performance. We were all impressed by his reflections and insights. No one wanted the discussion to end, and no one wanted to leave. Around midnight, I offhandedly said to Arnold, "So let's assume you'll keep winning these bodybuilding contests. Is that the end game for you? What are you going to do after you've won Mr. Universe a bunch of times?"

He thought for a moment, and then in his thick Austrian accent said, "After I win a few more Mr. Universes, I'm going to become the biggest movie star in the world." Thinking he was joking, we all cracked up. This big, muscle-bound guy had never acted. He could barely speak English. He hardly had the look of a screen idol, especially from this era of *Easy Rider* and *Annie Hall*.

I responded, "Really? The biggest movie star in the world?" We all laughed some more at the pure absurdity of his proposition. "Okay," I said, "and what about after that?"

In a heartbeat, he answered, "After I become the biggest movie star in the world, I'll go into politics. Maybe I'll become the governor of California." It was so preposterous, everyone in our group politely rolled their eyes as an otherwise interesting dialogue had turned a little silly. That was the cue for our evening to wind down.

In the years following that night in Boston, I watched Arnold Schwarzenegger from afar as he actually became the biggest movie star in the world. And he didn't just make muscle movies, such as *Conan the Barbarian*. He starred in some of the greatest and most thoughtful science-fiction movies ever made: *Terminator*, *Predator*, and *Total Recall*. And he became a great comedic actor in hits such as *Twins* with Danny DeVito and then *Kindergarten Cop* and *True Lies*. It was amazing. I watched as he became part of the Kennedy family when he married Maria Shriver, and things started falling into place. When he ran for governor of California, I knew he would win.

Young people often ask me, what do I think is the primary ingredient of success? Is it hard work? Is it your genes? Is it where you got your diploma? Of course, all these variables matter, but I believe it's a combination of vision, will, and drive—and of course, some good luck. This is what I have repeatedly tried to do with my personal and professional life. In this regard, Arnold has served as an unlikely but inspiring role model for me. If you want things to happen for you, you need to know what you want, and like Arnold, you need to be able to say it—and then pursue it—with confidence, regardless of how many people roll their eyes at you.

WHAT PRESIDENT REAGAN TAUGHT ME ABOUT AMERICA

Leadership is a potent combination of strategy and character. But if you must be without one, be without the strategy. —Norman Schwarzkopf

As I gained some more recognition as an author and as what used to be called an "idea guy" and then came to be called a "thought leader," I got to meet more and more powerful people. On February 6, 1990, Maddy and I found ourselves sitting within a few feet of Ronald Reagan, who was addressing an intimate group of fifty or so. February 6 also happened to be the former president's seventy-ninth birthday. We had been invited to a private island in the Bahamas for a four-day think tank focused on "understanding the future," and the former president and I were both on the faculty.

After lunch was served on an outdoor patio on a balmy Caribbean day, his birthday cake arrived, and we all joined in singing a rousing rendition of "Happy Birthday." The former president seemed to be in very good spirits as he posed for pictures with each of us. As Maddy and I stood beside him, I was struck both by his larger-than-life charisma and by the all-too-human frailty of an elderly man.

As we took our seats, we were informed that President Reagan would first deliver an informal speech on a variety of domestic and international issues. When he finished, we would be able to ask him a wide range of questions.

I was in my late thirties at the time, and Reagan was the first president I had ever met. Sitting with a small group of extraordinarily powerful and interesting men and women, I was going to participate in a private, no-holds-barred discussion with one of the most influential world leaders of the modern era. However, while he was completing his talk, Reagan's assistants discreetly handed out prepared questions to each of us on three-by-five-inch index cards. Apparently, the former president preferred to be asked questions to which he already knew the answers.

It's not my nature to go along with such prepackaged protocol. So, after he responded "astutely" to a handful of prepared questions, I raised my hand to catch his attention, which wasn't too hard to do, since Maddy and I were sitting directly in front of him, only about seven to eight feet away.

He selected me. I took a moment to stand up and face him, with respect. Although I hadn't voted for Reagan and had issues with some of his political and economic policies, I must admit that when he turned to talk to me, I immediately felt engulfed by his legendary gravitas. I steadied myself, took a deep breath, and asked, "Mr. President, as a long-lived American, and as a prominent leader of Americans, I imagine that you've given a great deal of thought to what makes us and our country special. Could you share your feelings and thoughts about this?"

He wore a slightly pained look as he realized that I was not working off the cue cards. Nevertheless, and to his credit, after first taking a moment to reflect and then fastening his eyes on me, he said, "Well, Ken, I have been thinking about that very question myself lately. Here is what I think makes America the greatest country in the world. In this day and age, you and your wife could move to Brazil, but in so doing you wouldn't ever be considered Brazilian. If you moved to Japan and spent the rest of your life there, and even became fluent in the language and culture, you'd never be accepted as Japanese. Similarly, if you chose to live and work in France, and even raised your family there, the French would surely never think of you as a Frenchman. But *anyone* who moves to America from countries like these and gains citizenship can become an *American*!"

A deep silence fell over our group as we all realized we had just heard something profound.

I was so moved by the clarity and passion of Reagan's extraordinary response that I may have only imagined his eyes welling up with emotion, but I was transfixed. He went on to say that in our nation, people from every conceivable religion, race, political persuasion, ethnic background, and nationality have joined together to undertake a historic social experiment: the creation of a living, breathing democracy—from scratch. And to raise the ante, we were doing so by capitalizing on the combined resources, creativities, experiences, and values of a truly diverse mixture of humanity.

In what felt like another dramatic moment, he said: "The other thing that I particularly appreciate about America is that in nearly all the nations of the world, each of their *constitutions* tell their *people* what they can do. In ours, the *people* tell the *government* what it can do."

When he finished, a hush fell over our group once again Democrats and Republicans alike let sink in the insightfulness of President Reagan's reflections and the intensity with which he was feeling them. While the idea of patriotism generally fascinates me, I'm put off when people use twisted versions of it as a self-aggrandizing contrivance.

In my everyday life I tend to spend a good deal of my time with professional cynics. Reagan was different. His love for America was pure, almost spiritual. As the president shared these comments with me and our group, it was apparent that he didn't just *believe* in America, he genuinely *loved* America.

With this encounter with Reagan, I also took note of the new territory that my networks of connections had begun to take me into—my world of influentials no longer comprised just psychologists, gerontologists, authors, and CEOs but increasingly included political leaders. Ultimately, I have, to date, met with five U.S. presidents. And perhaps because of what I was learning from all these encounters, I inched forward to try to become more of an influencer myself.

THE "GREATEST GENERATION" LOOKS TO THE FUTURE

THE 1995 WHITE HOUSE CONFERENCE ON AGING

Life is being on the wire, everything else is just waiting. —Karl Wallenda

On the night of May 4, 1995, I found myself in an odd, important, and truly uncomfortable situation. I was in Washington, DC, and I was about to address the three thousand delegates at the White House Conference on Aging on the last night of a five-day gathering. These delegates were outspoken, activist seniors who were chosen to participate in days of speeches, workshops, debates, speak-outs, and voting to decide the right road to an aging policy for the United States in the twenty-first century.

President Clinton was the keynoter that afternoon. He was thought-provoking and charming—but he was also kowtowing to the crowd every chance he had. He knew that older adults were the number one voting bloc in America. Who was the president? He was. But who had the power? They did. As a side note, I was dazzled by how smoothly Clinton worked the room: his almost overwhelming charisma was mesmerizing. I was also transfixed by how his security detail flowed seamlessly around him, as if performing a ballet.

During dinner, Dr. Bob Butler came over to me and asked me to leave the room with him. I'd known and admired Bob for years. As a physician, geriatrician, founding director of the National Institute on Aging, and Pulitzer Prize–winning author, Bob was unquestionably America's greatest thought leader and statesman pertaining to aging and public policy. I could see that he was very upset about something.

As we walked out of the ballroom and into a small adjacent room, he closed the door for privacy and asked me to sit down. Then he said, "Ken, we have a serious problem. As you know, these delegates have been asked to make decisions about what specific programs, policies, and services are needed for a coming century of healthful and purposeful aging. There are approximately forty-five policies that they have been debating all week and on which they will be voting tomorrow morning."

With a sad face, he explained that prior to the night's activities, he had been in his room reviewing the preliminary voting. Apparently, the delegates, the Greatest Generation—were throwing all their weight toward securing and wherever possible expanding their benefit programs and entitlements while not promoting innovative investments, medical research, or funding that could be beneficial for future aging generations. For example, he explained, funding research to beat Alzheimer's disease was currently ranked at number thirty-eight on their list of forty-five priorities, which meant it was not a priority at all. "I'm so disappointed," Bob said, and he implored me to use my speech—which would be starting in a few minutes—to challenge them to open their minds to their responsibility to the future and to all generations. My first reaction was to panic. How could I follow the president, and how could I possibly convince a group of thousands of strong-willed men and women (who were also more than twenty years older than me) to direct more of our nation's resources to strengthening critical programs such as Social Security and Medicare while also investing far more resources into much-needed scientific, medical, and social programs? Bob looked at his watch, got up, gave me a hug, and said, "You can do this. You must do this."

We reentered the grand ballroom, took our seats on the dais, and before I could think Holy shit! the evening program began.

Letting go of my planned speech, I steeled myself to impacting this White House Conference on Aging—the last of the twentieth century—and therefore, history. I took a deep breath, gathered my wits, and began. "Thank you. I am deeply honored to have been invited to speak to you this evening. While we've been busy battling to defend the important services and programs and funding that have been set in place over the past decades, I've been asked to have us take a flight of fancy for a bit and spend a few minutes looking at aging in the future. First, I'd like to share with you some of the forces that are changing our lives and will change this issue of aging for generations to come. And then I'd like to share some conclusions I've arrived at after more than twenty years of reflecting on this theme."

I proceeded to hammer the delegates about the importance of making big decisions pertaining to challenges our society was facing for the very first time—eliminating ageism, establishing a purposeful role for elders, and doing a far better job of matching our health span to our life-spans. I told them, "The whole world is watching to see how we tackle these problems. Indeed, history is watching us, too."

Because of Bob Butler's concerns, I focused the majority of my comments on future healthcare challenges due to the aging of America. I said, "We must have an appropriate aging-ready healthcare system. When Bob Butler says there are a hundred forty medical schools in America but only one department of geriatrics, and that most healthcare professionals currently taking care of you have never received any training whatsoever in dealing with older people, that doesn't cut it. I can't imagine that horrible mistakes aren't being made by well-paid health professionals. I can't imagine that we're getting the most effective and cost-effective treatment if our healthcare professionals are not properly trained and skilled. Also, we must commit to funding a great deal of scientific research. Please, please—I would hope that the future legacy to our children is not twelve million Alzheimer's patients. Although we need palliative and adult day care, we also desperately need enormous amounts of money so that we can put an end to Alzheimer's and other diseases of aging."

I closed my speech by imploring the delegates: "Let me once again say that you are the oldest, most long-lived, wisest, and most experienced generation in the history of the world. The decisions you make here this week will be your legacy. I turn to you now not only for your years, your feistiness, and your power. I turn to you for your sense of fair play and for your understanding that in order for America to be a truly great country, we've got to acknowledge that there's one pie and we've got to figure out how to best divide it up. When you cast your votes tomorrow for what issues and policies are needed to establish an aging policy for the twenty-first century, I know you will come to the right decisions."

My studying and practicing to become a persuasive communicator had paid off. The audience exploded in applause. The next morning, when the final votes were tallied, Alzheimer's research had surged from number thirty-eight to number four. It was a truly important moment in my career and in my life. In many ways what I chose to focus on that night—encouraged by Bob Butler—charted my course for the decades to follow.

BIG LESSONS ABOUT LIFE FROM JIMMY CARTER, ROLE MODEL

Go out on a limb. That's where the fruit is. —Jimmy Carter

In 1997 I received an offer to speak at a Rosalynn Carter conference on mental health in Americus, Georgia. I told the conference organizers I'd be honored to do it if, in exchange, I could have dinner with Mrs. Carter and President Carter the night before, which I knew was a bold—maybe even obnoxious—ask.

Several days went by, and I was thrilled when they called back to say, "The Carters would enjoy having dinner with you, and we'd all very much look forward to you giving a keynote speech on mental health and aging." However, the day before I was scheduled to fly to Georgia, I was alerted that something important and confidential was happening at the White House and President Carter and the other former presidents were all being asked to go to Washington to participate. He therefore wouldn't be able to join me for dinner. However, they said, "Mrs. Carter would still enjoy spending the evening with you." I said, "Count me in!"

That evening, Mrs. Carter and I spent several hours together eating, talking, and getting to know each other. She struck me as a very smart, honest, powerful, no-nonsense, and lovely woman. I remember at one point in our wide-ranging discussion, I asked her what it was like to *leave* the White House. She grimaced and told me she was "very angry" when her husband lost to Ronald Reagan sixteen years before. I asked her how she felt about it all now. In a somewhat controlled southern manner she told me, "I'm still angry!"

The next morning I was standing backstage in my suit and tie being introduced onto the stage at the conference. As I stepped to the podium, I could see there were around five hundred people in the auditorium—mostly academics and social workers—and they seemed like a very friendly crowd. I got to a point in my speech where I was talking about how our society hadn't created much of a purpose for older people, which contributed to their isolation and loneliness. I was explaining my views on the need for a national elder corps and how our society could benefit if more older people took a more active role in our communities. For some reason (perhaps the New Jersey wise guy in me), I paused toward the front of the stage, positioned myself in front of the section in which Mrs. Carter was sitting and said, "Mrs. Carter, when you see your husband, please tell him I've got a job for him." Chuckle, chuckle, chuckle. I think that these nice southern folks and mental health workers couldn't be sure if I was serious or kidding. I don't think I knew myself. Mrs. Carter smiled and waved at me from her seat, and I continued my speech. That night I flew all the way back to California and felt really good about my experience there, and especially about my special time with Mrs. Carter.

At that point in Age Wave's history, my administrative assistant was Rod McKenzie, a bighearted, funny, clever man who was also a bit dramatic. About a week after my Georgia trip, I was returning to my office from the bathroom in the hall and saw Rod standing there, waving his arms and shouting at me, "You've got to get in your office and pick up the phone right now. Pick up the phone! Pick up the phone!"

I asked him, "What's going on?"

"Just get into your office and pick up the phone!" he said.

I rushed into my office and picked up the phone and said, "Hi. This is Ken Dychtwald."

A playful voice replied, "Hi, Ken. This is Jimmy Carter. I hear you've got a job for me."

I was thinking it must be a gag. My good friend Jayme always loved to pull pranks—maybe this was him. Or maybe someone on my staff was trying to have some fun with me. I said, "Sure this is."

And the voice calmly said, "It is. This is Jimmy Carter. Rosalynn tells me you've got a job for me. I'd like to know what you have in mind." I took a deep breath as I realized that this was indeed the former president, and he was calling in response to my rambunctious shout-out in Americus, Georgia. We began talking, and in that initial discussion he shared with me that he was thinking about trying to write a book about aging, and maybe I could help him think it through. "Of course," I said. "I'd be honored."

I began flying back and forth to Atlanta to "mentor" him (I know it sounds silly) as his book *The Virtues of Aging* came to life. The very first meeting I had with President Carter, I arrived promptly at the Carter Center at 8:00 AM and his assistant said to me, "The president is running just a few minutes late. He hopes that's okay with you."

I said, "Sure. Is there a problem?"

She said, "No, but he just arrived at the airport."

"From where?" I asked.

"Well," he said, "he was a guest on the Jay Leno show last evening, and he's been flying across the country all night and he just landed a few minutes ago."

I said, "Would he rather go and take a nap and then—"

"No, no," his assistant said. "The president called on his way from the airport, and he's feeling great and is excited to meet you."

A few minutes later, when President Carter extended his hand to shake mine, a big smile on his face, he looked refreshed and energized and so very kindhearted. We sat down in a private office, and—this was before the selfie era—I asked his assistant to take a few pictures of us together; frankly, I didn't know if anyone would believe that I met the president. As we got to work, President Carter informed me that he had read all my books, liked what he read, and was eager to dig deep into a wide range of topics. I remember that he had a pad and pen and was ready to go. This blew me away. These days most people barely bother to Google you before a meeting. Here was a very busy, well-educated, former president of the United States who wanted me to know that he had done his homework and was ready to get to work.

During that year we had numerous meetings and many incredible discussions about family, work, purpose, success, faith, and death as he organized his personal views and reflections about aging. I loved these interactions because he was such a smart, decent, and curious man. During one meeting after we had gotten to know each other somewhat, I said to him, "President Carter, I have a personal question for you. I'm about the age now that you were when you were president. Have you come to any new perspectives about what matters in life, now that you're older?" He closed his eyes and thought for a few moments and then said, "Earlier in my life, when I was around your age, I thought the things that mattered were the things that you could see, like your car, your house, your wealth, your property, your office. But as I've grown older, I've learned that the things that matter most are the things that you can't see—the love you share with others, your inner purpose, your faith, your comfort with who you are, and your commitment to doing what is good and what is right." That was one of the most beautiful and life-steering lessons anyone has ever taught me.

Later that year, as our work preparing his book was near completion, he asked me, "How can I repay you for all of your help?"

I said, "Here's what I'd like as payment. I'd like to be your assistant on a Habitat for Humanity build. I'd like to be right there working next to you."

He responded, "Wait. That's something you'd be doing for me."

I said, "No. That's something you'd be doing for me."

He smiled and said, "Done. Why don't you join Rosalynn and me on the next one in Houston this summer?"

I asked if Maddy could join me, and he said, "Of course!"

In many ways, President Carter's greatest work has come after his presidency and has been mostly centered on giving back to the global community. Not only has the Carter Center led significant worldwide humanitarian efforts, President and Mrs. Carter have become the face of Habitat for Humanity since their first involvement in 1984. They raise funds and awareness and once a year take part in the Carter Work Project "blitz build."

So, in the summer of 1998, Maddy and I flew to Houston to take part in one of these massive home-building projects. It was a steaming Sunday in early June when we arrived alongside some five thousand other volunteers of all shapes, sizes, and ages (although the group generally skewed older). Some, like me, flew in. Others drove long distances. Others caravanned to Houston with church friends, while some came in buses sponsored by their companies. During the orientation that first afternoon, everyone piled into a large convention center, where we learned that the plan was to build a hundred houses in just five days. There would be about forty people working on each house. The rest—some one thousand volunteers—would cook meals, run errands, and haul trash.

President Carter stood before this crowd and respectfully reminded everyone that he was there to work, not to socialize. "I have a job to do," he told us, and asked that we all do the best we could, "but mind the heat and mind your health." Like all the volunteers, I had brought my own belt and tools and paid a $250 fee to be part of this unusual experience. President Carter explained that each house would be worked on by four skilled crew leaders, ten to fifteen construction pros, around ten some-what handy volunteers, and another ten or so folks who were like me—pretty much unsure which side of the hammer to hold. Maddy and I were thrilled to learn that we'd be working on house number one alongside

Jimmy and Rosalynn Carter. At the orientation, the reality of the endeavor was starting to make me anxious. Other than assembling a bookshelf or two, I had never built anything. In fact, my grandfather Max's nickname for me when I was a little guy growing up was "the Wrecker."

After a restless sleep, we showed up the next morning at the vast building site at six thirty. It was already 102 degrees, and fiercely humid. As the blurry Houston sun was rising, thousands of people were finding their way to the slab on which they were about to spend five long days building houses. President Carter gathered our team in a circle on the black tarmac next to the cement slab where the house was to be built. I noticed how because of skin cancer concerns, he was wearing a long-sleeve shirt, long pants, a neck scarf, and a hat. Not exactly a breezy outfit in 102 degrees.

Everyone bowed their heads, and President Carter offered a short prayer—then we got to work. Within an hour of working in that heat and humidity I felt like I was going to have a stroke. But I put my discomfort aside and joined the torrent of hammering, lifting, and nailing that had commenced. Within an hour I had already slammed four of my fingers and my work gloves were soaked with blood. I was thinking, Why did I ask to do this? I couldn't help noticing that there was an air-conditioned media truck right across the street from our slab, and I kept looking over to see how cool and refreshed the folks looked who were cycling in and out of it. I imagined that after lots of pictures were taken in the morning of the president working hard, he would glide off into the cool and comfortable greenroom. I was wrong, very wrong.

Wade and Shalina Gibson, the young couple who with their three children were going to live in house number one, worked with us on the build. You could see it dawning on this low-income, African American couple that they were soon going to have their own house, and that it was being built by a former president and his crew.

Remarkably, near sunset the entire frame was in place. I, however, was ready to go AWOL. It had been over 100 degrees for hours, and my arm ached from swinging a hammer all day. I glanced at the then seventy-something former president. He was banging away like a pro, and I wondered how long he could keep it up. After another work break, I was spent. But the president was still sawing and hammering.

Our first job the next morning was dealing with a lot of wood that needed cutting. With only two power saws on each site, some would have to be cut with a handsaw. You guessed it—President Carter stepped up and hand-cut 20 two-by-fours in the time it took me to cut only 10. It was another day of blistering heat, and by 4:30 PM the entire work crew was spent. Nearly all my fingers were now damaged, aching, and bloody. But President Carter kept right on toiling, well past the dinner hour.

House number one was proceeding so fast that by the third day all eyes were on us. I was fascinated that our pace was being driven by a gray-haired "old" man who said very little but worked so diligently. It became clear to me that President Carter's leadership style did not involve barking at people or being critical but rather quietly motivating everybody on the site to want to keep pace with him. For example, on the fourth morning one of the project leaders came to alert President Carter that the work pace was not where it needed to be on many of the one hundred sites, and there was a risk that many of the houses wouldn't be finished on time. I watched as the president thought about this and then asked me and several other crew members to join him on our roof. Once there, Carter picked up the pace of his hammering—as did we. People working on the nearby houses saw the president toiling and heard the pace of his hammering, and they in turn speeded up their pace. It seemed like within minutes all five thousand workers were working faster—propelled not by a bullhorn but by a role model.

While on the site, as we were all getting to know one another, I liked to ask my fellow volunteers why they were taking part in the build. Almost everybody had the same answer: they didn't feel whole inside unless they took some time to help others. And for this group, it wasn't about writing a check; it was about giving a chunk of their life.

One of my most memorable moments from the week was when the toilet needed to be installed. It was a tiny little bathroom, no bathtub, just a shower stall, sink, medicine cabinet, and toilet. The toilet had been dragged into the bathroom, but it still needed to be installed. The president asked me if I would help him do this. President Carter and I were crawling on the floor trying to bolt down the toilet in a very cramped space. At that moment, Wade was walking by the doorway and noticed what was going on. Clearly, this was not an ordinary home-building experience.

By twilight on the fourth day, we were laying sod and planting trees, then finally installing carpets and appliances. Then, at 3:30 P.M. on Friday— right on schedule—we were finished. We had built a modest but charming two-bedroom home! And all around us, one hundred other homes were receiving their final touches. President and Mrs. Carter brought our forty-person team inside the house for a ceremony. We were all sweaty, dirty, bruised, and worn out. But as our group of coworkers—and now new friends—stood together in a circle holding hands, I believe we all shared the feeling that we had just done a wonderful thing. Exhausted and filthy but with full hearts, we huddled as President Carter said a prayer, then turned to Wade and Shalina and gave them a white-linen-covered Bible— the first book for their first house. It was simply the most beautiful book I had ever seen. The gesture was so powerful, the emotional intensity in the room went up a notch, if that was possible.

President Carter then faced Wade and asked, "Do you know what Jesus did as a young man?" Wade wasn't so sure of himself and mumbled something about him being the son of God. Carter kindly explained, "He was a carpenter; he worked with his hands. By allowing us to build your house, in a small way you've allowed us to do the work of the Lord." Wade, a good three hundred pounds of brawn, started to cry like a baby, as did his wife, Shalina. Pretty soon we were all crying. It didn't even matter what religion any of us subscribed to—the feelings we shared in that moment were deeply spiritual.

Different from a beach vacation or a personal-growth workshop, by doing this work we all felt both loved and loving and deeply grateful for this extraordinary experience. President Carter then urged all of us who were fortunate in life to never forget those who were not. He spoke of the blessing of giving, how the harder he and Mrs. Carter worked, the more blessed they felt by the results.

Afterward I gave President and Mrs. Carter hugs and thanked them profusely for allowing Maddy and me to contribute to his efforts. Giving of himself, the president told me, makes him stronger. "Every time in our lives we thought we were making a sacrifice for others, it has turned out to be one of our greatest blessings," he said. Referring back to our discussions about the isolation of many older men and women, he went on to say, "More of America's elders should just try it, even if it's nothing more than going to a public hospital and rocking a baby for two hours a week. It's an expansion of life, an encounter with new people who are potentially friends. And it's a learning process, an exciting process that gives new and expanding life experiences."

HOW BILL CLINTON'S
WAYWARD PENIS RUINED
A GREAT OPPORTUNITY

Life is what happens to you when you're busy making other plans. —John Lennon

Powerful people can make powerful things happen. But then again, they can fuck up big-time too.

In late November 1999, Maddy, our kids, and I were in South Florida visiting my parents. Casey was twelve and Zak was nine. We were staying in my uncle Carl's apartment in the same retirement community my parents lived in. Since Uncle Carl was away in New Jersey, he had invited us to stay there and we piled in.

My administrative assistant, Rod, called me in a state of high urgency and said, "A letter just came to the office, and I have to fax it to you right away." I told him I didn't have a fax where I was staying. He said, "Get to a nearby hotel, and I'll fax it to you there." So I went to the local Marriott and waited anxiously at the front desk until the fax arrived. I was eager to see what Rod was so worked up about. The letterhead simply said, "The White House." No address, just "The White House," and under that, a picture of the White House. The note tersely stated, "President Clinton would like your input on his next State of the Union Speech. Would you be open to helping? Call this number: XXX YYY-ZZZZ." It was mysteriously signed "Speech Writing Staff."

After taking a few minutes to gather my wits, I called the number. It was like an espionage movie, because someone, a male, immediately answered the phone and said simply: "Speeches." That was it: "Speeches."

I said, "This is Ken Dychtwald."

The voice said, "We were expecting your call."

"What can I do to be of help?" I asked.

He explained, "The president has really taken an interest in the aging subject and is fascinated by your thinking and ideas. He would like for you to put together a briefing paper for him. He's thinking about doing a major portion of his upcoming State of the Union speech on this."

I said, "That's going to take me probably four or five days to prepare."
The voice responded, "Move quickly."

I drove back to the apartment and explained what was going on to my family and that I would need to excuse myself from our vacation to get to work. And that is exactly what I did—day and night for five days. I FedExed them a twenty-five-page document that I felt represented the best of my ideas.

They called to thank me for my efforts but explained that they were rejecting it. "What? Why?" I asked.

They explained, "This may be the first time you've been in a situation like this, but President Clinton prefers to read briefing papers that are smart and concise. Can you tighten this up?"

"Okay, " I said. "I'll distill this and get it back to you by tomorrow." I worked through the night to condense it down to five typed pages and sent it right off.

Again, they called me to say, "Sorry, but we can't submit this to the president."

Exasperated, I asked, "Why not? I did what you told me."

They explained, "Because the president already knows some of these things."

"What are you saying?" I asked.

"When you put a high-level teaching/briefing together for the president, you want it to principally cover ideas he hasn't already thought of," they said. "That way you can come up with ideas that no one else has ever had and he can learn something new. So that's what you need to focus your three to five pages on—great, innovative ideas that the president doesn't already know."

This meant that I had to first go through all of President Clinton's speeches—and Governor Clinton's speeches—to see what he knew and thought about the aging of America, and then match it up against what I was thinking... and take my ideas to the next level. It was insane, but I did it.

In the most carefully honed, four-page note that I had ever created, I focused on several key areas of opportunity. First, I encouraged President Clinton to take the lead and publicly recognize the ongoing postponement of old age and help facilitate the emergence of a widespread "cyclic life" paradigm. I explained that the growing longevity, combined with the boomers' propensity for personal growth and new lifestyle challenges, would soon be rendering the traditional "linear life" paradigm—in which people migrate in lockstep first through education, then work, then leisure/retirement—obsolete. In its place, a new cyclic life paradigm in which education, work, and leisure were interspersed repeatedly throughout the life-span was emerging. Phased retirements and "rehirements" would become common options for elder boomers, who'll either need to or want to continue working. And it would become normal for fifty-, sixty-, and seventy- year-olds to repeatedly re-invent themselves through new careers.

Second, I implored him to reshape our scientific and medical communities to focus more on "healthy aging." Age-related chronic conditions such as Alzheimer's, arthritis, heart disease, prostate and breast cancer, osteoporosis, and diabetes were beginning to reach pandemic proportions. Unfortunately, America had not oriented or equipped our healthcare system to provide excellent geriatric care, nor had we directed sufficient scientific resources to eradicate these mounting horrors. For example, a five-year delay in the onset of cardiovascular disease could save an estimated $69 billion per year. Postponing the onset of Alzheimer's disease by five years would reduce the incidence of this disease by 50 percent and would empty half of all the nursing home beds in America. I warned him that without a dramatic shift in scientific priorities and healthcare skills/competencies toward healthy aging, costly epidemics of chronic disease could become the social and economic sinkhole of the twenty-first century.

I then suggested that he create a new *purpose* for maturity. I explained that in some ways, the biggest challenges facing aging Americans would be psychological. America had always considered itself a young nation, a new society—not an old one. Although medical science had focused on how to prolong life, political and community leaders had not yet created a compelling vision for what tens of millions of long-lived men and women might do with those additional years. While we had created a wonderful new third of life, we had done a far less effective job of envisioning a new sense of purpose to go with it.

I explained that at the dawn of the new millennium it was ironic that our society faced two parallel problems: one was the growing wasteland of so many older people sitting idle in their homes, and the other was that we had tens of millions of young people considered "at risk," and without enough funding or human resources to help them. What if we took these two dynamics and brought them together through a national elder corps? The seeds for such a social invention were planted in 1963 by President

Kennedy as he envisioned a National Service Corps, and since then many wonderful programs such as Foster Grandparents, Green Thumb, Service Corps of Retired Executives, and Retired and Senior Volunteer Program had grown. However, progress had been hamstrung by an absence of an overarching vision and strong national leadership. If the public and private sectors joined forces to recruit and sponsor retirees in order to create a full-blown Elder Corps, millions of elders could become mentors in the workplace, friends to latchkey children, teachers' helpers in our schools, and leaders in their communities.

I thanked him for the special honor of allowing me to share some of my thoughts directly with him, and of course I ended my note by asserting that if he found any of the thoughts or notions I had presented intriguing, I would certainly welcome the chance to discuss them with him in greater detail.

The very next day I was absolutely thrilled to receive a very positive response from the White House. President Clinton, I was told, loved my letter and ideas. Specifically, he was extremely enthusiastic about the idea of envisioning and launching a national elder corps. His team explained that he had immediately seen that this kind of bold social innovation could become a key part of his legacy, similar to Kennedy's announcement of the Peace Corps in 1961. I imagined that this would be the best alley-oop pass of my life. An idea that I dreamed up was going to be introduced to the world and brought to life by the president of the United States.

Over the next several weeks I worked with him and his staff to help him think through this initiative and how he would launch it during his State of the Union speech the following month.

As fate/luck/fortune/destiny would have it, in the week before this speech, Clinton's sexual misbehaviors, particularly with a White House intern, blew up in the media. I was at the World Economic Forum in Davos, Switzerland, and was following all of this from afar. (While there, I was again looking around in an attempt to see if there was some sort of deep-state, mysterious cabal that the world leaders were secret members of. There wasn't.)

I thought, Oh shit, how is all of this controversy going to impact his speech and our project? I knew where his Elder Corps announcement was situated within the overall architecture of his planned State of the Union speech, so I stayed up all night to watch it live from my hotel room in the mountains of Switzerland. It started, he talked, and then it was over.

Apparently, he had chopped the State of e Union speech down. There was no mention of a revolutionary new approach to joining young and old, no mention of introducing a new role for retirees, no mention of elder anything.

And so a potentially life-changing, nation-changing, generation-changing, world-changing idea didn't happen because of President William Jefferson Clinton's wayward penis.

What the fuck?!

IN SERVICE TO AMERICA
JOHN MCCAIN'S HANDS

I fell in love with my country when I was a prisoner in someone else's. I loved it for its decency, for its faith in the wisdom, justice, and goodness of its people. I loved it because it was not just a place but an idea, a cause worth fighting for. I was never the same again; I wasn't my own man anymore; I was my country's.
—John McCain

My dad—and nearly all of my friends' dads—served in the military during World War II. At that point in history there were no deferments for college students or other easy means for people to dodge the draft. If you were an able-bodied man, you served. When I was in my teens, my dad would often tell me how proud he was to have been in the army and helped win the war against the Nazis and the Japanese. He always spoke glowingly about how his military experience had shaped him as a man and connected him with other young Americans from every part of the country. I always imagined that I too would one day sign up and spend several years in the military in service to our country.

However, during my era, there were easy deferments for those of us in college. And the war that was raging at that moment in history was a strange one—entangled in the jungles of Vietnam and the geopolitical tensions between the United States and the Soviet Union. Several guys from my high school who were a little older than me had not gone to college but instead had enlisted to fight in Vietnam and had come back fucked up on drugs and feeling conflicted about whether we should have been over there fighting in the first place. To compound their misalignment after having done their duty, they received very little respect and appreciation from the media, the masses, and their fellow boomers. During that strange moment in time, a massive generational rebellion was raging, centered on a peace movement, which made many young people think about whether we should be sacrificing our lives in Southeast Asia, in a war that didn't quite make sense, on behalf of a government we weren't sure was telling us the truth. When my time approached, a new selection system had been introduced in 1969 that was supposed to be more fair and just than the drafts of previous generations. It was called simply the lottery, and it worked by the 366 birthdates of the year being put into blue capsules, which were placed in a glass jar at Selective Services Headquarters and drawn one by one to determine the order of call for men born between 1944 and 1950. On the night of the lottery around nearly all young men—and their families—tuned in to both TV and radio coverage to watch as birthdays were randomly pulled. Whoever had a low number had to serve, and those with higher numbers did not. My number was a high 268, and when I and a few close friends all realized that we were not going to be called to military service, we celebrated all night long.

In the years since, I have found myself feeling that a major mistake was made during that era in that I, my friends, and most of the popular culture never really showed the deserved deep respect for the brave men and women who gave up their safe and secure personal lives in service to America. For whatever it's worth, I'm ashamed of this and I would like to profoundly apologize to my generational brothers and sisters for this terrible and unkind demonstration of disrespect. During a 2013 interview I conducted with presidential advisor and political analyst David Gergen he stated that the Vietnam War "put an axe right down the middle of our generation. Because some people served and some people didn't, and the people who went will always resent those who didn't."

I arrived at the legendary Biltmore Hotel in Phoenix to give a speech to the senior management of Ford Motors. In addition to the chairman and CEO, there were a hundred senior executives of the company who had been brought there to spend several days discussing the state of their company and to be exposed to the ideas of a few outside speakers.

During my rehearsal, the conference organizers confirmed that I would be speaking from nine o'clock to ten the next morning. They told me that I must end exactly on time and when I was done, I needed to exit through the curtain behind me. Knowing that I sometimes float a few minutes over my allotted time, I asked why the precision scheduling? They said, "Because there's another speaker after you. It's a secret, and there will be security behind the stage." I thought, Cool, I wonder who the surprise speaker is going to be. Near the end of my speech, which was going well, I began hearing some talking and rustling right behind the curtain.

I finished my remarks exactly on time. As directed, I turned around and walked through the curtain to the back of the stage. Who do I see standing there but John McCain, flanked by his bodyguards. I walked toward him and made sure his bodyguards were okay with my doing so. I extended my hand and said, "Senator McCain, what an honor to meet you. I'm eager to hear your comments this morning." As he extended his right hand to shake mine, I was startled because his hand was unlike any hand I had ever felt before. Having spent decades as a public speaker, I have shaken thousands of hands, but none like McCain's. It was a grown man's hand with a baby feel to it. It was a hand with absolutely no musculature. I learned that even though he covered it well, he simply could not use his arms beyond lifting them a few inches—and so he couldn't perform the activities that would naturally build strength in his hands.

I had been to Vietnam a few years before and visited the infamous Hanoi Hilton where McCain and other captured Americans had had grisly things done to them. During the roughly two thousand days he was held prisoner, McCain had both of his shoulders and arms broken repeatedly when the Viet Cong hung him from his arms tied behind his back. As he hung in this horrible position day after day, his tendons snapped, the bones splintered, and his shoulder joints were destroyed. As a result, he had hands that he couldn't use for anything. They felt so tender and vulnerable, I immediately knew I would never forget them. As he awkwardly shook my hand, he looked at me and said, "I'm glad to meet you, Ken. I've been following your work since I read *Age Wave* a few years ago."

And then I went into the audience and joined the group to listen to Senator McCain. He was absolutely terrific. He was smart, charming, funny, and masterfully insightful about the use and abuse of power in Washington. Because the session was private and off the record, the barrage of questions were blunt, tough, and sharp. McCain's responses were equally blunt, tough, and sharp. Even though some of the Ford executives were former military, I noted that he didn't mention anything about his nightmare in Vietnam or his disability—he soldiered on with dignity. At the end of his comments, this group of tough automobile executives gave him a standing ovation. Then he disappeared behind the curtain and was whisked away by his handlers.

I was mightily impressed with John McCain. He was a brave man, a decent man, a patriotic man. He was a leader.

QUITTERS, FIGHTERS, WINNERS AND LOSERS
BLUNT ADVICE FROM EUGENE KLEINER

Age wrinkles the body; quitting wrinkles the soul. —Douglas MacArthur

Toward the end of the 1990s, expectations at Age Wave were high, and I was experiencing tons of pressure from my investors, who wanted me to do what I said I could do. I wasn't sure if I was effectively balancing my career and my family, and I guess I was going through one of my grumpy-with-my-life phases.

One of the people to whom I mentioned my situation was a wonderful older woman named Rose Kleiner. I knew Rose from her groundbreaking work in the aging field. Years before eldercare caught on as a service and a business, Rose had started an innovative program called Older Adults Care Management. She was a compact, Jewish-grandma type woman, and extremely kindhearted. One day at a conference I was bemoaning my life to Rose. She listened to me patiently and then said, "My husband's got some experience with these kinds of things. Maybe he would visit with you and could give you some counsel. Why don't you first come to our home for dinner?"

So I went to dinner at their lovely redwood home not far from Stanford University. As we looked out the windows at a particularly beautiful sunset, they seemed like two very thoughtful and nice elderly people as they shared pictures of their children and grandchildren. Eugene didn't say a word about his work, and at the end of the evening he suggested we schedule a time to meet one-on-one and discuss my work/life dilemma.

Several weeks later Eugene Kleiner and I met for breakfast at a restaurant near their home in what is now known as Silicon Valley. It was just the two of us. He was a tall, hulking guy who wore glasses and two large hearing aids. In a grandfatherly tone he said, "So tell me what's going on with regard to your work and your company." I can remember thinking he probably didn't know much about business and dealing with investors, but what did I have to lose? And so I began my diatribe, telling Eugene about the coming age wave and how it would affect nearly everything. I went on for nearly an hour, nonstop, as he quietly ate his scrambled eggs and listened patiently.

As I was running out of steam, I said to him, "But here's my problem. I've got all these employees and a long list of responsibilities. I've also got these shareholders who are breathing down my neck." I told him that the pressure was getting to me and I was thinking of just walking away. "Why? Why would you do that?" he asked. "So I could be free again. Not too long ago I was a broke but free-spirited hippie, and now I go to sleep worrying about shareholder value. I told him. Why am I pushing myself so hard? I could be liberated from all this pressure and other people's expectations." Finally, I had the good sense to stop babbling and say, "So what do you think, Eugene?"

There was no easily available Internet at that time, and I hadn't done any homework on Eugene Kleiner. I imagined that his primary assets were that he was Rose's husband and now he knew me. He paused for a few moments and then said, "Okay, so this is a company that you created and in which you have enlisted many people to support your vision. And now you're feeling stress. Well, someday you may want to have a partner or raise money or hire someone or many people, and they'll take a look at how you handled yourself *now*. If you walk away, you'll probably feel pretty good at first, but understand that you'll be known for years to come as a quitter. On the other hand, if you stay at the helm and battle your way through this—even if you fail—you'll be known as a fighter. So, do what you want." And that was it. He put some money on the table to pay the bill, shook my hand, said good-bye, then got up and walked out the door.

During that era many people were talking about "following your bliss" and doing whatever felt good. What this Zen-like elder was telling me was that you sometimes must fight for what you want, and if you want people to be willing to affiliate with you, you may have to struggle through really unpleasant times that don't feel blissful at all.

His profoundly simple guidance jolted me. On the drive home from our breakfast, I decided to stay—and to fight. Because I gave it everything I had then, in the years since, many incredible people have chosen to work with me or join my causes. Encouraged by Eugene Kleiner, I wasn't a quitter then and I'm not a quitter now.

Several years later, while reading an article about the incredible success of the pioneering Silicon Valley venture capital firm Kleiner Perkins, I gasped when I realized that Eugene was the Kleiner. As I stared at his picture, I felt so foolish that when I had met him for breakfast I didn't have a clue that this humble man had been the visionary co-founder of one of the world's most successful and respected venture capital firms. I had not known that this kindly elder had almost single-handedly given birth to much of the tech revolution—with investments in hundreds of pioneering firms such as Netscape, Amazon, Compaq, and Genentech— while transforming the modern world in the process. I also didn't know he was one of the wealthiest and most highly respected men in the world of finance and investing. Eugene Kleiner had given me some of the best advice of my life. He had also demonstrated a level of humility, generosity, and wisdom I hope one day I can come close to matching.

At that point we were improving the lives of tens of millions of older adults, and as a wonderful added benefit, Maddy and I felt like we were living the American dream. Our personal holdings were worth more than $25 million and doubling every year.

Like the sorcerer's apprentice, I thought I was learning how to master the magic of entrepreneurialism, leadership, marriage, and parenthood.

Then everything fell apart.

PART V

SELF, SUCCESS AND PURPOSE RECONSIDERED

If you succeed, who are you?

·

If you fail who are you?

·

When you're hurting, who helps you?

·

When those you love are sinking, will you help pull them out?

·

Have you ever thought of ending your life?

·

Does growing older make you feel the urgency of life?

·

Do you believe the idea that "what doesn't kill you makes you stronger?"

THE COLLAPSE

Success is not final, failure is not fatal: it is the courage to continue that counts.
—Winston Churchill

Then, in the late 1990s, something new appeared on the nascent technology scene. At the time, personal computers were little more than glorified word processors; but from that world something that no futurist had accurately predicted was rising: the World Wide Web. As I sit here in 2020, it is hard to think of anything else that has so altered the face of the world during my lifetime. And as wrapped up as I was in my own interests and persuasions, I didn't see the enormity of the tech revolution that was coming—and how it might impact our work and my life. I should have been more curious about this other reality that was emerging. That was a big and costly mistake.

When you're launching a start-up business, you need a compelling idea that meets a market need, early capital, and a strong management team, which we were able to achieve. But you also need continuing capital for additional rounds of funding. But in 1999 as interest in the Internet exploded, all of a sudden every potential investor we talked to told us they were no longer interested in funding old-fashioned ideas. The Internet was the future, and that's where all their money would be going. The sad irony is not lost on me that although I was considered to be quite the visionary futurist, I didn't see this disruption coming.

When we tried to secure more funding for our publishing business, investors said, "Wait a minute, you spent all this money buying up local senior-oriented magazines and newspapers. There aren't going to be any magazines or newspapers in the future. Forget it."

And so that business, with hundreds of employees in offices in twelve states and its hundred-plus people in our headquarters in Emeryville, was looking at about ninety days, then sixty days, then thirty days before it would have to go belly-up. Everyone kept saying, "Ken's a rainmaker, and he has surrounded himself with talented executives. They won't fail." But we were definitely failing. As the chairman, I had to get on planes and fly to all our offices and tell people we were closing everything down.

Everyone was stunned, and many cried. Telling people that they no longer had a job, their families no longer had medical insurance, that their company stock was worthless, broke my heart. I cried myself to sleep every night on the road. For a guy who liked to be the bearer of good news, it was a nightmare, a terrible nightmare.

The next to fail was MedMax. We had to raise a lot of money just to take out leases, build out the stores, and secure tens of thousands of different products. It was very expensive, so we raised money first from the Baxter healthcare company and then from Blue Cross/Blue Shield of Pennsylvania, who had been one of our consulting clients. They became the majority shareholder because they believed that having a retail presence would be a perfect match for them. They'd be not only in the insurance business but in the health and wellness business, too. Then, due to some additional scrutiny of the health insurance marketplace by the media, Blue Cross/Blue Shield became concerned about the perception of conflict of interest. By guiding customers to get their home health products at stores they owned, maybe they'd be open to criticism. Thinking that wouldn't be good for their brand, they decided to shut them all down. Business number two gone.

It was a good thing our marketing communications firm, Age Wave Impact, was on such solid ground—or so I thought. Soon after the MedMax news, the CEO I had recruited and whose family I had relocated to the Bay Area came into my office and said, "I hate to tell you this, Ken, but I'm leaving."

"What do you mean you're leaving?" I asked.

He explained, "I've been made an offer by a start-up Internet marketing company, and I'm not alone. Pretty well everybody in the company is being plucked up by Internet start-ups." It was like another gold rush in Northern California. The stock offerings and the valuation multiples were so crazy in these Internet companies that if you had a semi-appealing business idea and you had some staff—even if you didn't have many customers or any profit—your market value could jump to hundreds of millions of dollars in no time at all. It was nutty, but it was the *new* new, and these start-ups were taking the most talented people in the Bay Area and giving them unbelievable compensation packages. Nearly everyone, from traditional executives to cabdrivers and nannies, was getting lucrative jobs at these companies, Suddenly working in a company that was dedicated to marketing to older people didn't seem quite as sexy.

There I was, trying to raise more money for a marketing services company with no CEO and no creative director and an unraveling staff. That business went bankrupt, with creditors coming at us from every angle.

I remember—it's eerie how you remember a specific day—the day I got a call from our one remaining potential investor. "You know what?" he said. "This is a different era, even more so than it was a couple of months ago. This World Wide Web is the future. Your businesses, we can't get there from here." That day I said to my assistant, Rod, "This is a horrible, horrible day. It looks like soon we'll have no companies, we'll have no employees, we're not going to have any offices." I told him, "I've got to get out of here to clear my head. I'll be back tomorrow or the next day."

Rod nodded, and said, "Oh, you just got a call from your doctor, and he wants you to call him back right away."

I said, "Oh shit. I'll do it from my car." I called my doctor back while driving. "Well, there's two things," he said. "Your cholesterol is a dangerously high four hundred forty, and you may have prostate cancer."

Maybe for the first time in my life I felt totally overwhelmed, and all the bad news was just jumbling together in my mind. The parts of me that were used to seeing the glass as half-full were nowhere to be found. Instead, terror rose up inside of me. Terror of illness, terror of failure, terror of my inability to get through what I was now faced with, and terror that my wife—and kids—would abandon me. And surrounding the terror was deep sadness—my first encounter with full-on despair.

The bad news just kept on coming. My board said, "This has become a house of cards. This Internet revolution, it's going to change everything we know about investing. All the businesses you got us excited about, they were good ideas, but now they're yesterday's news. Oh, and what you're trying to do with Tithon in this brain-health space, forget it. We're out." So, one by one, my board members moved on. I had tried my best, but I had failed. However, my chairman, Charlie Lynch, remained by my side and counseled me through all the tough times to come. Some of my left-leaning friends like to banter that businesspeople are heartless. My experience was otherwise. Charlie, who was an in-demand, seasoned executive, had just put in almost ten years with me and Age Wave, and he came out with nothing. Yet he remained compassionate and helpful through the collapse and for years after the demise of these companies. He is one of the finest human beings I've ever encountered, a truly kind and honorable man.

In the year leading up to this mess, I was on magazine covers, I was being hailed as the human potential guy, then the social science guy who had crossed over into business, taken an original theme, and turned it into numerous exciting enterprises. I had been on a steep rise, and it wasn't just a personal rise. There were thousands of people who contributed to our ascent, and they had relied on me, as did their families. Now it was indeed collapsing like a house of cards. What a way to turn fifty. Maddy and I had taken very little money out of the company—we had rolled the dice, and everything we had was in Age Wave stock. Suddenly we had nothing. We were completely broke. Our big dreams had crashed and burned. I sure felt a lot like Mickey Mouse in "The Sorcerer's Apprentice." I had tried out the wizard's wand and conjured up all sorts of cosmic magic. Then it all came apart. I blamed my incompetence, inexperience, and ambition. Oh fuck.

Did I feel badly about losing a lot of money? I did. I felt horrible. Did I feel badly about having tried so hard and failed? I did. I felt miserable. Did I feel crummy about having health problems —especially since to much of the world I was Mr. Bodymind? I did. I was ashamed. By then my parents were kvelling over all of my accomplishments, with framed magazine covers adorning their living room walls. As I tried to explain what was happening, they couldn't quite make sense of it all. They were alarmed but remained supportive. But what I felt the worst about was letting so many people down. I guess I learned something about my entangled nature: on the one hand, I like to think I'm curious, bold, and courageous and enjoy trying new things. On the other hand, it pains me to my soul to disappoint those who are counting on me.

But wait, it gets worse. The failed companies owned my intellectual property—my ideas, my speeches, even my slide carousels and videos. Oddly, as all this was coming apart, I received a message from a guy named Wally Amos. "Hey, Ken. I've been hearing about your troubles. I'd like to come and talk to you. Maybe I can be helpful."

I called him back and asked, "Aren't you the Famous Amos cookie guy?"

He said, "I used to be the Famous Amos cookie guy. I'll explain when we meet. I'm in San Francisco this week—how about I take you to lunch?"

We met for lunch, and this lovely man said, "I've just written a book and I'd like for you to read it. Maybe it can be helpful to you." The name of the book was *Man with No Name*. Wally Amos explained to me that utilizing his auntie's recipe for cookies, he put himself, his panama hat, and his attitude on the packaging of all his products. The business had gone through a rough spell, and his investors took control. When they did, as unimaginable as it might seem, Wally Amos lost the rights to his Famous Amos image, so he could no longer talk like Famous Amos, look like Famous Amos, or act like Famous Amos. He could no longer appear in public as Famous Amos. He said, "It looks to me like you're going down that same street." All my speeches, my ideas, my books, my information, and my slides were owned by one of these individual companies that was either bankrupt or shut down. I had lost the ability to be Age Wave, and maybe to ever do any of the work I loved again because it was all tied up in the companies. Wally advised me to talk to a lawyer—or several—and find a way to be able to work in my field and earn a living again. I had become the "artist formerly known as Age Wave."

ON THE LEDGE

Our greatest glory is not in never failing, but in rising every time we fail.
—Confucius

I was deeply unhappy and depressed. Who was I now? So many people had put their trust in me, had owned equity, and now had nothing. Hiring people had been exhilarating, but firing people was terrible. I no longer felt proud or invincible. I was overwhelmed by feelings of embarrassment, humiliation, and shame—and ultimately deep, deep sadness. The cancer report had been a false positive, but my heart was both broken and unhealthy. Would I ever not feel this way? What was I going to do? Did I really have the inner strength to go forward?

I had never really failed before. Oh sure, I had screwed up a few times, and not everything I had tried worked. But this was a very public total failure and humiliation. Maddy and I were left with no money and no obvious way of making money. We had no clients. Mentally, I went to a very dark place and felt like I might never get out of it. For days, weeks, months, I was drowning so deep in the swamp of failure that I thought about whether I wanted to continue living. I wondered if the best years of my life had already passed, and maybe my plot line should come to an end.

I started seeing a psychiatrist. He said to me, "How you doing? Can you describe to me how you feel?"

I told him "I feel ashamed, I feel like a total failure. I feel like I have let everybody down—Maddy, Casey, and Zak and all the people and their families who had put their faith in me." I did not tell him I was thinking about ending my life—I think I was simply too embarrassed to even mention it. He then asked, "When in your life have you felt this way before?"

I said, "I've never felt this way before."

He thought about this for a few moments and then said, "You are obviously depressed. You know, there are a lot of people who feel this way a lot of the time. You'll work your way through this, and it may even make you a more caring and overall better person." He reminded me that Carl Jung, whose thinking I admired, had said, "Knowing your own darkness is the best method for understanding the darkness of others."

And yet, perhaps for the first time in my life, I wasn't interested in trying to understand. I felt so very sad, so beaten down, not stronger at all. In the months that followed, I sort of moved downstairs to the guest bedroom in the basement below our house—to be left alone and cry. I regularly and sometimes matter-of-factly thought about the relief I'd feel if I could simply go lights out. I looked up the Hemlock Society on the Internet, which provided recommendations for ways to end your life painlessly. I didn't tell anyone about these thoughts, not even Maddy. As I considered my options, I didn't fantasize dramatic scenarios; rather, I rationally considered the pros and cons of choosing to gently and swiftly end my life. And since Maddy and I were now totally broke and on the verge of complete bankruptcy, I thought about the $4-million life insurance policy that I had and even quietly checked around to make sure that such policies paid out, if a suicide was involved. Turns out, they did. With an aching heart, I was thinking that I'd put Maddy, Casey, and Zak in such a shitty situation, maybe if I was gone they'd have some funds for a fresh start, a secure home, and college tuition downstream. But I seesawed on that theme and cried myself to sleep when I imagined the guilt and loss they'd feel if I took my life.

It was a year of sadness and shame. I didn't know if I'd ever be able to work in my field again. I didn't know if I'd have the confidence to do anything again.

Maddy was rattled by our losses: money, time, energy, and dreams. She had repeatedly warned me that I was taking on too much. I had fucked up and fucked up *big-time*. She was frightened about our predicament. Would we have to leave our home? How would we ever be able to pay our mortgage? How would we be able to send our kids to college? Was I the guy she still wanted to be married to? But through it all, she tried her best to remain strong and supportive. Our kids were clueless, and that was great. I would wander into ten-year-old Zak's room, and did he know that two of my businesses had just collapsed? Not a clue. He just wanted to wrestle and be goofy and have me cuddle him. Casey was thirteen and fully immersed in her early-teen lifestyle, trying to be her own version of Britney Spears. We'd talk and play. I'd watch her make collages, and it lifted my spirits. I read her stories before she fell asleep. She told me she loved me.

Maddy, Casey, and Zak were my medicine. They were like my bridge back to some kind of a sane place. I truly can't imagine how so many people go through periods of depression alone. I was fortunate to have my family love and nourish me so much, notwithstanding my fuckups.

It was my brother who helped me truly appreciate this. Having struggled for years with agoraphobia, Alan had had a tough time of it, and so our conversations were important, even a lifeline for me at times. Alan could relate. "So tell me, how's Maddy? Does she still love you?"

I said, "Yes, she does. She's very rattled by what has happened to us, but I believe she still loves me."

Alan then asked, "And how are those great kids?"

"They're healthy and they're terrific."

"Then you have everything you need," he said. "You are a fortunate man. You have more of what matters than most." And that was my turning point, my brother reminding me what was really important.

I knew that I needed to reboot my mental and physical health and pull myself out of the hole in which I had been spiraling downward. I changed my diet, restarted my yoga practice, did two hours of exercise a day, got myself on statins, and brought my cholesterol way down. I continued my psychotherapy work and, in time, began to feel the sadness recede. But although little bits of confidence were beginning to reemerge, I no longer felt invincible. I felt as though my armor had been pierced—permanently. Even today, decades later, there's a part of me that's still haunted by the despair of this period. I came to realize that I could learn to work around my damaged protective gear and my wounded soul, but that's all it would be—a work-around. I am a guy who, for a while, thought about the pros and cons of ending my own life. I'm not alone, and I obviously came back from the ledge, so to speak. But once you've been there, you're not the same anymore. It's now become commonplace in medical exams to be asked if a person is thinking of "hurting themself." That would have been a misguided phrase for me back when I was in the pits of despair. I was already hurting. I viewed the idea of possibly ending my life as a potential solution to the pain and sadness.

BREATHE, LEARN, TEACH, REPEAT

Be willing to be a beginner, every single morning. —Meister Eckhart

The next year, psychologically hobbled and surviving on credit cards, Maddy and I had one employee—our administrative assistant, Rod—and we were given some free office space in San Francisco by a kind friend and business associate, Chip Baird. I picked myself up and started all over again. As the bankruptcies settled down and it was clear that I had given Age Wave everything I had and was not snookering anything out of the companies, my investors grew sympathetic to me. They let me get access to my pension, which was maybe $20,000. And after consulting with lawyers, per Wally Amos's suggestion, I realized that no one could own my ability to think, ideate, and speak out. So Maddy and I reemerged as Dychtwald & Associates, and I reemerged as a more sober, focused version of myself. When I looked in the mirror, I realized that I was not the business mogul I had imagined myself to be. I was not a brilliant business developer, and I was definitely not a multimillionaire. But I was still healthy and, even more important, I had a loving wife and two wonderful children. I asked myself, What do I really love to do? I'm just going to do that and find a way to earn a livelihood again.

I reflected that I didn't love having shareholders or boards of directors. I didn't love the pressure of meeting quarterly targets. What I really loved was to think about the implications of global aging and longevity and communicate about them. I loved being a public speaker and storyteller and a big-picture strategic advisor to companies, nonprofits, and governments. I loved working on a team with caring, loyal, talented, and high-minded people. And then, like a rebirth, things started up again. The world was definitely continuing to get older, and I had a unique body of understandings in my head.

All of what we had gone through had surely knocked the wind out of Maddy, but she was strong, supportive, and downright badass when she said, "Let's try this again, but let's not make the same mistakes. No more start-ups. No more juggling acts. Let's do good for the world, make money when we can, and put it in the bank."

People such as Chip, the founder of the private equity firm North Castle Partners, called to say, "We'd like for you to work with us on our investment portfolio, and we'll pay you X, Y, and Z."

I said, "You know, I just failed at everything."

But to my surprise, he and his partners said, "Yes, we know that, but these challenges you've lived through have made you smarter, less pie-in-the-sky and more level-headed. Before, you were principally an enthusiast, but now you're a lot more grounded. You're far more valuable to us now." I also learned something seminal at that time. I had thought that people in my field had really cared about my success and now, my failures. For the most part they didn't care at all; instead, everyone was swimming as fast as they could to keep their own lives afloat. That was a BIG learning for me. We all worry so much about our hairdo, our work title, our dance moves – as we're trying to impress others. Most of the time, however, they're too busy worrying about their own hairdos, work titles and dance moves to even notice.

With the advice of my lawyers, I double-checked with all my former investors and said, "Let me again tell you how deeply sorry I am to have failed. I believe I tried as hard as I possibly could. I'm trying to pick myself up and start over again. Can I please take back the Age Wave name?" They all said okay, and so I reemerged as the CEO of Age Wave, but with just a couple of employees to start. Central to this metamorphosis was Elyse Pellman, who had been the head of our speakers' bureau in Age Wave Communications. A former New York marketing and advertising professional, she was tireless, fair-minded, honest, trustworthy, and most of all, massively kindhearted. Elyse, Maddy, and I were determined to create an even smarter and better Age Wave with a small but mighty crew of employees and associates. In truth, I felt a little like Akira Kurosawa forming the *Seven Samurai* when we started reaching out to our favorite former Age Wavers (many of whose Internet start-ups had pooped out) and asked if they'd like to rejoin a small team of people trying to do both good and well.

Over these past two decades, out of the ashes of the old Age Wave, the new Age Wave has emerged—led by Maddy and me and Elyse, who became our president—and in many ways these have been our finest years.

Since our corporate rebirth, we've been doing the things we love to do and are really good at: newsmaker studies, strategic consulting, documentary filmmaking, book writing, professional training programs, and keynote presentations (to more than one million people). Instead of my attention being so diffuse, I decided that I would try to make every single speech the very best one of my life and every consulting project a breakthrough. We loved producing the PBS special *The Boomer Century: 1946–2046* and were giddy when it aired 2,200 times on PBS stations nationwide in 2007 (as I covered earlier in this book). We are super proud of our thought-leadership position and the excellent clients who have retained us. For example, the Future of Retirement newsmaker studies we conducted worldwide with HSBC Bank have transformed the global narrative about aging, longevity, and retirement. The recent suite of ten studies titled The Seven Priorities of the New Retirement, conducted in partnership with Bank of America Merrill Lynch—which involved more than seventy thousand hours of hard, mind-bending work—have garnered more than twelve billion media impressions. One of my absolutely favorite relationships is with the Virtuoso travel company and its magical chairman and CEO Matthew Upchurch. Together we have thoroughly enjoyed conspiring to envision the future of travel experiences, while Matthew has further convinced me of the spiritual need for people of the world to get to know one another better. And of course, there's the work we've done pro bono in partnership with Peter Diamandis's XPRIZE Foundation in an attempt to crowdsource a solution to the problem of Alzheimer's disease.

Through these and many other initiatives, we continue to try to do good in the world. As we promised each other, Maddy and I have been taking the money we're making and putting it in the bank. The truth is, we've all been having pretty much of a blast. There's so much to be thankful for. In the years to come, as we dream up new initiatives and cultivate new business relationships, we hope to continue to unravel the mysteries of our aging world, in partnership with both the for-profit and nonprofit sectors, in the United States and abroad.

I continue to enjoy the challenge of trying to do good while doing well. Our blend of fee-based and pro bono work feels right to me—about two-thirds/one-third—and I anticipate that in the coming years, making money will become less and less important to me.

When I was trying to make rational sense of what I'd been through, someone told me this Chinese fable about getting through unpredictable times, and I have kept it in mind ever since. It's a fable without any clear beginning or end, but here's how it goes:

A long time ago in China, there was an elderly man who lived on a ranch with his one son. They loved and respected each other deeply. On their modest spread, they had only one horse, and it needed to be broken in, so the old man asked his son if he'd go out to the corral and take care of that. The son respectfully went out of the house and into the corral and got on the horse. The horse immediately threw him off and then jumped over the fence and ran away. The young man tumbled to the ground, breaking both of his legs.

Is this good or bad?

In the following months, as the young man was mending from his broken legs, the country went to war and the military came to recruit all the young men into their fighting crews. They obviously couldn't take this young man because his legs were broken.

Is this good or bad?

As it turned out, all the young men who went off to fight in that battle were killed.

Is this good or bad?

Meanwhile, back at the ranch, the old man and his healthy-again son are sitting on the porch, and they see that the horse who had run away is returning, bringing back with it five hundred wild stallions.

Is this good or bad?

In this modern age, we often think we can imagine the future and then just chart a course straight toward it. There are lots books, workshops, and films that propose that the way to manifest the life you want is to envision it clearly and then it'll just happen as planned. However, what I've come to realize is that we can't really know the ultimate outcome of any action, decision, or encounter. Who's to say when something good or bad happens what the downstream effect will be? While I remain a *big* fan of curiosity, I'm a lot more skeptical about downstream certainty.

With early Age Wave and its various iterations, we had an exhilarating ascent, which I loved. I loved coming up with new ideas, I loved being joined by terrific and talented people. I loved the growth. But then it all fell apart—and I didn't like that at all. And to quote Rosalynn Carter: "I still don't!" I had a dark come-to-Jesus period and then I went back to doing what I really love most—envisioning the future, speaking out, breaking new ground, working with a professional team that often feels like a family, and partnering with high-minded companies and nonprofits. I guess I got to learn what my superpowers are and what they are not. I also learned that I could break and still survive. I think I came through all of it a bit more real. I guess that what didn't kill me did make me stronger—or maybe just a little wiser. In many ways these past two decades have become both the most vulnerable and the most powerful years of my life. What I thought I was hoping for didn't happen. But I am better for it. My destiny, it seems, continues to unfold.

Throughout all of this, Maddy and I continued to get remarried. In 2008, our twenty-fifth anniversary was approaching. We decided to do a trio of ceremonies. First, we had Maddy's mom and stepdad marry us at our home. Then we traveled to Florida so that my mom and dad could marry us there. And then we went to Bora Bora with our close friends Kenny and Sandie Dorman to have a formal Polynesian wedding, including beautiful hula-dancing women and fully adorned tribal chiefs arriving in canoes.

Although each of our weddings has provided a romantic break from our normal lives, our "normal" lives have kept us on a bit of a roller coaster. We have lived through the death of Maddy's dad and then, over the next twenty-five years, struggled with and supported her mom, my mom, and my dad through their illness, disability, dementia, and death. We have found it all both disheartening and heartening. As I'll describe elsewhere in this book, for a while, due, I guess, to my big dreams and more limited business skills, we experienced exhilarating successes as well as devastating failures. Our lives have been at times smooth and easy but more often intense and messy. When Maddy and I fight or disagree, it's usually because I'm being an ass and/or she's being self-indulgent. But on the night of our original wedding, Maddy's grandma Anea told us to never go to sleep angry with each other and without kissing each other good night. Solid advice that we have followed religiously. And through it all, our relationship has endured, evolved, occasionally backtracked, and ultimately deepened.

Over all these years, one of the things that has always struck me is that no matter how kooky or sophisticated the situation is, when I stand there facing Maddy at our weddings, my memories roam back over the countless experiences we have shared, the successes and failures, the births and deaths. My heart always fills with emotion when I'm asked to tell her "I do." And every single time, as I look in her eyes, I'm taken by how she is a bit different, a bit older, and a bit wiser. I imagine that she too is reflecting on how I am a bit more weathered (and hopefully seasoned) by another turn around the sun. I always feel how fortunate I am to have her as my soul mate and how much I love her. I also notice how much she loves and admires me. I can be more than a bit anxious and needy at times, and my confidence regularly needs a boost. Before I fell in love with her, I was independent—but overwhelmingly self-focused. In Maddy's eyes, smile, and embrace I see her belief in me as a man, a son, a brother, a father, and a husband. Her faith in me gives me great strength and resilience. Through the evolution of our relationship, I have come to care about her more and more deeply. I don't ever want to hurt her, and I want to help make all of her dreams come true. These remarriages never fail to reboot my core feelings for Maddy.

In truth, we have come to view these remarriage ceremonies as punctuation points. When I was a young man, I really felt the most important part of the sentence (and probably, life) was the noun, the thing: "chair," "table," "house." And then when I entered out my human potential period, I thought, No, it's not the noun. It's the verb. You know, it's the being. It's the living. And then for a lot of years I thought I had this great insight that what really mattered in life was the adverb, the way you did what you did. But through these ceremonies with my Maddy, I'm coming to believe that the most important part of the sentence (and life) may be the punctuation points. It's the moments when you stop and are aware and appreciate who you are and the life you're living. And for Maddy and me, the lives we are living are inextricably entwined.

TRAVELING LIGHT AND LIGHTENING UP

If what you've done is stupid, but it work... then it really isn't all that stupid.
—David Letterman

When people learn that I've given talks to more than two million people around the world, they often comment about what a fantastic way to earn a livelihood I've conjured. I agree. I love the chance to impact the way people think about subjects such as aging, longevity, demography, and communications, and I get to meet so many interesting people—both the clients and the other speakers. I know this life isn't for everyone. The travel is rigorous, sometimes disorienting, and sometimes flat-out infuriating

One year, after my reemergence, I was doing a huge amount of back-to-back traveling and had become pretty good at organizing my clothes for each trip and packing my bags accordingly. I had a gig coming up in San Diego during the summer months—a big keynote for Mass Mutual.

Because there were going to be thousands of attendees, the main conference sessions would be held in the San Diego Convention Center, right next to the Hyatt Hotel, where I'd be staying. My speech was to be the first thing on Monday morning. When I got to the San Francisco airport and was walking toward my gate, I noticed that my suitcase was pretty light, and I reflected on how much easier it was to travel in the summertime because I didn't have to bring heavy coats and sweaters. Since I'd only be on the road for a couple of days, I hadn't even brought my sweat suit and sneakers. I was traveling light and feeling good about it.

My flight arrived in San Diego around 9:00 PM. Since I'd be speaking at eight o'clock the next morning, my A/V rehearsal and sound check were scheduled for seven. When I got to my room, I opened my suitcase to unpack and discovered that, other than my toiletries, it was empty. There was nothing else in it—no suit, no tie, no shoes. I had forgotten to pack it: that's why it was so light. All the clothing I had were the jeans, T-shirt, and sneakers I was wearing, not at all appropriate for a major corporate event. That's not who they hired me to be. They were paying me to be a professional. That was on me to deliver.

I said to myself, Yikes, if this happens again, I'm going to need to slow my life down a bit! Then I switched into problem-solving mode. It was Sunday night. Where could I possibly get a suit, dress shirt, tie, and shoes? I felt like a complete idiot and called Maddy to see if she could get on a flight that night and bring my stuff down. But it was too late.

I called the hotel manager and, too embarrassed to tell him the truth, said, "My suitcase got lost in baggage, and I'm giving an important speech early tomorrow morning. Is there any chance that you've got a spare suit here or maybe somebody left one and it's in lost and found? Oh, and are there any men's shoes I could borrow?"

Understanding my predicament and trying to be helpful, he said, "Let me ask around. I'll call you right back." A few minutes later my phone rang, and he reported, "I am so sorry. We don't have anything like that."

I asked, "Are there any stores open?" By then it was almost ten thirty.

He said, "Sorry, but even Kmart and Walmart are closed now, and neither will be open in time for your session in the morning. However, we have a fairly large gift shop in the hotel, and I think they may have some shirts and maybe even a sports jacket or something."

Desperate, I asked, "What time does the gift shop open?"

"Eight AM," he replied, and when I told him I had to be at the convention center at seven, he said, "Let me call the manager of the gift shop. I have his home number. Hold tight." A few minutes later he called to tell me, "The store manager is willing to meet you at the hotel's gift shop at six AM."

So after a restless night, at six o'clock in the morning, wearing my jeans, sneakers, and T-shirt, I met the still-waking-up store manager and began hunting around his gift shop. I almost immediately found a dark sport jacket. It was actually sort of like a rain jacket, but it looked okay and I bought it. Then I spotted some gray golf pants, but they were two inches too long on me. So I bought a roll of masking tape and folded the pant legs up on the inside and taped an internal hem onto them. I still didn't have a shirt or a tie, but he told me he might have a tie in the storage room. When he brought it out, I saw that it was red, with pictures of Santa Claus on it, and it was a clip-on. But I was desperate. Last, he found a white shirt for me. It was short-sleeved, but it was going to have to work. Because it was too small and fit so tight, I wouldn't be able to take my jacket off while I was presenting.

I took stock of my situation. I had a rain jacket that from a distance looked like a sports jacket. I was wearing a red clip-on Santa Claus tie, a pair of gray pants that were hemmed with masking tape, and, to complete the look, a pair of dark golf shoes. While ringing up my bill, the store manager couldn't stop grinning at me. He was obviously getting a big kick out of my efforts to patch it all together.

I looked at my watch, saw that it was almost 7:00 AM, and quickly walked next door to the convention center, completed my A/V check, grabbed a glass of juice and a slice of toast from the buffet in the green-room, got introduced, and stepped onto the stage, flanked by big cameras and mega IMAG screens. I took a deep breath and proceeded to give what I consider one of the very best, most engaging presentations of my life. I received a rousing standing ovation. No one mentioned anything about my attire!

The show must go on, whether I've packed my suitcase or not.

FROM SUCCESS TO SIGNIFICANCE

You must be the change you wish to see in the world. —Mahatma Gandhi

In 2005 I was winding up work on *The Power Years: A User's Guide to the Rest of Your Life*, which I co-authored with Dan Kadlec, a highly talented *Time* magazine journalist. The message of this book was simple: later life is evolving into an extraordinary period of good health and extended opportunity for people to do whatever they want to do with their new-found time affluence. What would they do? Would they be more self-indulgent or more giving? Writing this book, I had loved exploring the future of relationships, leisure, learning, and work—and making sense of how people were going to pay for it all. But for me the heart and soul of that book was the final chapter, "Leaving a Legacy."

As a side note, in addition to what I've been trying to say to my readers, each book I've written has in one way or another been a note to myself. I don't know if other authors feel this way, but I sure do. In our *Power Years* book, Dan Kadlec and I had concluded that both leaving and living a legacy—not necessarily just the financial kind but doing something memorable that fixes a problem or lifts others—could emerge as the centerpiece of a true retirement revolution. With hundreds of millions of men and women around the world approaching a period of life when they would have unprecedented amounts of discretionary time, many might be looking for a new purpose. Maybe they haven't achieved what they thought they might in their career and would now be looking for something totally new to get involved with. Maybe it's the opposite: they have achieved what they set out to do and now find at age fifty-five or ninety that they're looking for a fresh reason to get up in the morning.

These were the thoughts filling my head as we prepared for the book launch that was scheduled for mid-September 2005. I was excitedly ramping up to full promotion mode, clearing my schedule and getting ready for a big publicity tour, imagining the news and talk shows I'd be on and dreaming about how well the book might sell. Could it be the great book of my career? If I received a lot of media coverage, could I help change the public view about the purpose of longevity? Anyway, it was at this exact moment that the massive Hurricane Katrina hit the Gulf Coast with all her fury. I, like many Americans, sat in front of the TV for hours, horrified by the destruction of buildings, cities and lives I was watching in real time. I was stirred by the incredible devastation being brought down on the city of New Orleans and dismayed by our nation's slow response.

As those hours became days and those days became weeks, my family and I watched as so many good people had their homes and lives destroyed and so many struggled without relief. Because this crisis was so massive, it absorbed all the media's attention and my publicity tour was canceled. That was that.

However, as I watched the relief efforts begin, far too slowly, I still had the "Leaving a Legacy" chapter in my head. I decided to donate all the future earnings from *The Power Years* to help rebuild New Orleans by supporting Habitat for Humanity. This wasn't a PR stunt: I didn't talk about it with anyone but my family. I wanted my teenage daughter and son to one day measure me not by what I said but by what I did. So, I wrote a letter to Jonathan Reckford, the executive director of Habitat for Humanity, telling him of my intention. A few days later Reckford called me to thank me for my pledge. Then he shared with me a simple, yet life-clarifying observation: "Ken, I see and hear a lot of people your age [mid-fifties] going through what you're going through."

"What do you mean?" I asked.

"You know, you've got that gnawing feeling," he said.

"What gnawing feeling?" I probed.

"You know, you're trying to make the transition... from success to significance," he replied.

Every now and then a clever or poignant idea grabs a hold of you, gets inside your mind, and creates an identity shift. Jonathan Reckford's comment about the need to go from "success to significance" stirred me deeply and remains an ongoing guiding force in my life. Ultimately, it's one of the reasons I decided to write this book.

LESSONS ABOUT THE URGENT DANCE OF LIFE
A DISCUSSION WITH ANNA HALPRIN

We make a living by what we get, but we make a life by what we give.
—Winston Churchill

When I think of significance, Anna Halprin immediately comes to mind. Several years ago I had the very special experience of conducting an intimate interview with Anna, one of the most interesting women in the human potential field. Living a full life of ninety-eight years at the time of this writing, Anna Halprin has been a teacher and role model to tens of thousands of women and men in search of their authentic selves. Blending classic dance with the movements and practices of psychodrama and Gestalt, she has almost singlehandedly transformed the flowering fields of movement and expressive therapies into postmodern dance. What follows are elements of that exchange.

Ken: You were born Anna Schuman in the year 1920. You were a teenager in the Depression; you experienced the arrival of antibiotics and other medical breakthroughs that took the life expectancy from about fifty or so—when you were young—to almost seventy-nine by the end of the twentieth century. During the 1940s, as you became an entertainer and performer, you were a bit of a renegade, fusing comedy and serious issues. And then you experienced the Holocaust. During World War II, you married a man who was in the navy. You experienced the dropping of the atom bomb. You saw the birth of modern Israel. You experienced the Salk vaccine breakthrough and saw the horribleness of polio put to the side. You contributed to the baby boom with your two wonderful daughters. Television appeared, the civil rights movement exploded, and you were a part of it, and it was a part of you. Psychedelics came along, and you took the trip. The women's movement came along, and you became one of its leaders. You've lived through the exponential multiplication of modern technology and have tried to help people find their spiritual center in this modern high-tech world. All the decades of your life, you've always been a renegade, battling for authentic personal liberation and social justice.

Yours has been a long life, fully lived and fully felt. Every step of the way, rather than pulling away, you did your best to feel the issues, to make sense of what mattered, and to be on the side of right. It's so hard for me to be an unbiased interviewer, because I've got a great love for you and have for decades. I can't even tell you what an honor and delight it is for me to be here with you tonight in your tenth decade of life.

Anna: I love being here with you too, Ken and I've really been looking forward to seeing you and to this discussion.

Ken: Let's jump right in. So, there's your life as a daughter, wife, mother, and grandmother—and then there's what you simply and respectfully call "the dance." How does that all work for you?

Anna: Remember, dance is the mother of all the arts and your body is your instrument. It can sing, it can draw, it can write, it can dream, it can heal. I've been able to find a way of dancing that connects to my life. So, when challenging things happen around me and I've struggled to deal with them, when difficult feelings come up, I dance. And that's been my way throughout my life—being able to live my life as a continual dance.

Ken: Years ago, you went through a very difficult—nearly deadly—period with cancer. I've heard that in 1972 when you were working on a self-portrait, you intuitively drew a large black mass in your abdomen. When you went to see your doctor, you were diagnosed with colorectal cancer. During that dark period, did you step away from the dance?

Anna: No, Ken. That's when I danced the most. And for those of you who have cancer or who've had cancer, you know how life-threatening it can be. You're unprepared suddenly to face the possibility of dying and all the terror that comes with that. It was an overwhelming emotion to deal with. I was frightened both for myself and for my family: what would happen and what would the future be for them? Rather than let the cancer run my life, I chose to do a lot of drawing of my cancer to express how ugly it was—yet still a part of me. And then I did a lot of dancing of my drawings.

All of that really helped me recover, and I continue to do these kinds of honest and expressive processes with everything that happens to me in my life, whether it's good or bad, perplexing or joyful. My most effective way of really dealing with any of my life issues has been to use the arts, and dance happens to be the most welcoming of the arts for me. That helps me literally "move on." It helps me from just being stuck. Life is about movement. Stuck is not who I ever want to be.

Ken: As a young woman you trained for a while with the legendary Martha Graham. How did that go?

Anna: It didn't work for me. Rather than teaching us her experience as a dancer, she was teaching us to dance like her. I could never dance like Martha Graham, and I didn't want to. But the experience with Martha Graham propelled me to explore more organic ways of moving—walking, reaching, climbing, rolling. Rather than dance in a theater, I moved many of my classes to the woods and beaches to improvise and engage with nature. Rather than viewing the body as a disciplined instrument for making pretty shapes, I experimented with encouraging dancers to speak, sing, growl, or make whatever sounds they felt like.

Ken: In the 1960s, before the controversial show *Hair*, before all sorts of other things that occurred in theater and culture and style, you started getting naked onstage. In some ways it was you that brought the whole issue of nudity into the public dialogue during a very revolutionary period in American history.

Anna: Oh, yes. I sure did!

Ken: And you and your dancers were in their bodies and nothing else. What were you thinking?

Anna: Well, perhaps you could say I wasn't thinking, because it created such an uproar. That was in the late 1960s. My husband, Lawrence Halprin, had designed a magnificent dance deck behind our home on Mount Tamalpais. My dance classes usually took place on our dance deck, so we were always outside. You could feel the wind and the sun and the sky and the trees. Everything was so beautiful and so natural. There were times when it was hot, and we'd just take off our clothes; that's all. It was as simple as that. We were hot and we took our clothes off. The trees didn't wear dresses. Why do I have to wear a dress? That was our attitude. For us it was very natural and, in a way, not only natural, but in a way almost sacred that the body could be accepted as an authentic extension of nature. We weren't mechanical forms, and women weren't just sexual objects— we were all sacred beings and our bodies were naturally beautiful.

In a way, it was a statement, a very strong statement, particularly during the sixties and the early seventies when we had the hippie revolution. To me, the hippies were beautiful. They wore their hair long and very natural, and the women went without bras. And many of us didn't shave our underarms—everything was natural. We thought the human body was very beautiful.

We were invited to dance in Sweden, and during the performance, all of our clothes came off. The dance critics said, "It was like a ceremony of trust." And then they had us on national television, and I got a letter from a farmer, and he said, "Oh, when you were naked it just made me think of my newborn calves, it was so sacred." I remember thinking, "Great. Perfect. Good. Everybody understands our respect for the beauty of the natural human body." After that, I came home, and they wanted us to perform in New York. Oh, my. New York.

We went to Hunter College and did our dance—and began to remove our clothes. I could hear people shouting out, "Oh, my God. What are they doing? Oh no, they're not going to! Oh, my God, they did it." Because we got a little naked, the police arrived, and I was arrested for indecent exposure. Our company was blackballed. Can you believe that? I couldn't go back to New York to perform for ten years!

Ken: At Esalen, where you and I first met years ago, there was lots of cross-fertilization taking place; you somehow took what was an era of stylized dance and formula dance and made it psychological, made it personal expression. What drove that? What made that happen?

Anna: Fritz Perls, the father of modern Gestalt therapy, lived at Esalen in the 1960s. He loved theater and he loved working with actors. He heard of my work and invited me to come to Esalen to bring movement into his sessions. At first I wouldn't go because I said, "I'm a serious artist, not a therapist, and I don't want to be confused with all the touchy-feely stuff going on." But ultimately, I was so moved by Fritz Perls's work in Gestalt therapy that I came to Esalen. Thanks to my interactions with Fritz, the use of emotions and how to process and work with them is a big part of what we do at Tamalpa Institute and in our programs all over the world. We call it the "life/art process." For example, one of the things that grew out of my daughter Daria's and my interest in dance and movement as a healing force took place right after the Watts riots. I wanted to use intimate rituals and movement to do reconciliation between whites and blacks. So, back then I trained two sets of dancers—an all-white group in San Francisco and an all-black group in Watts—and then brought them together for an improvisational dance piece that we named "Right On." At the beginning of the dance, interactions between the groups were tense, electric, and angry, then ultimately worked their way into fusion and harmony. It was a thing to behold. I believe the documentary of these sessions can now be viewed on YouTube.

Ken: You've had a boldness and willingness to break new ground, to change the world of dance, to be naked publicly, to get attacked in the media. What is inside of you that has given you either the neuroses or strength to push so many boundaries?

Anna: I don't really know. I grew up with two older brothers and all male cousins. Maybe I just had to develop a little push to keep up with them. I don't know. Maybe I'm just a stubborn Jew, or maybe I'm just a feminist. Maybe it's a combination.

Ken: When the feminist movement arose, did you feel this was your song? Your tune? Your cause?

Anna: Oh, yes, definitely. Feminism is empowering, and I think women are more comfortable in the emotional realms than men. Nowadays, there are many more men dancing, but I think the feminist movement is an outcome of more and more empowered women, and dance is one path to power.

Ken: In your work you've created an impressive spectrum of performances, expressions, and partnerships. Of all the things you've crafted in your work, which is the one you feel the most proud of?

Anna: I think what my legacy will be is the "Planetary Dance," which is a dance about how people can come to a common pulse and common purpose the way dance used to be. If our ancestors wanted rain, they did a rain dance. If they wanted the crops to grow, they did a dance to make the crops grow. If you wanted to have courage in a hunt, you danced it. Somewhere along the way, we lost that connection between purpose and ceremony, and ritual and dance. Our "Planetary Dance" has a purpose. It started out very real. We had a trailside killer on Mount Tamalpais near my home who killed seven women. We could no longer walk our trails for fear of this danger. The purpose of the dance was to reclaim the mountain. One week later, after two years on the loose, the Trailside Killer was caught. Did the dance catch the killer? I don't know. But we danced and the killer was caught.

And so, every year we've chosen a different problem in our community. One was bullying, another was the Oakland terrorism of young people killing each other, another was breast cancer. This began to grow. Now people all over the world participate in our "Planetary Dance"—in Poland, Germany, Switzerland, Scotland, Korea—it's in forty-six different countries. People around the world are dancing for peace. I am so proud of this.

Ken: And now, my last question. Do you think of yourself as an old woman?

Anna: Yes, I do. But I'm not an "old woman" in the sense that I'm a cartoon character of a bent over, crotchety old woman. I will never allow myself to be that. Rather, I think of being an old woman in terms of what am I doing with my life. There's an *urgency* I increasingly feel that every day has got to count. What's the right thing for me to be doing right now? Becoming old for me is a way of being urgent about life. [Note to self: There's that paradox again—just as I had learned about it way back in the SAGE Project.]

For example, last year I tripped on something and fractured my pelvis. I was furious. I went to bed and thought I'd be all right in the morning. But in the middle of the night I was in excruciating pain, so I called 911 and was taken to the hospital. The doctor there said, "Mrs. Halprin, you've got a fracture. It's going to take six to eight weeks to heal." So I said, "Well, too bad," and he said, "What do you mean? Aren't you going to check into the hospital?" I said, "No, I've got to leave now because I have a class to teach at ten AM."

THE BOOMER CENTURY
ON PBS

IT'S GREAT, IT STINKS. HE'S GREAT, HE STINKS.

There is only one way to avoid criticism: do nothing, say nothing, and be nothing.
—Aristotle

As I was hoping to spread the word about the coming age wave more effectively, while carefully rebuilding my work life and my state of mind, I became obsessively curious about television. I got it into my head that I could learn how to be a documentary filmmaker, and I wanted to do it with PBS. I had been interviewed on everything from *Good Morning America* to *60 Minutes* to *The Oprah Winfrey Show*, and I had been involved with several other documentary films, including CBS's *The Age of the Future* and *Ageless Heroes* for PBS. Now I wanted to know what it would take to create a two-hour documentary, something that I could shape from idea to airing. And, having grown up in awe of J. Bronowsky's *Ascent of Man* series and Carl Sagan's *Cosmos*, I dreamed I could share my ideas and learnings with a much larger audience than I'd had before, which might open people's minds to a different way of viewing not only the boomer generation but their own futures.

Every time I met with Age Wave clients who had the resources to fund it, I asked if they might be interested. I received a fair number of "Thanks, but no thanks." However, in a meeting with Vanguard, their president happened to ask if I had any out-of-the-box ideas that might be a fit for them. They're an excellent firm, and I immediately said, "Well, I really want to do a multi-hour PBS special about the past, present, and future of the baby boomer generation." He said, "If you can make that happen, we'd consider sponsoring it."

I immediately reached out to my longtime friend, collaborator, and talented producer Neil Steinberg, who then contacted his friend, experienced documentary producer Joel Westbrook. Joined by Age Wave president

Elyse Pellman, we together called Mark Harris, a three-time Academy Award–winning filmmaker, journalist, and professor at USC, who also agreed to join our team. Mark was uncomfortable with my desire to present such a predominantly positive image of aging and maturity. He was skeptical that people would take this work seriously if we were not willing to show the disease, the loneliness, the loss, and the fear, as well as the upside of aging. He was right: his wise and seasoned point of view was far less perky than mine, and he became a great collaborator and mentor.

In previous documentaries, boomers had primarily been portrayed in terms of the Vietnam War, rock and roll, or Woodstock. We sought to examine the generation from both a sociologic and, most important, a psychologic point of view: who we are, how we got to be that way, and who we might become as we aged. During the next two years we gathered input from a diverse group of thinkers, experts, academics, and activists to learn all we could about boomers—from many different perspectives.

For example, the feminist and writer Erica Jong said, "You have to see the boomer generation in opposition to the Depression generation, or you can't understand it at all. Children who are adored grow up with extreme self-confidence. Some of them are a little spoiled. Some of them really believe in themselves in a way that's terrific. They had a lot of 'I can do anything.' That's the boomer generation." Jong believed that not only were boomer women quite different from previous generations, but boomer men were as well. "We gave men a great gift. We said you can be close to your children and we won't think you're wusses. And now we have a whole new generation of men who are close to their children… and that is a gift."

Actor-director Rob Reiner provided some interesting insights on the emergence of new media and technologies. "I was born in 1947, and my father Carl was on television before we had a television. When I tell my kids that I was born at a time there was no television, they can't even imagine that."

Civil rights leader Julian Bond commented on another role that TV played in our lives, especially in the lives of people of color. "All these shows were about families that could have been yours, except you weren't them, they weren't you. You never saw yourself there, except as a maid or a janitor, or some person doing menial work. So, you liked it and it repulsed you at the same time." Atlanta Mayor Shirley Franklin added, "I remember the first time I saw a young black woman on television. It was Cab Calloway's daughter, and she was dancing. She was in a dance program on Ed Sullivan, I think, and everyone in the neighborhood went home to watch that show because it was such an unusual occurrence."

Feminist and *Vagina Monologues* playwright Eve Ensler reflected on the pros and cons of free love—and feminism's future. "I think the fact that women finally had reproductive rights, that we could protect ourselves, that we weren't going to get pregnant when we had sex absolutely freed women to begin to experiment with sex. I'm so happy not only that I lived through it, but I survived, because there was a period right after where people didn't survive that kind of lifestyle."

Futurist Alvin Toffler bemoaned the "sex, drugs, and rock and roll" lifestyle: "As a parent of a young woman then a child growing up in the sixties, I felt that the society was making my life difficult, like when *Time* magazine glorified drug pushers on their front cover. I am trying to get my kid to stay away from drugs. That's no great help to me as a parent."

According to director Oliver Stone (who smoked a huge joint right before his interview), "I grew up in Manhattan as a conformist. I was a Republican and attended private schools. But when I ended up in Vietnam at that young age of my life and found myself at the bottom of society's barrel, my eyes were opened to the wide gulf between the haves and have-nots in our society... Years later, when I made *Platoon*, it was all based on that feeling of division in every military unit I was ever in."

Psychologist Daniel Goleman shared fascinating insights about the connection between the hippies and, later, the techies, "There's been a direct line drawn sociologically and historically between the Haight-Ashbury and Silicon Valley. They are only thirty miles apart, but in spirit, they're very much the same, because they were both groups that didn't respect the old rules, and that were creating new ways, new means, and new methods. And I think the spirit of creativity and innovation and the entrepreneurial strengths of this generation relate to the fact that authority didn't have to be listened to; you could think for yourself." Goleman, the developer of the idea of "emotional intelligence," was sanguine when envisioning the future of the boomers. "The legacy of the boomer generation won't be the 'me first' image of their early years... It's not how you begin the act; it's how you leave the stage that people remember."

United States Under Secretary of Aging and polio survivor Fernando Torres-Gil shared a prediction: "For baby boomers, our biggest challenges could be at the end of our lives. Our grandparents and parents faced adversity when they were young with the Depression and World War II, and then they were able to live out their lives and enjoy what they had accomplished. For baby boomers, our greatest test is going to be in our old age as we confront loss and disability."

When we asked genetic scientist Craig Venter—the man who decoded DNA—what he believed about the prospect of future science lengthening our life-spans, he said, "Increasing life-span should not be a goal of science. We're already having some very serious problems with the six-plus billion people we have now on the planet. If we can improve health and quality of life during normal life-span, those are totally reasonable things to do."

With input from so many visionary thinkers, I was energized by everything our production team was learning—and that we were going to share with PBS's viewership. It was my job to go into the various studios with sets that had been built to film my segments and connecting parts. I must admit that going from behind the script to in front of the camera was a challenge. While I enjoy public speaking, I found that I was not very good at either acting or reading lines from a teleprompter. I got some emergency coaching and tried my best to learn how to repeat a paragraph and walk toward the camera again and again and again until I got it right.

When it was finally completed, PBS suggested that it be named *The Boomer Century: 1946–2046*. All there was left to do was to wait until our air date. During that quarter of a year, I started head-tripping about our film. Was anyone going to even watch it?

On the Friday before the special was scheduled to air, the *Christian Science Monitor* published our first review in an article entitled "Tubegazing: *Planet Earth* and *The Boomer Century*." I was alarmed. I had seen *Planet Earth*, and it was magnificent; how could our work compare? The reviewer gave *Planet Earth* some decent commentary and a B+ grade. But to our amazement, *The Boomer Century* was given a great review and an A. Yay!

There were still four days before airtime. Then, late on Sunday night—March 26, 2007—my Internet news search revealed that the *New York Times* had just posted a review of our documentary, which would be featured in the morning paper. Written by Felicia Lee, it was prominently featured at the top of the Television section and was titled, "Boomers: Whimpers or Bangs?" I was quoted throughout the review and referred to as a "leader, pioneer, expert." This is fantastic, I thought. I have tried my hand at filmmaking, and we have contributed to the master narrative of the past and future history of my generation. Our hard work has paid off! I was filled with pride and excitement.

However, the night before the show was to air, I was jolted by a second *New York Times* review, this one written by Virginia Heffernan and titled "Apart from Wanting It All, What Makes Boomers So Special?" It was blunt, mean, and negative. She wrote: "Its host is Ken Dychtwald, a pleasant and suntanned gerontologist whose book titles—*Age Power, Age Wave,* and *Bodymind*—suggest he might have a knack for motivational seminars. Indeed, he rarely stops smiling here. The ideology of the Baby Boomer, in his telling, is a George Foreman Grill, something to be sold."

Ouch! While I was exhilarated by the first reviews, I was wounded by this one. It made me think about how hard it must be to be a public figure and have to contend with critics admiring or shaming you. I realized that I didn't have tough-enough skin for that kind of role.

But then, on Tuesday night, March 28, 2007, *The Boomer Century* aired to a strong viewership. I received enthusiastic calls and emails from friends and family all night. However, predating #OKBoomers, the generational aftershocks that followed the airing of the documentary were dramatic and unexpected. In response to the Heffernan *New York Times* piece, there was a flood of reactions in print and online. People—mostly boomers—were challenging whether she was attacking the documentary or our generation. "What's your beef with the Boomers? We have given the world rock and roll, women's liberation, social activism, the sexual revolution, and countless technological innovations." However, an equal number of Gen Xers jumped into the debate and basically said, "I'm sick of your generation. Shut up already." And to liven up the discussion, many Greatest Generation folks weighed in: "You boomers are a bunch of spoiled crybabies. Stop being such drama queens and drama kings." In an era before social media, within a week of our first airing, according to LexisNexis, there were more than 190,000 different websites and chat rooms debating our show. I followed as much of this as I could, twenty-four hours a day, and was struck by two things: (1) We boomers generally think so highly of ourselves that we can hardly imagine anyone thinking otherwise; and (2) Younger and older generations have lots of issues with us. Many think we're jerks.

During the coming months, the show received so much attention that PBS stations in all fifty states aired it again and again: 2,200 times in total. With nearly 5 million viewers, it slightly outpaced Al Gore's theatrical release of *An Inconvenient Truth.*

The reactions to this program provided a Zen lesson to me. You just have to try your best and hope for a positive reaction, and you cannot control how people are going to react to what you do. Notwithstanding being told I smiled too much and that I should be selling George Foreman grills, I also learned that while I very much enjoy trying to shape the public narrative about aging and longevity issues, it hurts to be publicly shamed. I do not know how anyone can endure the modern era of media assault.

WHOSE DREAM AM I IN?

I have had dreams and I have had nightmares, but I have conquered my nightmares because of my dreams. —Jonas Salk

I am unrelentingly curious about the roles that luck, fortune, planning, and serendipity play in the unfolding of each of our destinies. Here's a story, within a story, within a story that captured this particular paradox for me.

In the spring of 2007 I was in the middle of a five-day personal retreat at Esalen. It had been a high-combustion year, and I needed some time off the grid, to take a lot of deep breaths and try to remember which way my life was pointed. During my fifties, I would usually take these "return to Esalen" (or maybe better stated as "return to myself") personal retreats once each year. Going off by myself in this fashion allowed me time to rest, recharge my batteries, and sometimes dream up new ideas. The days had been flowing smoothly, and I was beginning to feel calmer and stronger.

At mealtimes, I usually liked to sit off by myself and watch the interplay of workshop seminarians, very much enjoying the feeling of not having to do or say anything. However, on this day I sat down for breakfast across from one of Esalen's more colorful characters, Mr. Ronnie Hare. An elder hippie—and proud of it—at seventy-five, he had a full head of long white hair crowned by a cowboy hat. His handsome, wrinkly old face was covered with a rock-and-roll white beard. Short in stature, he was usually nattily attired in a pair of gray farmer's coveralls hanging down over his beat-up cowboy boots. No question, Ronnie was a cool old guy; he looked like he could have played bass in the Grateful Dead. While I didn't know Ronnie well, I had always admired his character and style. In a room full of individualists and nonconformists, Ronnie stood out.

It was around 9:00 AM, and Ronnie and I were both eating oatmeal. I had a glass of fresh juice, and he was playing with the lip of his coffee mug. With a big shit-eating grin on his face, Ronnie pulled out a piece of sketch paper and said, "Hey, Ken, you've got to see this." I looked at the drawing: it was a portrait of Ronnie, and it was magnificent. It wasn't like one of those Coney Island caricatures. It was a masterfully expressed, finely crafted portrait. I was stunned by how deeply and fully this simple drawing portrayed Ronnie's essence. I asked, "What's the deal with that? Where did you get it?" He said, "Oh man, there's a guy visiting this week, and his name is Dave. He's tall, artistic-looking, he's got long white hair, and he's been sketching and painting scenes here in Big Sur."

The drawing of Ronnie was so good, so intense, and so accurate that I asked Ronnie how long he had sat for the portrait. He told me that Dave met him the afternoon before, asked if he could sketch him, and then got right to work. He had finished the whole thing in fifteen minutes. Ronnie had been looking around and now almost jumped out of his seat as he pointed across the dining room and said, "There's Dave." He went on to say, "Ken, you two have got to meet because you and Dave are going to do something important. I have a feeling about this."

I thought, What do I have to lose? You never knew what kinds of characters you might meet at a place like Esalen. Carrying the portrait, I walked over to Dave, who was sitting at one of the lodge's dining tables with his sketchbook open. I said, "Hey, are you Dave? My name is Ken. Ronnie was just showing me this fine portrait. Did you do this?"

"Yes, I did," he said with a smile. "Ronnie is such a great-looking subject, I couldn't miss the opportunity to draw him."

"What else have you done while you've been here?" I asked.

"With the wonderful light, beautiful nature, and colorful people, my sketchbook is nearly bursting with images," Dave said. My curiosity piqued, I looked at his oversized, leather-bound sketchbook and was amazed by what I saw flowing on every page. At that point I'd been coming to Esalen for thirty-five years, and I quickly realized that Dave was drawing things most people don't notice. I sat down to talk some more and learned that his last name was Zaboski. He was forty-five years old, married with one young daughter, and he had been a senior animator for Disney, where he had worked on such incredible films as *Beauty and the Beast*, *The Lion King*, and *Pocahontas*. Although he had been classically trained, he had loved his years at Disney, but now he was branching out on his own.

Let's take a pause for a side story. In the 1970s, one of the people whom I met, learned from, and was impacted by was Joseph Campbell. Joe believed that the stories we learn, the fables we grow up with, the myths we live by, start out as stories but ultimately become the tracks on which ideas, possibilities, and even civilizations move forward. As Maddy and I were raising Casey and Zak, we'd read children's books to them all the time. Because during the day we were doing all we could to promote a new, more positive image of aging, we couldn't help but notice that none of the children's books we were reading to Casey and Zak had any positive examples of old people in them. Quite the opposite: when elders appeared, they were usually presented as geezers or crones who were hiding under the bridge to grab children, throw them into a sack, and take them home to fatten them up before putting them in the oven. For years Maddy and I thought that one day it would be nice to do a children's book that was not ageist. We wanted to write the book Aesop would have done if aging and longevity had been more commonplace during his era. We thought we could create a fable about what was possible at the end of a long life. Our story should include some kind of reinvention or metamorphosis in adulthood. Knowing that children's books are jointly driven by their story and the pictures that bring the narrative to life, we had repeatedly reached out through our networks for an illustrator, but we hadn't found one whose worked we liked.

Back to that week in Big Sur ... As I was driving home, I called Maddy and blurted, "I think I might have just found our illustrator." Maddy was captivated by my enthusiasm and when I got home I showed her some of his work. We reached out to Dave the next morning. Within days, he flew up from LA and we brainstormed all sorts of ways to go about creating an impactful and enjoyable children's book. In preparation for our meeting we had all spent hours at our local Barnes & Nobles to get a feeling for how the very best children's books were crafted, illustrated, and written. We learned that children's books worked best when they had a simple story line, weren't too filled with nuance and subplot, and leaned heavily on the illustrations to make the point. We felt we were up to the task and got to work. During the early goings we were unsure of ourselves, since none of us were between the ages of five and ten. However, Dave's wonderful daughter Grace was seven, so we enlisted her help—for an equal share of the writing credits and the earnings, of course. Our team decided that rather than have our story be directly about aging, we would handle it metaphorically.

Together we created *Gideon's Dream: A Tale of New Beginnings*, about a hardworking caterpillar grub who one day falls off a leaf and has the experience of flight. He first becomes terrified but then finds himself loving the feeling of being airborne. So much so that he starts to dream about being able to fly, even though all his grub friends think he's a bit foolish. He also wonders if maybe he's too old to learn to fly, until his wise best friend, Grace (named after our coauthor) tells him that you're never too old to learn something new. What does Gideon do? He packs his things and goes off into the meadow, where he builds a cocoon around himself. When the time is right, he sheds his cocoon and emerges as a beautiful butterfly. After flexing his new wings and marveling at his transformation, he takes flight and soars off to his new beginning.

We envisioned this to be a story that grown-ups, teachers, parents and grandparents could read to young children and instill in their minds a hopeful and even magical story of metamorphosis in adulthood. Dave and I flew to New York, met with editors at HarperCollins, and were delighted by their interest in being our publisher.

Over the year that this was all happening, I visited Big Sur for a meeting, and when I saw Ronnie Hare I explained all that had happened since he introduced me to Dave Zaboski. Ronnie was thrilled by the story of Gideon and that the book would be available in around half a year. He made me promise that as soon as the book was published, he would get the very first copy. "Of course," I told him. "If not for you, this would not have happened."

When publishing day arrived, we authors received a box of beautiful copies of *Gideon's Dream*. As planned, Dave, Grace, Maddy, and I signed the first copy and FedExed it immediately to Ronnie in Big Sur. Although I knew he lived in a truck parked near Esalen, I believed that it would get to him through the folks at Esalen. It was a Tuesday, and Ronnie would hopefully be getting the book in Big Sur on Wednesday. We all hoped he would love it as much as we did. As it turned out, I was scheduled for one of my five-day personal retreats starting that coming Sunday, and I couldn't wait to see Ronnie and the look on his face with his copy of *Gideon's Dream: A Tale of New Beginnings* in his hands.

On Saturday morning I received an email from a Big Sur friend. Ronnie Hare had passed away the day before. He had apparently been diagnosed with a terminal illness and had been living in his truck; he felt he wanted to be in control and not be a burden to his family, So he ended his life on his own terms—not in a nursing home somewhere. Our book collaboration seemed to shrink in significance.

I arrived at Esalen on Sunday and checked into my room, feeling sad that I would never know if Ronnie had received his copy of *Gideon's Dream* and, if so, what his reaction to it was. Then on Monday evening at around nine o'clock I walked down to the natural sulfur-spring hot baths hanging on the edge of the cliffs high over the Pacific Ocean. Although each of the stone-enclosed tubs can fit around a dozen people, I was soaking by myself that night under a sky bursting with stars. No one else was there, as most of the guests at Esalen were in evening workshops. Eventually a woman stepped into the tub. In the quietness of the night, we nodded to each other as she settled in and closed her eyes to adjust to the warmth of the water. She looked to be around fifty years old. After a while, I asked her, "Are you here for a workshop?"

"No," she said, "I'm here for personal reasons. What about you?"

I said, "Me, too."

About twenty minutes later she spoke up and said, "To tell you the truth, I came here this morning because my dad just passed away and I'm gathering his belongings. I'll be heading home to my family in Sacramento tomorrow."

"What?" I asked. "Was your dad Ronnie Hare?"

"Yes," she said. "Did you know my dad?"

I explained that I didn't know him well, but I had known him over many years and that he was a great guy. I also said I could tell her a story about her dad that nobody else could tell her. Although weary, she wanted to hear what I had to say. I began: "There had been a book project—"

She interrupted: "Wait a minute, were you involved in *Gideon's Dream*?"

"Yes," I said. "I was. How do you know about the book?"

She said, "My dad sent *Gideon's Dream* to my teenage children, his only grandchildren, whom he dearly loved, on Thursday, the day before he passed away."

So, Ronnie had received the book on Wednesday, and on Thursday he had mailed it to his only grandchildren, the day before he ended his life. I asked her, "Did he send anything else to his grandchildren?"

"That was it," she told me. "But in the front page of the book he had written them a note explaining that *Gideon's Dream* was a book about Grandpa. That it was *his* story of leaving his body to go to heaven. And that he would always love them, no matter what form he was in."

So, was this fable my and Maddy's dream? Dave's and Grace's? Gideon's? Or Ronnie's? I'll never know. Maybe it belongs to all of us.

A HUMANE APPROACH TO DEATH

Death exists, not as the opposite but as a part of life. — Haruki Murakami

When Casey was five and Zak was two, Maddy and I decided we should get a dog, mostly for the kids. But what kind of dog would make sense? A big dog? A little dog? What kind of personality? Zak and Casey decided they wanted a dog that looked and acted like the movie dog Benji. A week or so later we were having dinner with some friends who had a dog that looked a lot like Benji. It was not the same breed as Benji, but a Tibetan terrier. We asked our friends what they could tell us about Tibetan terriers, and they told us that they were smart, lively, and playful, and they're good watchdogs. Apparently, even though they're small, they're protective.

On the drive home, Maddy and I decided that all signs were pointing to a Tibetan terrier for the Dychtwald family. We looked in the newspaper (that was when there were newspapers) and saw that a family not far from us was selling Tibetan terrier puppies. We took our kids to the home where these people lived. Running around the living room floor, going crazy, were six cuter-than-cute Tibetan terriers in an assortment of colors—caramel, white, black, spotted. One of those little puppies, dark with a white nose and paws, jumped right up on Casey's lap. Zak walked over and played with her, too. There was no question that was going to be Casey and Zak's dog, so we bought her and brought her home. We named her Corrie, and as Casey and Zak grew up, Corrie was their playmate around the clock. She'd play with them, cuddle with them, eat breakfast with them, and tirelessly run around the yard with them. Corrie became an integral part of our family.

I must admit, Corrie was not very responsive to any of our attempts at training her. She pretty well lived by her own code of behavior, and we'd have problems with her from time to time. Because in her genes she was both a watchdog and a herding dog, she'd aggressively snarl and yap at any workers who came to the house, and she'd chase cars up and down the street. She'd try to bite tires and would not let up as she attempted to corral the unruly vehicles. Every now and then a jogger would come by and we'd hear them yelling, "Get out of here, you crazy dog!" and we'd realize that little Corrie was after them.

When Corrie was older, maybe thirteen or fourteen, her vision started failing. Then, during the next year, she became incontinent from time to time and we'd have to clean up after her. Our vet informed us that she had some internal organ problems that sometimes caused her pain. Then one night when she was seventeen—Zak was a senior in high school but was away on a field trip, and Casey was off at college—Corrie went outside and didn't come back. We called out for her, but she didn't return. With a flashlight, Maddy and I went walking around our property and found her way out back, caught under a metal fence. Corrie had dug her way halfway under that fence, and there she was, stuck and whimpering. We managed to get her untangled, but she couldn't walk. Maddy and I took her right to the local twenty-four-hour vet. We'd never been to this vet, but the receptionist was very kind. It was probably around ten o'clock, and we sat for a little while before the vet came out to take Corrie with him to an examination room.

About half an hour later, the vet came out and explained to us that Corrie had serious internal problems and that she had probably reached the end of her days. It was conceivable that she could have surgery on her eye and maybe also on her bladder, and that might help her live a few more months. Maddy and I looked at each other. We turned to the vet and asked, "If this was your dog and you loved her, what would you do?"

He said, "If it was my dog, I don't think I'd put her through all the surgeries for just a few more months of painful living." He also explained that sometimes when animals know they're at the end of their lives, they will go away from a home or from the family with whom they've lived to be at peace with the end of their lives. Perhaps that's why Corrie had gone out that evening and tried to dig under our fence.

"So how does this work?"

The vet explained, "We have a comfortable and private sitting room. I'll bring Corrie in and you can sit and talk with her and hold her and do whatever you want. Feel free to take ten minutes or ten hours—we're open all night. Then, when you feel it's appropriate, let me know and I will come back into the room and inject Corrie and she will pass peacefully."

Maddy and I went into the private room, and then Corrie was brought in. She had been such a sweet part of our lives, and now she seemed so vulnerable. We spent about an hour holding her. We told her how much we loved her, and we reminded her of times she had played with Casey and Zak and their friends, and vacations we had taken together. We took about an hour for that and then we just held her for another little while. When we felt complete, we let the receptionist know. The doctor came back into the room and asked us how we wanted this to unfold, and we said we wanted to both be holding her. We lovingly held her, and she looked at us tenderly.

This kind vet stroked her, took out a small needle, and injected her in her side. There was no pain to the injection. Corrie was looking at us and seemed totally and completely comfortable and at peace. After a few short moments, her eyes closed, and she passed.

As we were driving home, we talked about how this process was referred to as a "humane" way to treat one's dog. Hmmmm, humane, not canine. We reflected that it was far more humane than the way most human deaths occur with our modern, hyper-institutionalized approach, with its extreme use of Frankensteinian technologies to prolong the dying process.

At that point in my life, I hadn't had anyone (other than my father-in-law) close to me die. A few years after Corrie's passing, I was involved with my dad's and then my mom's deaths. As you'll see, some of a sizable portion of how I approached these deeply important transitions I learned from Corrie's kindly vet. Those teachings proved both practically and existentially helpful.

WE ARE OUR
BROTHER'S KEEPERS

Strive not to be a success, but rather to be of value. —Albert Einstein

My brother, Alan, is three years older than me. Our paths have been quite different, yet we have an extremely close bond. I'm married; he's not. I have two children; he has none. My career has been a roller coaster; his has been more steady. I turn to him for counsel; he turns to me for counsel. We love each other deeply and talk every day; we share the ups and downs of our lives. In many ways he's my biggest supporter, and I try my best to be that for him. I'm lucky to have him in my corner, and I believe he feels the same way about me.

When we were growing up, he was the cool older brother. He was very smart, a great athlete, played drums in a popular band, and enjoyed lots of friends and romances. But then in his late teens, something got twisted up inside, and he became agoraphobic. It was quite severe, and for decades the agoraphobia constrained him in every imaginable way. It made it hard for him to travel, sustain a relationship, and work steadily. Since panic attacks were never too far away, all of this damaged his self-confidence. Nevertheless, he tried his best to live a good life with good friends and productive work. Throughout all his trials and tribulations, he always remained kind, caring, and loving to me and, later, to our parents, when they were in need.

I'll give you an example of what a dear soul my brother is. Years ago, after over a decade of painful shoulder problems, I called him to explain that I had just been to the Mayo Clinic and learned that I needed to have my shoulder replaced. Without even a second to think, and not quite understanding what my surgery entailed, he said, "It would mean a lot to me if I could give you one of my shoulders." I cried. He was selflessly offering to have his shoulder and arm amputated to replace mine. He laughed and was relieved when I explained that they were going to remove my shoulder joint and replace it with a titanium-and-plastic replica.

On that day, and on so many days, I was touched by how huge Alan's capacity to love me was. I am truly fortunate to have him as my brother.

A few years later, in 2010, Alan called me to report that he'd just come from his doctor's office and his PSA level was very high, requiring some additional tests on his prostate. I said, "Let's be sure to get you to a great doctor, and make sure you go about this process in the best possible way. Count on me to help you every step of the way." I reached out to some friends in the medical field in New Jersey, and everyone lent a hand to get Alan properly diagnosed. It turned out that he had prostate cancer and would need to have his prostate gland removed.

At that point there was a lot of excitement about the da Vinci surgical robot and how effective it was at prostate removal. Previously, the best prostate surgeons had to rely on their scalpels and dexterity to remove the gland without doing too much damage to the bundle of sensitive embedded nerves that control both urination and the ability to have erections. Before the precision of the robotic surgeries came along, many men who went through a radical prostatectomy then struggled with incontinence and impotency for the rest of their lives. But with this new technology, using joysticks in another room, the surgeon precisely guided two surgical probes through Alan's belly to remove his prostate while doing minimal damage to the nerves. I learned that the doctors who had been the finest traditional surgeons were getting left behind when that robotic surgery came along, because it required a totally different set of skills.

Since Alan was living alone in New Jersey without much of a support system, Maddy and I canceled our work commitments and flew east days before the procedure to support him emotionally and make sure that everything went smoothly. He asked me to come to his pre-op doctor's meetings with him, because he was nervous and scared. On the day of the surgery we arrived at the hospital and he was in pretty good spirits. He repeatedly told us he was glad that he wasn't alone. Alan, Maddy, and I were briefed by the surgical staff and were told that his procedure was going to be relatively routine. In a day or so he'd be home recuperating. They explained that he'd have to wear a catheter for maybe three or four days and then he'd be retrained to use his bladder without a prostate gland, and within around six months everything, hopefully, would be healed and back to a "new normal."

The surgery went just fine, although it was hard for me to stay relaxed in the waiting room, with calls coming in from our mom and dad in Florida every few minutes. Maddy was less shaken up, so she was very helpful in comforting me during the hours of waiting. Before we knew it, Alan was in post-op looking okay. It appeared that everything was going to be all right. He stayed in the hospital until the next day, when I brought him home. Things seemed to be so on track that Maddy headed back to California. However, as I helped him walk up the stairs in his apartment, he said that something was wrong, and he felt like he was swelling up inside. A little while later, Alan started having a panic attack like I'd never encountered. We called his doctor, who told us that this might be a normal reaction to the surgery and anesthesia and post-surgical anxiety and that we should call him in the morning if things hadn't improved. That night, with a catheter in his penis and a bag on his leg, he called out to me from his bedroom (I was sleeping on his couch in his living room), "Kenny. I'm scared. Would you please come in and hold me?"

Although we had hugged from time to time, I had never held my brother before. I took him in my arms and rocked him, and he started to cry. It was not a sob or a whimper, it was a terrified, frightened, sad cry from the deepest part of him. It felt like a lifetime of sadness was coming out. It was a profound "Why is this happening to me?" sadness. As I held him and felt him coming unglued, it struck me that throughout our lives, even though we don't usually think about it, we feel a sense of indestructability. Then when something scary happens, particularly with our bodies, our boundaries are pierced, the rules of control no longer apply, and we feel our own mortality, our own aloneness, our own vulnerability. It all hit Alan that night like a firestorm. It hit me, too. We were both so shaken and scared by the fragility of being human, we wept together for hours. I just held my brother with all my love and sympathy for him, and this went on through the entire night.

It was the saddest I had ever felt.

At sunrise Alan felt even worse, so we tracked his doctor down and he met us at his office. As soon as the doctor saw the condition Alan was in, he rushed us to the hospital. When we arrived at the emergency room, Alan was in full panic mode. The emergency room doctor quickly took stock of what was taking place and gave Alan a strong shot of lithium (a powerful mood-stabilizing medication), just to settle him down. Alan's lifelong best friend, our cousin Ira, showed up to lend support. And then finally, after a four-hour wait, they put him through a series of tests. It turned out that indeed, one of the robotic arms had inadvertently punctured his intestines, and all his intestinal toxins had been flooding into his body, which could be fatal. He wasn't imagining this; something terrible was really going on.

Alan was then admitted to a room in the hospital, and a doctor showed up to interpret all of the tests for us. Because Alan was under the influence of drugs and in a panicked state of mind, the doctor addressed me: "Your brother's body is filled with nearly a gallon of toxic waste. Before we operate on his intestines, we're going to have to pump all of the released toxic fluids out of him."

I asked, "How do you do that?"

"We're going to put a hose down his throat," he bluntly said.

"Will he be asleep during that procedure?" I asked.

"No. That would be too risky," he replied.

I told the doctor, "I don't think he can handle that."

He said, "He's going to have to handle that, or he could die."

Although Alan was only semiconscious, he asked me what was going on. I gently told him, "Here's the situation, Alan. You were exactly right. When they did the robotic surgery on your prostate, they accidentally punctured your intestines. They're going to have to operate on you to fix the problem, but first they're going to have to drain all the toxic stuff out of you."

Alan looked at me, trusted me, and asked, "Kenny, what do you think?"

I said, "I think it's what's necessary right now. I'll be right here to make sure everything is okay."

He responded, "Have them do it right away."

While I was holding Alan's hand, they inserted a thick tube down his throat and sucked more than a gallon of ugly-looking liquid out of him into jugs beside his bed. It was a horrible thing to watch. After that gruesome process was completed, they quickly sedated him and rolled him off to another surgery, in which they opened his abdomen and stitched his punctured intestines back together.

Alan steadily settled down and recovered in the hospital. But it wasn't smooth sailing. The previous week had shaken him to his core. One night when I stayed late with him in the hospital, he was having trouble breathing. He started calling out, "I can't breathe, I can't breathe," and hit the help button. We waited a few minutes, but no one showed up. Then a few minutes more, and no one showed up, so I ran to the nurse's station to find someone to help him. They adjusted several of his tubes and monitors, and he settled down. Over the next several days, friends and family members came by to visit and give Alan some encouragement.

Finally, I brought him home again. Although we arranged for nurses to check in on him each day, I wound up staying there with him for almost the entire month.

Finally, Alan seemed to be through the worst of it, so I decided to fly home. It was so good to be with Maddy again and sleep in my own bed after such an ordeal.

Today Alan is better than ever. After caring for our parents in their final years, he relocated to Florida, where he's healthy, happy, and socially involved – although still a bit agoraphobic. And after a fifty-year break from music, he got back behind a set of drums. He now spends most of his time playing in his popular, in-demand band, named Still Jammin.

GOD OF DAY, GOD OF NIGHT

If God did not exist, it would be necessary to invent him. —Voltaire

On a clear, beautiful day, when the light is bright, how far can you see? When you look up into the clear blue sky, you could be taking in a stunning distance of up to several hundred miles, where the envelope of the earth's atmosphere stops. And what can you see at the absolute farthest distance, way beyond our atmosphere? Our sun, which is a vast 93 million miles away. And what about time? Most of us would agree that one hundred years would be a very long time to live and a thousand-year period is difficult to grasp. A million years—nearly inconceivable.

Within those parameters and that scale of space and time, we each establish the relative gravitas of our own individual lives and personal power. How much impact can one individual have on the world? For example, if I work at it, I may be able to create some ripples and influence some of the people in my life: my wife and kids, my community, and thanks to modern media, maybe even people who are hundreds, even thousands of miles away. My own database has several thousand connections, and my interactions with this many people provides a sense of my level of power and influence in this world. From time to time, I imagine that my contributions may even ripple forward in time.

However, if there's a God that oversees this earthly domain, it's breathtaking to imagine this being's ability to track billions of human lives - continually. On top of that, could such a being precisely intervene from time to time to help make wishes come true and limit humanity's misbehaviors in quantity and impact, while also deciding every election and which basketball team will triumph in the NBA? Maybe. And what if this singular God also determines who will ultimately be eligible to live with him or her in eternal bliss in heaven or burn in the everlasting fires of hell under the control of God's evil alter ego, Satan? That's quite a lot of power and responsibility. It would require an omniscient, omnipresent, and omni-capable being. So, within the context of what we can see and imagine from the surface of our wonderful planet Earth on a bright sunny day, the God that is believed in by many appears to be quite a towering figure.

However, on a clear, moonless night, if you look up and see the massive and radiant Milky Way galaxy in which we're spinning, and beyond that, billions of other galaxies erupting, rippling, and swirling through nearly infinite time and space, all bets are off.

Three or four times in my life I have been in extremely isolated locations where there was no artificial or ambient light and no moon, and I have witnessed the universe in all its blazing glory. On those nights, distance and time are so vast as to be completely incomprehensible to my own limited perspective. What did I feel? Awe.

Around a decade ago, as Zak and I gazed upward from the starlit cliffs of Big Sur, we saw what looked like comets streaming across the sky and realized that what we were seeing might actually have been stars erupting fifty million years ago. And although shimmering clusters of stars appeared to be near one another, they may actually have been dancing billions of years apart. Within this cosmic framework, we discussed how very hard it was to reconcile that there is a singular God—and that the only place that this God would pay much attention to is our tiny Earth, which is busy rotating with a few other sister planets around an ordinary, middle-aged sun. Like the mayor of a very small town who might have great authority in the town square but becomes far less impressive in the wider world, the God who knows all our names, has preferences for certain entertainment and sports figures, enjoys certain kinds of architecture, gets agitated about gender roles and whether we've been bad or good, appears quite provincial.

Instead, Zak and I concluded that God is the entirety of the living, pulsing, swirling cosmos we're all a part of, which I feel more deeply lying beneath a brilliantly starry night sky than I have ever felt in a synagogue, church, or any formal place or worship, whether it's the Sistine Chapel (spectacular), the Blue Mosque (fantastic), or Newark's Temple B'nai Jeshurun, where I was bar mitzvahed.

Does this cosmos have a purpose? I don't really know. However, I do imagine there is some sort of a cosmic consciousness—not an elderly white man with a white beard—with both physical and nonphysical dimensions (maybe thousands of physical and nonphysical dimensions) that, on our earth, formulates into plants, animals, and human beings. I believe our human purpose is to either hone or liberate our potentials and better ourselves—by working to advance our awareness of our interconnectedness with all of life, our mindfulness, our heartfulness, our kindness toward others, and as the Buddhists suggest, to try to become more godlike in our hearts, in our consciousness, and in our actions. In time, our bodies die and disassemble and return to their earthly elements, maybe to become a plant or a bowl of dirt or a tree one day. And perhaps, hopefully, when we drop our bodies, our essences have been made better and a bit more conscious and return into the grand ocean of cosmic consciousness. And if we're all doing that—and by "all" I mean all beings in all universes—then perhaps the cosmos's core essence is evolving and awakening, too.

Maddy and I went to hear John Cleese, of Monty Python fame, give a talk called "Spirituality and Religion" in San Francisco. He said, "I think there are two paths to religious experience. The first is the pursuit of direct experience of the divine, the sacred, and I'm all for that. The rest is crowd control."

I agree.

Note: For the record, I don't track with many of my New Age, reincarnation-believing friends who'd have all of our various lives moving in one-dimensional time (who were you in your last life and who will you be in the next?) and repeatedly, on this modest speck of a planet versus throughout the cosmos. Rather, if we incarnate into different beings, it could be forward, backwards, sideways in time, and potentially anywhere in the universe.

PART VI

ELDERHOOD

Have you made peace with the aging or passing of your parents?
·
Do you think of your own aging as an ascent or descent?
·
Have you considered your new purpose in your life beyond work?
·
How do you fund your peace of mind?
·
What are the upsides to aging?
·
Have you helped your kids make peace with your eventual passing?
·
What will be your legacy?

LIFE'S THIRD AGE

If you can let go of passion and follow your curiosity, your curiosity just might lead you to your passion. —Elizabeth Gilbert

A new stage of life has been emerging, the "third age," a concept borrowed from the European tradition of adult education. In life's first age, from birth to approximately thirty, the primary tasks of men and women center on biological development, learning, partnering, and procreating. During the early years of human history, the average life expectancy of most people wasn't much higher than the end of the first age, and as a result, the predominant thrust of society was oriented toward these most basic drives. In the second age, from about thirty to sixty, the concerns of adult life focus on the formation of family, child-rearing, and productive work. Until the last century, most people couldn't expect to live much beyond the second age, and society was centered on the concerns of this age.

However, with our longer lives, and the coming of the boomer age wave, a new era is unfolding, the third age, which brings new freedoms, new responsibilities and new purposes to adulthood. First, with the children grown and many of life's basic adult tasks either well under way or already accomplished, this period allows the further development of emotional intelligence and maturity, wisdom, and one's own personal sense of purpose. The third age has another appealing dimension: there's an abundance of free time and opportunity to try new things—and to contribute to society in new ways. In the next twenty years, boomer third agers will have 2.5 trillion hours of leisure time to fill in the U.S. alone. Worldwide, we're looking at fifty trillion hours of time affluence. I've noticed that there's a lot of confusion among many retirees regarding what they should be doing with their free time. Last year the average American retiree watched forty-eight hours of television a week. Maybe if we all cut a few hours off that and gave more of ourselves back to our communities, we'd all be better off. The historically unique combination of longevity, time affluence, and wisdom produces unprecedented potential for elders to be seen not as social outcasts but as a living bridge between yesterday, today, and tomorrow—a critical evolutionary role that no other age group can perform. In this third age, we need to focus not simply on striving to be *youthful* but also to be *useful*. How can we be most helpful to our children, to our communities, and to the future?

And there surely is a need, particularly during this high-anxiety period in history: so many in our communities really need more involvement from grown-ups. They need us to share—not hoard—our life experience and perspective, as coaches, mentors, teachers, guides, and surrogate parents and grandparents. We should also reach out to people in other neighborhoods and even other parts of the world. And taking a cue from Greta Thunberg, it would be wonderful if we elders also concerned ourselves with future generations, not yet born. They deserve a planet with a healthy environment, readily accessible drinking water, the opportunity to learn and grow and as many chances to unleash their curiosity and explore their potentials as possible.

AGING, DEATH, AND BEYOND
LESSONS FROM HUSTON SMITH

Life is a pilgrimage. The wise man does not rest by the roadside inns. He marches direct to the illimitable domain of eternal bliss, his ultimate destination.
—Swami Sivananda

In late 2009 I found myself in a challenging but fortuitous situation. I had become friendly with the husband-and-wife documentary filmmakers Jon and Anna Monday, whom I had met while they were filming a number of very special annual fund-raising gatherings I was leading at Esalen. Jon and Anna are smart, kind, thoughtful practicing Buddhists and very high-minded in everything they do.

One evening they called and explained that they were working on a passion project—a documentary about the life and work of legendary religious scholar Dr. Huston Smith. Raised as a Christian by Methodist missionary parents in China and having also studied and practiced Vedanta, Zen Buddhism, and Sufism throughout his life, Smith wrote *The World's Religions*, which stands as an iconic reference to the role different religions play in people's lives worldwide. He wrote another ten books along the way, including *Why Religion Matters: The Fate of the Human Spirit in an Age of Disbelief* and *Tales of Wonder: Adventures Chasing the Divine*. He was also somewhat renowned because while chairman of the philosophy department at MIT in the late 1960s he became involved across town at Harvard with Drs. Timothy Leary and Richard Alpert (later to be known as Ram Dass), who were conducting investigations into altered states of consciousness through everything from meditation to LSD. They approached the extremely straitlaced Smith because they believed there might be shortcuts to the religious experience.

In any event, Jon and Anna Monday explained to me that as Dr. Smith, who had entered his tenth decade of life, had grown quite frail and weak, and they believed he only had enough strength to conduct one more interview, which they wanted for their film. They asked me if I would be willing to do this. My first reaction was to decline, as I was only superficially knowledgeable about his theories, writings, and philosophies about religion. I just did not feel I was up to the task. That kind of thing should be left to folks like Bill Moyers, who had previously produced a five-part series for PBS about Huston titled *The Wisdom of Faith*. I had seen Huston Smith speak several times but didn't really know him or his work well.

However, the Mondays explained that they were hoping for an interview that wouldn't reexamine his theories and studies but rather probe his personal views about aging, death, and beyond. I thought about it for several days and realized that this was a singular opportunity—to talk to an elder religious scholar and glean his personal reflections on the complex and extraordinary life he had lived. "Yes," I said. "Definitely yes."

Several weeks later, at the Buddhist seminary in Berkeley, Huston Smith and I—along with the Monday film crew and Zak, who was on a break from college—met for our one and only visit and what turned out to be one of the most soaring lessons of my life. What follows are elements of what we covered in our discussion: his honest and open reflections about life, loss, aging, death, and the afterlife.

Ken: Dr. Smith, it is such an honor to meet you. With your permission, I'd like to ask you a variety of both philosophical and personal questions.

Huston: It's a pleasure to meet you as well. And please call me Huston.

Ken: Okay, Huston, how old are you today?

Huston: Well into my ninety-first year.

Ken: With your own aging process, do you think of it as an ascent or a descent?

Huston: With the body, it is very clear; it is a descent. Yes, old age sort of creeps up on one, so incrementally that you don't realize that you crossed the line and you're old. Do I feel old? Yes. There is evidence. I've been very fortunate in my health, but I was stricken nine years ago with osteoporosis, and as you can see, I can't sit upright, as my spine cannot support my back. I played college tennis when my body was okay, but to walk and to steady myself now, I have to hold on to my friends' arms. I also sleep a lot more, and I'm a good sleeper. And another way I feel old is that deafness has approached me, and for many years I could barely hear anything. But since I had a cochlear implant installed on the side of my head a few years ago, I'm very grateful to technology for keeping me in the communications circle.

But with the mind and the spirit, it's easy to say that aging is an ascent. It has provided an increase in understanding, and this has recently become the more important part of it for me—also an increase in acceptance. I love Saint Paul's statement in one of his letters: "I have learned whatsoever condition I find myself in therein to be content." I think that's wonderful, and I am practicing that, and I must admit—without bragging—I think that I am, on balance, more content at this stage in my life, with fewer ups and downs. I'm more on an even keel.

Ken: You have invested a great deal of your life in a desire to live it consciously. You're in your tenth decade of life. Has it been worth it?

Huston: Of course.

Ken: Why?

Huston: Well, you have to excuse me, but I feel I'm developing a certain rapport with you that I can sort of make a joke out of your question. Let me ask you in turn: Do you like to be happy? And you'd answer, "Sure," and then I'd ask you, "Why?"

Ken: So, for you, it's as simple as that. You don't question whether or not this pursuit of a conscious life was the right path or not.

Huston: Well, it was Socrates who said "The unexamined life is not worth living." I agree one hundred percent.

Ken: So much of the literature on aging is about loss, fear, nostalgia. While you have been twisted by osteoporosis and you can't play tennis anymore, and you might not hear well, do you feel that the screen between your perception of life, of God, has been more opened with aging or more closed? Do you feel that your "doors of perception," using Aldous Huxley's phrase, have grown wider?

Huston: Yes, opened. In terms of horizons, mental horizons. Yes, definitely.

Ken: The quality of your thinking seems extraordinary to me. I have studied aging and older adults now for thirty-five-plus years, and usually, if I sit down with a ninety-year-old, the quality of their mind is diminished. Yours does not seem to be.

Huston: Well, use it or lose it.

Ken: If I were to ask you to provide simple advice about how to age well and you'd give five suggestions to younger people based on your life experience, what would you advise?

Huston: First, take care of your health. Second, keep your mind alert and occupied. I recently reread *The Brothers Karamazov* by Dostoyevsky. It's complicated, but it is an amazing book.

Third, friendships are very, very important. I'm picked up for lunch about three days a week to go out, and we have an enjoyable time. Just being with friends and catching up on what's going on in their lives is so nourishing, at so many levels. Fourth, do not overlook the beauty of this world. And the fifth one would be: listen in order to understand the lives of others that you are associated with because they too have their story.

Ken: Do you ever wish you could be young again?

Huston: You know, I have been interviewed maybe five hundred times, and once in a long while, someone comes up with a question I've never thought of, and my knee-jerk response is, "Darn you for asking me a question I've never thought of!" Do I wish I were young again? No. No, categorically, no. Being young was fine then, but I've done that, and there's no wish to repeat it. Life is like an arch, and the arch has been completed. This is not like one of those bridges where you have arch after arch. I mean, after a wonderful dinner, you don't need three desserts.

Ken: There is a great deal of attention spent with trying to put off aging, to look young, act young, be young, feel young. What's your point of view about all that?

Huston: That it's denial and it's tending to appearance without getting down to the real question of coming to terms with it and making the most of it.

Ken: And making the most of it, of one's life, of one's aging. How is that done?

Huston: How do you make the most of your life? By making the right choices and trying, from experience, to cultivate wisdom. I have sought out His Holiness, the Dalai Lama, Gerald Heard, Aldous Huxley, and so on, and I have been rapacious in trying to assimilate as much wisdom as I can from them. I think I've gleaned almost ruthlessly from wise people.

Now, I think there is another thing that comes into this matter of aging that we have not mentioned yet, and this is one's attitude towards death. If one is not afraid of death, then aging, which slopes inevitably toward that moment, holds no great fear. I happen to have been born and raised a Christian. So that's what I am. But far be it from me to pass judgment on what it would be like if I had been born a Buddhist or a Hindu. I have some information of that because I have friends in all the seven other major religions. So over the years I have learned to pick their minds for their understanding.

The Christian view regarding death is that if you have lived your life reasonably well, you will go to heaven. And I think that it's basically right, whatever words you want, and it's very interesting that now science is confirming that point because one of Einstein's three greatest discoveries is that matter cannot be annihilated. It can transform into energy or something, and then come back to matter and then goes the other way. But there's no way to annihilate it. Well, we're matter and there's no way to annihilate it. It may go into that other mode, but the "light on the television screen never goes off." We have no idea of what the image on that television screen will be after we—and this is a useful phrase, and it's from the Indian—after we drop the body. We don't know, but the light's never going to go off.

Ken: What would a Buddhist view be about what comes next?

Huston: Reincarnation. They see death, simply, analogous to changing your clothes. You change the clothes of your body, but the essence of you takes on a new body, and how it is reborn depends on how you have lived your life. Each life is only one chapter in a very thick book, and the virtues and merit one has obtained in this life will be cumulative through your future lives.

Ken: Do you find yourself, as you age, altering your view about how much fear you have about dying?

Huston: Well, now, you will not let me weasel out, but I'm going to put it slightly differently. How does one feel about one's life when one nears the end of it? And this is also another recent realization, namely, that if you're happy about your life, then you're content to just let it drop away like a leaf falling from a tree.

Ken: You have a far bigger bank of knowledge than most people have, particularly about what the different religious traditions think happens at the end of this physical life, and I'd like to know what you personally believe is going to happen to Huston Smith at the end of this life.

Huston: Well, his television screen is not going to go dead, but part of what makes it interesting is that at this stage, I have no idea what the images will be.

Ken: Are you curious to see that next chapter?

Huston: I am content with the pace and arc of life. If I were to learn that I would die tomorrow, I would hope that there would be time for my family to gather around me. But otherwise, the acceptance would be there.

Ken: When you personally envision the transition out of this body, do you perceive it as something that's abrupt? One moment you are this, and the next moment you are in some other form. Or do you see it as something that is fluid?

Huston: No. It will be abrupt, and it will come as a surprise. But I have pondered this a little bit. Let me make my point by way of a cartoon. Cartoons are intended to be funny, but they can also be very wise at times. I remember a cartoon of a man on a cliff looking out over a beautiful sunset, and the caption ran: "Man enjoying himself enjoying the sunset." In other words, the attention was on his enjoyment, rather than on the sunset. Now, that carries over and that creates a little wondering on my part about when I drop the body. I am at peace and persuaded that it will be as glorious as heaven is supposed to be, but what I don't know is whether that glory will totally absorb my attention or whether there will still be some remnant of attention on Huston enjoying the glory of heaven. I hope it's not that, but who knows.

Ken: Do you have an expectation that there will be a reincarnated you that will appear somewhere, sometime?

Huston: Reincarnation is sure, but where or when, not so sure. The classic Indian doctrine of reincarnation is you are reborn in a new body on this earth. Well, possibly, but I'm not invested in that. It may be in an unknown land, if land even... well, it's a metaphor.

Ken: So, if you were to find yourself, to the extent that you were taking note, of yourself in some far-off galaxy or with some other metaphysical realm. Would that be okay?

Huston: Sure. Now, there is one question about whether I want to not totally be ... my attention not totally on the sunset but on myself, and that is that I find myself wondering whether I will know my loved ones still in the body when I'm not in the body. And I find myself saying to myself, "Yes. I love them, and I'm invested in their lives and in their future, and I would like to continue to be aware of them." But if that's not the way it is ... I can take it or leave it.

Ken: If you knew your life was coming to end, this life, or this body that you might drop soon, what would you regret the most?

Huston: That I wished I had listened more to my wife. I heard the words, but I did not always pick up the feeling behind that word, those words. So, that is a regret that I wish I had done differently.

Ken: If you were to think of one song that best tells the story of your life, what song would that be?

Huston: "How Can I Keep from Singing?" Do you know that song? It's a wonderful song. It goes like this:

My life flows on in endless song above verse limitation.
I hear that sure but far off tune that spells a new creation.
Amidst all the sorrows and the strife, I hear that music ringing.
It sounds and echoes, oh, in my soul. How can I keep from singing?

Well, you asked for it, so you got it.

Ken: If there were one prayer that best reflected your deepest wishes, what prayer would that be?

Huston: God, please increase my love for my fellow companions and my understanding of life with its profound mysteries.

Ken: And that prayer comes from?

Huston: Me! I made it up just now.

Ken: Please imagine that it's one hundred years from now and you and I are long gone. People are studying the life and work of Huston Smith. What would you wish in terms of how people might think of you, your studies, and your teachings?

Huston: He did the best he could.

Ken: As it turns out, you've lived longer than many of your teachers. Many of the individuals whose work you admired and studied lived far less long than you've lived. What have you made of these additional years beyond what your teachers could make of their sixty or seventy years of life? What shines through more clearly from these extra decades of life?

Huston: It's common knowledge that I was a close friend of Aldous Huxley. Once when I was driving him home from a lecture, he said, "Huston, you know it's rather embarrassing to have spent one's whole life pondering the human condition and come up with nothing more profound than 'Try to be a little kinder.'" Aldous was a very wise and modest person, but

I think that's exactly right. So, with each passing year, it becomes more evident that this is the basic human project: to be a little kinder in one's dealings with other people.

Ken: Before we end our discussion, what would you like to ask of yourself?

Huston: I would like to ask myself what I would hope my last words would be, and there's a little story behind this, little in the sense of short, but momentous. Saint John of Chrysostom, a Christian saint in the fourth century, crossed a Russian czarina for neglecting the poor. And she, in her absolute power, ordered him to be dragged to death behind a chariot. He was deeply loved by the people, and so in that scene throngs of people on both sides were mourning his death. It is said that one of them picked up his last words: "Thanks, thanks for everything; praise, praise for it all." I would wish those could be my last words.

Ken: I have so enjoyed our discussion. Thank you for allowing me to visit with you today.

Huston: You're most welcome.

ON HIS OWN TWO FEET

If there is any immortality to be had among us human beings, it is certainly only in the love that we leave behind. Fathers like mine don't ever die.
—Leo Buscaglia

About twenty years ago, my father started to lose his vision and with it, control over much of his life. At first, his diabetes-related macular degeneration made it hard for him to read. But as the disease progressed, he no longer could write, balance his checkbook, drive his car, or find his clothes. Sadly, during that exact same period, my mom was being decimated by Alzheimer's disease. He loved my mom so much that he railed against the dissolution of her memory and her mind. He got depressed and angry. And when he felt this way, he sought out people to argue with about politics.

My father had always been a contentious and activist Republican. Even when I was a teenager, I remember him writing edgy letters to the editors complaining about this or that left-wing liberal. As he got older and more visually disabled, he stepped up his game and would unleash his views on everyone. When his home health aide drove him to the eye doctor, my father would start arguing, battling with the other patients in the waiting room. He did the same thing at the heart doctor, the diabetologist, and the dentist. More, he stirred up arguments at the supermarket, the deli, in the dining room of his community center, and even in his home when the repairmen would come to fix a leak in the plumbing. None of these people had a chance because among other things, my dad was a world-class political grappler. He had a storehouse of knowledge and biting questions, and he modeled himself after outrageous right-wing radio/TV hosts Joe Pyne and Alan Burke and then their offspring Rush Limbaugh and Sean Hannity; his intention was to take you to the ground.

His style of political confrontation reminded me of the Gracies, the legendary family of martial artists from Brazil. There were maybe ten of them: a grandfather, father, kids, grandkids, cousins, who knows. They would come out before each fight lined up one behind the other like train cars, each one with his hand on another's shoulder. While most mixed martial artists would focus on punching or kicking, the Gracies had perfected a style that first got their opponent to the ground. Then they'd destroy them, because there wasn't anyone who could grapple on the ground like they could.

Not having gone to college or spent time within polite society, my father was a grappler when it came to intellectual combat. He would ply you with complicated facts, extreme propositions, and edgy questions. By the time you realized what was going on, intellectually he'd have you to the ground and you couldn't win. This was tricky for me because I loved my dad deeply, respected his thought processes, but disagreed with much of what he concluded and promoted. As you can imagine, over the decades this led to many, many lively discussions, debates, and arguments.

In any case, around 2007, after he had become totally blind and my mom's mind was rapidly dissolving, during our nightly phone call, my father started talking to me about suicide. He'd say, "Kenny, I can't stand the state I'm in. I'm no good for anybody. I can't look after your mom. I'm costing money. I don't want to be alive anymore. I'm going to end my life." Night after night, I'd do my best to comfort him in his depression. And every few months I'd fly to Florida to take stock of the situation and try to shower my mom and dad with love and support.

But the nightly suicide discussion continued unabated. Finally, realizing how serious he was about this, and after consulting with my own therapist, I said to him. "Dad, I love you. Mom loves you, Alan loves you. Maddy, Casey, and Zak love you, and we all want you around as long as possible. I love talking to you, and I love being with you. I'll be back in Florida in a couple of weeks. But you are living your own life, and you have to do what you think is right for you and Mom."

As time passed and my mom became more confused, he began telling me that he was thinking of committing suicide in partnership with my mom. "We have always loved each other, but the wheels on both of our carts are falling off. If I die before Mom, she'll struggle terribly, and if she dies before me, I'll go crazy. I'm going to end my life and take her with me. Just as we've lived together, we want to die together." That was quite a lot for me to digest. One night he asked me, "If I take my own life and Mom's, would that be brave or cowardly?"

I said, "I sure don't know, Dad. If I was in your situation, I can't imagine what I'd think or do. But I might come to the same conclusion that you have." So for almost a year, every night I'd go to sleep not knowing if my parents would be alive in the morning. But he never took this action.

In the spring of 2013 my brother reminded me that our parents' seventy-first anniversary was coming up in August. We realized that there might not be that many more anniversaries they would experience together. We decided to fly our whole family to Florida to celebrate their anniversary—and their lives—with them. My brother's girlfriend, Mary, flew in from Peru; Zak and his friend Liz were coming from New York; and Casey and her boyfriend, Tyler, would come from LA. The weekend was truly wonderful. Everyone showered my parents with love and respect. My dad and mom were beaming with happiness with every touch and toast at the celebratory dinner. When it was time for everyone to say good-bye on Sunday, , I could see tears rolling down both of their faces as they hugged each of us.

There's a side story to this anniversary that's worth mentioning. When I realized my parents had very few friends left to celebrate their seventy-one years together, I half-kiddingly said to my dad and mom, "Just tell me anyone in the world who you'd like to call you on the day of your anniversary, and I'll see what I can do." In truth, I wondered if they'd pick President Obama, since he was the leader of the free world. I didn't know if I could get this request to Obama, but I'd sure try. However, in response to my question, my dad had an immediate request: Fox News host Sean Hannity. "What?" I said. "Of all the people in the world, the one you'd most like to hear from on this grand occasion is Sean Hannity?" "That's right," my dad said as my mom nodded her consent.

I had met Rupert Murdoch a few years before when I had the great privilege of speaking at a gathering of global leaders, alongside Bill Clinton, Tony Blair, Bono, Arnold Schwarzenegger, and Al Gore. Hoping that he might remember me, I reached out to Mr. Murdoch, who was kind enough to pass my note to Bill Shine, who at that point oversaw much of Fox News. Shine wrote me an email asking for particulars: my parents' names, when and how they met, what they had done in their lives, how they felt about each other now, and so on. He also asked me what date and time they'd like the call from Sean Hannity, in case he was able to make it happen. "Ten AM on their wedding anniversary," I told him.

When their anniversary rolled around, at exactly 10:00 AM their phone rang, and Sean Hannity was on the line, calling to wish them a happy, happy anniversary. My mom graciously thanked him for calling, and then my dad jumped in and began a lively argumentative exchange with Hannity that lasted almost an hour. It was truly a dream come true for him. For weeks afterward, everywhere he went, he proudly proclaimed that Sean Hannity had called to talk with him on his anniversary!

Although I can't stand Sean Hannity's perspectives or attitude on the air, I appreciated how kind and caring he was with my parents that day.

One month later Alan called me in a state of distress to report that our dad's blood sugar was going haywire. Usually, it's around 120. That day it was 600. And to make things worse, he couldn't get his balance and had fallen on his face, giving himself a big gash on his forehead. Alan was already on his way to Newark Airport to fly to Florida and take charge of the situation.

The next morning Alan went to the doctor with my dad, while my mom was looked after by Lorna Dalrio, their wonderful home care aide. I was boarding my plane to Florida when my brother called to tell me that the doctor had taken one look at our dad and immediately had him admitted to intensive care. They discovered that not only was his blood sugar out of control but he had internal bleeding and had suffered a mild heart attack. His body was shutting down. As soon as I landed, I raced to the hospital to find my father in intensive care with my brother beside him. There was a tangle of wires and tubes all over him, and he was aggressively pulling them all out. As a sightless man, in a state of extreme agitation, not knowing what had happened to him or who these strange people were who were putting tubes and needles in his wrists, his mouth, his chest, and his penis, my dad was clearly going mad. When he realized that his two boys were there for him, he called out to Alan and me, "Take me home! Please get me out of here! Get me out of here!" Unfortunately, while most of hospital staff was kind and considerate, the head nurse was an asshole. My dad needed to take pain and anxiety medication, but because he was so unruly and upset, the guy pushed him on his side and stuck the medication in my father's ass while my brother and I looked on dumfounded.

My dad settled down a bit, and Alan and I went home to see our mom. Then at around 10:00 PM my mom's phone rang. It was our dad, and he had gotten someone to dial the number. He was pleading with us to come back and rescue him. Alan and I shot back to the hospital and went into our anguished father's room. We held him and tried to calm him down. He was calling out, "Where am I? Who are all the people around me? What's happening?" His arms, chest, face, and hair were covered with blood because he kept pulling out his IV lines. The same mean nurse from earlier said to me and my brother, "Your father is really losing it. I can't deal with him. One of you guys is going to have to stay here tonight and hold him down."

Seeing how exhausted I was from just having traveled across the country, Alan said, "I'll do it." I returned to be with our mom for the night. When she asked, "Where's Dad?" I explained that he was in the hospital and he wasn't doing very well at all. Although confused by her Alzheimer's, my mom could understand that something was very wrong, and she quietly retreated to her bed, where she lay awake all night.

In the morning, after a torturous night for both my dad and my brother, and a sad night for my mom and me, I returned to the hospital and we asked, "Dad, what do you want?"

"I'm scared," he said, "but I know this: I've lived my whole life on my own two feet, and I'm not going out on my hands and knees. Help me, Kenny and Alan. Help me. Please help me bring this to an end."

Shortly after that exchange, Alan and I met with our dad's physician. He was a kind and decent man who asked us if we wanted our dad to remain in intensive care or if we preferred to shift him to a hospice care ward in the hospital. What an emotional and yet simple decision to be made. Were we going to battle to keep our dad alive for a few more days, albeit in a ghastly, ghoulish fashion, or were we prepared to make him comfortable and allow him to die a good death?

We immediately had him transferred to the hospice floor, where the kind nurses and aides removed all the IV wires and tubes, lovingly sponged all of the blood off of him, and even gave him a shave and combed his hair. They asked him what his favorite music was, and they put a Frank Sinatra album on the CD player. They began a low dose of morphine to ease his anxiety. Maddy, Casey, and Zak all dropped what they were doing to fly to Florida and be with my dad.

Not knowing how I should handle my dad in this truly extreme situation, I called one of my closest friends, Stuart Pellman, who was a bit older than me and had already dealt with the death of both of his parents. He wisely told me, "Get one-on-one time with your dad, and tell him everything you need to tell him. Even if he's unconscious, tell him you love him, ask him to forgive you for anything you may have ever done to trouble him. Tell him you forgive him for anything he might have ever done to upset you, and then tell him you'll always remember him."

And that's what I did. I sat beside my dad and held him and told him how much I loved him, and he came awake and kissed me. He told me how much he loved me, and then we forgave each other, and we even laughed about all of the times we had fought over the years. I told him I'd always remember him. We held each other for a long while, and then I left the room and encouraged my brother to do the same. He did, and it seemed to provide massive relief to him that our dad told him how much he had always loved him. Then my mom came to his bedside and we all left the room, but we could see that she was holding and kissing him, and he was telling her how much he loved her. She asked us to take a picture as she gave him her final kiss good-bye. Later that day, as Maddy, Casey, and Zak arrived and entered his room, he awakened and each of them got private time with Grandpa. Zak spent hours sitting there with his grandfather.

Later that night, after the other members of my family had gone home, I joined my dad for a very intense and private conversation. I said, "Dad, you've never asked me what I think happens when a person dies."

"I'd like to know what you think about that, Kenny," he responded. "Because I have begun to see my brothers and sister and Marty Marcus, and they're reaching out to me."

My dad had no religious beliefs, but I had some. So I said, "Dad, I don't know this for sure, but I believe when a person passes there is another plane that presents itself. In that place are all the people you have known and loved." As I began to describe this to him, he calmed down and started to cry. Then he turned toward me and told me he was ready. I asked him if I could record the rest of our exchange on my phone so that I could always have it to watch when I missed him. He said okay, and this is what transpired. (I have since watched this short clip with my dad more than a hundred times.)

Ken: Dad, you know that what's going to be next is going to be beautiful, and your vision's going to be back, and you're going to be a beautiful young man again.

Dad: I'm ready for that, Kenny. I'm ready.

Ken: And you know we all love you.

Dad: I know it, Kenny.

Ken: And you've always loved us.

Dad: Right. That's true.

Ken: So, what you'll need to do is to let go, and just surrender, and not worry about anything because Alan and Mom and I and Maddy and Zak and Casey, everything is going to be looked after. All we need is for you to be relaxed and calm and just drift off into the white light. Can you do that, Dad?

Dad: Absolutely.

Ken: I love you, Pops.

Dad: I love you, Kenny.

My father died peacefully that night. With help from all of us, he went out on his own two feet.

Ultimately, even with all his frustration, anger, and talk of suicide, my dad died a good death. At the end, his pain was minimal. His mind was calm. He knew how much we loved him. He found a way to think about leaving his body as not being frightening. He had even thought he was catching glimpses of his siblings Milton, Carl, and Ethel, and his best friend and brother-in-law, Marty Marcus. And although he had been blind for years, at the very end he began to describe beautiful waterfalls, flowers, birds, and castles. When my time comes, I hope that Maddy will kiss me good-bye and at least one of my kids—maybe even both—will be there to lovingly guide me out of my body.

There is no doubt for me that those last moments with my dad represented the culmination of my radical curiosity practice. He and I were both teacher and student at once, each reflecting the other and ready to continue growing. *Breathe, learn, teach, repeat.*

ZAK'S DECLARATION OF INDEPENDENCE
A LETTER TO MOM AND DAD

Parents can only give good advice or put them on the right paths, but the final forming of a person's character lies in their own hands. —Anne Frank

Forty years after I wrote a letter to my parents in my mid-twenties—a declaration of independence that was also a major first step in beginning to understand who I actually was—Maddy and I received the following letter from our son.

5/4/2015
Dear Mom and Dad,

The fact is I need family support right now, and I think I deserve it.

I know that I live in China—very far away from you both and Casey. I know that this choice is mine. I am doing it because I want to make a contribution to the world at a young age, because I don't want to be ordinary. It has been a very difficult road. The work has been hard, and the extreme loneliness of being here that sometimes sinks in, is the worst. It is the loneliness of holding onto a dream.

I have busted my ass harder than ever to speak the language fluently and am trying to write a book reinventing the way people see a global superpower. I'm also 25, alone, and have no experience writing. This is hard for me. I think it would be hard for anyone. What hurts me the most is when I call either of you and you both spend more time asking me about when I'm coming home, expressing your longing for me to come home. Do you think it is easy for me to go against both of your wishes? It's not. It's very hard.

On the phone you said you want me to come home because you miss me and I'm your boy. You want to hold and cuddle me. I love you and will always be your son. I miss you, too. But I am doing something called dream chasing. I am trying to make something of myself that my father, my mother, my sister, uncle, and grandparents can be proud of. I am trying to make something that I will be proud of. Please don't stop me from trying to do that so I can go home and make you feel good.

You often ask me how you can help, how you can be better parents to me. The answer is, fortunately, simple and easy: support me. When I say it is hard work, say, "It's okay, son, we know you can do it. We're here for you," and then maybe share some tips. Make me feel good, like I can take on the work. Don't over-compliment me as being this super-smart whatever guy. I am not looking for that kind of thing. Finish calls on a warm note. Make me feel like you have my back, and then have it. That is what I would like my parents to do.

Next month, I'm taking a major test to prove that I am fluent in Chinese, the highest language fluency test they have in Mainland China. I hope you can be supportive with this book, because it is the hardest thing I've ever done and I would love to have your help and support, even if it just means helping me feel like I can do it. It would mean so much to me.

With love,
Zak

After Maddy and I finished reading Zak's letter, we took a moment to collect our thoughts. We had a choice about how to take this as parents. We could be defensive, or angry, or deny his position. Or we could learn a little more about who our son really was—clearly he was doing his best to figure that out for himself as well.

Breathe, learn, teach, repeat.

THE DEATH OF A PEARL

I loved you every day. And now I will miss you every day. —Mitch Albom

My mom, Pearl Dychtwald, died on October 1, 2016, at the age of ninety-three. Overall everyone was very kind to me upon learning of her death: their reaction was generally, "How sad." Maybe I'm deluding myself, but although I miss her deeply, her death didn't feel sad to me at all.

My mom was always, always, always a caring, kind, and loving human. When I was a child, she was the mom that my friends would come talk to when they were having trouble at home. When I was a teenager, she taught me to dance the cha-cha and to do gymnastics. Then, in my hippie years, as my dad and I regularly battled it out to determine who was "right," my mom never lost her gentleness and perspective. She'd say, "You'll be fine. You and your dad love each other so much. Everything's going to work out, I believe in you." She was always this way—her belief in me never faltered. Her positivity about everyone never faltered.

When she reached around eighty years of age, my mom's memory started to fail, and over the next dozen years she was slowly decimated by Alzheimer's disease. Every time I'd see her, which would be every several months, she'd be less there. Although raised in poverty and never educated beyond her high school diploma, she was always a very wise and elegant woman. When she was growing up, she was trained as a dancer, in everything from ballet to tap. She was poised and graceful both in her movements and in her nature. Even into her seventies she practiced her dance steps and choreographed routines daily, and she had even begun teaching tap classes to the retired women in her community as well as to the low-income kids who lived in nearby neighborhoods.

But Alzheimer's chiseled away at her mind and her memories. After a long flight from California, when I'd come in the front door of their home in Delray Beach, Florida, she'd always rush toward me and greet me with a big hug. But I couldn't help noticing that her makeup would be askew, or she would have two different socks on, or she'd have forgotten to zip her slacks. At the same time—as I've discussed earlier in this book—each year my dad was becoming increasingly blind due to macular degeneration, and more and more distraught because my mom, the love of his life, was clearly losing her mind. In her final years my dear mom also struggled with chronic obstructive pulmonary disease, and for three hourlong sessions a day she had to wear a nose mask and breathe through a nebulizer connected to a big oxygen tank to help her lungs stay clear.

After one terrible fall, we learned that she had fractured her pelvis and would need to spend six weeks in a rehab facility. This terrified her, as she didn't know where she was, couldn't figure out who the people orbiting her were, and was so sad to be away from my dad, who sat beside her all day, every day, and held her.

Alan and I flew to Florida to support them, and I made a point of meeting with the director of services at the facility where my mom was a patient. She was aware of my work, and I was assured my mom would receive extra-special attention. That was just fine with me. However, one night my mom awakened, unsure of where she was, and needed to go to the bathroom. She cried alone until she figured out how to push the button beside her and call for help. After a while, an aide showed up and lifted her to the toilet seat in the bathroom. Then he forgot about her and just left her there. In the morning, when we arrived, we found my beautiful mom still sitting on the toilet seat, confused and crying uncontrollably. She didn't deserve to be treated this way. Nobody's mother deserves to be treated this way. Nobody's mother deserves to be in this situation in the first place. Nevertheless, with each blow to her mind and body, my mom kept bouncing back. No matter where I was or what I was doing, I always made sure to talk to her every single day for decades. I loved her so much, and the sound of her voice, however unsure of itself, warmed my heart.

In the period before my dad's death in 2013, his macular degeneration was infuriating him, making him increasingly cranky and moody. My kids came to think of him as an eccentric, grumpy old man. They hadn't know him before he'd gotten beaten down this way. Of course, I had. I knew him to be a smart, tough, and caring man, but in his final years he raged against his and my mom's disabilities. He had become tormented.

When my dad died in October 2013, my mom at first became totally disoriented. It was understandable, as they had been married for seventy-one years and were like old trees whose roots and limbs had grown entwined around each other. She'd walk around the house looking for him in his usual spots—in front of the TV watching Fox News or next to his radio, listening to the stock reports. She'd call out, "Seymour? Where are you, Seymour?" Alan and I wondered, What's going to happen now? Our family had discussed this potential situation in advance, and we had a game plan. Alan was fully committed to becoming our mom's caregiver. We thought she'd live a few more months. In fact, her doctor had told us that her vital signs were beginning to fail and that we should swiftly put her affairs in order. My kindhearted brother gave up his apartment and lifestyle in New Jersey and moved into the guest bedroom in my mom's home, stepping into a role that we all thought would be intense but temporary. As a single man in his sixties, he had never really cared for anyone before, and he poured himself into it. As he attended to all her needs, just as Alan and I had promised our dad several years before, he assured our mom that she would never be frightened and would never be alone and that she would never be put into a nursing home. We both repeatedly told her that she would always be cared for in the comfort and familiarity of her home—no matter what it took or what it cost. Between us, we would do everything humanly possible to protect our mom while honoring our dad.

In the final years of her life, because she had to be watched every second of every minute of every hour, we needed to have aides helping out twenty-four hours a day, two to three shifts a day. They'd clean the house, bathe my mom, prepare her meals, and make sure she didn't wander or fall. These women, especially Lorna Dalrio—a warm and loving Jamaican American woman who had begun helping my dad and mom years before—became part of our extended family. They were massively helpful of course, but the whole situation was stressful and unrelenting for my brother, especially when an aide would arrive late, leave early, or not be able to show up at all. He never was really off, and even when he left the house, he was on call and on edge, worried about our mom. But my brother didn't think of this caregiving as a burden; he saw it as an honor.

Even after our dad's death, and even after much of her mind and memory had disappeared, my mom kept moving forward in a wobbly but positive fashion. Whenever I asked how she was doing, she'd say, "I'm doing marvelous." When I'd follow up and ask, "Really? How come?" she'd respond, "I'm just so lucky, I'm so fortunate to have Alan and you and Maddy and Casey and Zak. I'm the luckiest woman in the world!" Even when she became incontinent and had to wear a diaper, she didn't complain. The aides all thought she was like an angel. They would say, "Mrs. D., it's time for your medicine," and she'd say, "Thank you so very much. You're so kind to me." And when they put her socks on, she'd thank them profusely.

Over the last year of her life her mind and body were shutting down and she began losing the ability to walk. Then, in the last few months, she could barely use her arms anymore. Whereas she'd always wanted to go to the beauty salon once each week, now her hair was stringy, and her lipstick, which she insisted on putting on herself, was tilted. Her clothing, which she had always taken great pains to have look nice and neat, was sloppy. During that period, for the first time, she began to ask my brother, "Why am I still alive? I had a wonderful marriage and a marvelous life. But I don't know if I should be alive anymore." This upset Alan, but over the months that she was broaching this issue, he began to realize that in her own way she was signaling that the end was getting nearer.

By then her short-term memory was nearly nonexistent. For example, one time when I came to visit, we sat and held hands while she watched the TV show *Jeopardy*. She kindly asked me if I'd like some watermelon. I told her, "No thanks." Several minutes later she again asked me if I'd like some watermelon. I told her again, "No thanks, Mom." Then only a few moments later she asked me if I'd like some watermelon, and again I told her no This continued over and over again through the night, until she went to bed.

One of my biggest challenges during those years was to not lose patience with my dear mom. I had to continually remind myself that she wasn't being rude or inattentive, she simply could not remember anything from moments before. The Alzheimer's was taking away everything except her essence—her kindness and appreciation of life. There were times when I thought that this must be what enlightenment is like: to be kind, caring, loving, and totally in the now.

As her ninety-third birthday approached, we didn't know if she'd make it, but she was sort of keeping an eye on the date. "Isn't my birthday coming soon?" she began to ask.

"Yes," we told her, "and we're going to throw a wonderful party for you."

"I hope I can be there!" she said.

I kiddingly told her, "I hope so, too! Without you, it wouldn't be as good a party!"

And so, on the eve of her birthday, Maddy, Casey, Zak, and I joined Alan and his girlfriend—and of course, Lorna Dalrio—for a festive birthday dinner. She was as happy as could be and insisted on leaving her bed and wheelchair in order to sit upright at the head of the table. She fed herself, which she hadn't done for months. We sang "Happy Birthday" to her, with her joining in to sing to herself. It seemed to take all her strength and focus to blow out a solo birthday candle and make a wish. Then she gathered herself and told us all how much she loved us and how thankful she was to have all of us in her life. It was a wonderful night. The next day, Maddy, Casey, and Zak left, but I decided to stay to give my brother some extra backup.

In the week immediately following her birthday dinner, my mom she took a nose dive. She just couldn't do anything; she couldn't even drink water. The hospice aides were called in. One night Alan had plans to go out for a few hours with some of his musician friends, but he wasn't sure if he should leave the house. I told him to go out and get his mind off of things. I'd be there with our mom. That night she was lying in a little hospital bed that had been placed into her bedroom by the hospice aides. It had side railings because she didn't know where she was and she might try to get up on her own or fall out of her bed.

I asked the aide and hospice nurse if they could leave me alone with my mom for a while. She seemed zonked, but I wanted to just hold her hand and kiss her cheeks. She looked beautiful—radiant really. I said to her, "Mom, I'd like to try to talk to you a little bit, and I'm not sure how much you can hear me." She turned to me and gave me the sense that she was trying to pay attention to what I was saying. I asked, "Mom, how are you doing?"

She said, "Kenny, I'm doing the best I can."

I looked her in the eyes and said, "I think we're coming to the end of this life here."

She nodded. "I only have a little bit left. It's been a marvelous life."

I told her that I wanted her to know how much I loved her.

"Oh," she responded as she gripped my hand, "I know how much you love me, and I have always loved you with all my heart."

"Mom, are you frightened at all?" I asked.

"What would I be frightened of?" she responded.

"What can I do for you?" I asked. She was foggy, but she was sort of tracking me.

She said, "You've done so much for me, what can I do for you?"

I'm thinking, Here's my mother, she's on her deathbed, she can't move her arms or her legs, she's wearing a diaper underneath her pink sweat suit, and she's asking me what she can do for me. I held her close and said, "Mom, you've done everything for me. I'm going to be fine. Alan's going to be fine. Maddy, Casey, Zak, and I are all going to be fine. We're going to think of you every day forever. It'll be all right, and you can let go anytime you want."

And then, not being sure if she could hold her mental focus for any more questions, I said to her, "Mom, I'd really like to know... when you think back over your life, what part of your life was your favorite part?"

She closed her eyes, and I thought she had totally spaced out because nearly thirty minutes went by. Then she opened her eyes, looked at me, and said, "Every part of my life was my favorite part." Then her eyes closed, and she never talked again.

My brother came home later that night, and I said, "Look at Mom. Have you ever seen anything like this?" She was glowing. We both sat together for a long while and just stared at our mom, remembering how loving she had always been to us and what a special human being she was.

The next day, with both of us holding her, she passed away. She hadn't been frightened. The two boys she had given birth to were holding her as she left her body.

And when she died, rather than becoming unglued, Alan felt at peace. He felt that he had done the best he could. For an intense three years he had devoted himself around the clock to creating a world in which our mom felt secure, safe, and most of all, loved. In many ways we had been mourning our loss for years. In her final months she wasn't frightened; Alan had surrounded her with love, respect, and kindness. Her final days were beatific.

The next day Maddy, Casey, and Zak flew back to Florida for a small, intimate memorial service. After we gathered with a local rabbi and shared our stories about my mom, we returned to her home, now Alan's home, to clean out her bedroom and her closets. Because of my dad's blindness and my mom's Alzheimer's, her closets were overflowing with stuff, stuff, and more stuff. Apparently neither my brother nor the aides had felt comfortable throwing anything away, and so there were decades of clothing and memorabilia to be sorted through.

Then something quite unexpected happened.

As Maddy, Casey, and Zak were digging around in the back of their grandmother's belongings, they found a large shoe box filled with little scraps of paper. Zak brought the box out to the living room so we could all see what was inside. There were hundreds of notes, written on scraps of paper or on the back of envelopes. They were simple love notes, written over the years from my dad to my mom. Written in his sloppy handwriting, they read:

"I almost drove away without telling you I love you."

"It's been too long since I told you how much I love you."

"Let me count the ways I can tell you I love you. Your not-so-silent admirer."

"Why waste words with much ornate prose. All I want to tell you is I love you."

"I don't know if the ginseng or me upset you last night. I hope I'm the lesser of the two. I love you."

"I have an eye problem. I can't take my eyes off of you. I love you."

"I don't have to get on a helicopter to look at you with amazement. You're a star at any altitude. I love you."

"You may miss when you swing at a golf ball. But whatever you do, you go right to my heart."

"I tingle with anticipation at the thought of being alone with you tonight."

"I said goodbye to you only minutes ago, but it seems like hours. I love you."

"I'm late for work, but I always have time to tell you I love you."

"I looked for you and found you—right next to me, where we belong."

No two were the same. These were notes that my father had apparently put on my mom's car windshield or on her pillow or on the kitchen table when he was rushing off to work. As I read them, I kept thinking, Oh, Dad, look what you wrote. Look how much you loved Mom. Look how sweet you were. Until these notes appeared, I had been inclined to think of my dad as he had been these last years—depressed, angry, and unhappy, with a mean streak.

But as we finished reading them—all of them—Alan, Maddy, Casey, Zak, and I completely recrafted our narrative of my mom and my dad and who they were in this life. Before my dad had become so unhappy and tangled up in his fear and worry, it was clear that he was crazy in love with his beloved Pearl. My dad was surely beaten up by the disabilities of later life. However, there was also this: a seventy-one-year love affair.

And so, when people, upon learning of my mom's passing, commented on how sad it must have been for me, I think, It wasn't. It was a tender, loving "good death." I hope that when I die I'm not frightened, and my family is holding me and my endless love for Maddy continues to soar.

ENTERING THE TWILIGHT ZONE

THE FATHER/SON ACT

When a father gives to his son, both laugh; when a son gives to his father, both cry.
—William Shakespeare

In 2019 I received a note from Matthew Upchurch, the chairman and CEO of Virtuoso, one of the world's largest networks bridging travel advisors and the hotels, tour operators, and other travel suppliers that serve them. Matthew was exploring if Zak and I might like to be dual keynote speakers at the most powerful and influential travel conference in the world, the World Travel & Tourism Council (WTTC) Global Summit, which in April 2019 was to be held in Seville, Spain. Heads of state, nearly all of the world's ministers of tourism, heads of the major travel and hospitality firms, and heads of global media would be attending. This would be, as you can imagine, a once-in-a-lifetime opportunity. Zak and I immediately checked our schedules, locked down the dates, and got to work gathering the research and ideas we'd each need to give home-run keynote presentations on this world stage. During the months ahead of the summit, Zak and I had numerous phone meetings with the conference coordinators and became increasingly excited about the chance to impact such a high-level group with each of our respective fields of interest. And, of course, a "dual" keynote with your playful but competitive son can slip in and out of a "duel" keynote, as Zak and I joked about storming the stage and seizing the crowd with each of our powerful topics and delivery.

Then in March I received a phone call from the head of WTTC. She explained that Zak and I would each need to cut the length of our presentations in half, as another speaker had joined the program as a keynoter during the same block of time as ours. That annoyed me, and as I tried my best to temper my frustration, I asked, "Who is this new speaker, and why is he or she cutting into our time?" I was told, "The other keynote speaker we have just secured is former President Barack Obama." What? Yikes! I immediately tracked Zak down somewhere in China to tell him whom we'd be following in Seville. From ten thousand miles away, I heard him gulp, and we agreed to reconnect to discuss strategy.

After letting the "Obama factor" percolate for several days, Zak and I talked. First, he boldly proclaimed, "Let's crush this!" Followed with "But Dad, when the Obama, Dychtwald, and Dychtwald evaluations come in, I intend to be ranked second." Over the phone, I could hear his smile as he added, "Whoever comes in first or third, that's between you and President Obama."

This became a running joke with us, probably as an antidote to the nervousness we were feeling about being compared with President Obama—or each other. Every time we talked, Zak reminded me that he was shooting for the number two spot and teased me that I'd wind up in third place. Zak and I each worked around the clock to tighten, trim, and strengthen our sessions. When we arrived in Seville, me via San Francisco and Zak via Cairo, where he had just given another keynote speech, we were so excited and happy to see each other, but we were also jet-lagged and exhausted.

Over the past forty years I've spoken to more than two million people at meetings and conferences around the world, but following my son, who would be following President Obama, would be a singular experience. My son was on par at the young age of twenty-nine. My little boy, now a handsome, world-traveled, charismatic, athletic, bearded, grown man (how did that happen so fast?), had spent much of the last decade living in China, not only pursuing his "hero's journey" in a way that would have made Joseph Campbell smile but, with the publication of his book, *Young China: How the Restless Generation Will Change Their Country and the World,* he had swiftly turned himself into a highly respected "expert" on China, one of history's most mysterious and increasingly influential cultures.

As President Obama was completing his remarks about the power of travel to unite people from different backgrounds and cultures—all the more valuable in a world that is becoming increasingly nationalistic—Zak and I were backstage trying not to panic while dodging heavily armed Secret Service guards. As the president offered his concluding comments, Zak and I hugged each other, double-checked our mics, and prepared to be introduced. Zak asked me what my nervousness level was. I told him mine was a high 8 a scale of 10. When I asked him the same question, he said, "A comfortable three." "And Dad," he reminded me, "I'm aiming for the number two spot when the evaluations come in." Then Matthew

Upchurch, the session sponsor and moderator, stepped onto the massive stage at the Seville Convention Center to introduce us.

Zak went first. After bowing to the audience and saying, "Zūnjìng de gèwèi lǐngdǎo, géwài láibīn, gèwèi péngyǒu, dàjiā xiàwǔ hǎo," he proceeded to mesmerize and educate the audience.

As I stood at the side of the stage, hiding a bit behind the curtain so the audience couldn't see me, I had a clear line of sight to my son. I was transfixed by his strength and his high-mindedness, and he was mesmerizing this powerful and influential audience with his big ideas and big heart. And I was transfixed by the surreal fact that he was my son. I was feeling as though I had truly entered the Twilight Zone.

Then I was jolted out of my reverie when I felt Matthew Upchurch's hand on my shoulder. "Your son just crushed it," he said. "Are you ready to take the stage?" I heard Zak say, "And now I have the unique honor of introducing Ken Dychtwald, my father."

I tried my best to turn everyone's attention to the fifty trillion hours of leisure that boomers worldwide would be seeking to fill. The next thing I knew, Zak and Matthew were standing beside me and the audience was giving us a standing ovation.

The next day, when all the evaluations of the more than twenty-five conference presentation sessions were tabulated, including President Obama's, Zak and I were evaluated as one session. We were blown away to learn that ours was the highest rated of the entire conference—in fact, it was the highest-rated session in the decades-long history of WTTC meetings.

SEARCHING FOR THE FOUNTAIN OF HEALTH

Every human being is the author of his own health and disease. —Buddha

My always curious daughter Casey (currently thirty-three years old) has of late become a critic of Western medicine and a vocal proponent of alternate approaches to wellness. Casey, in general, is nobody's fool. After completing her undergraduate degree from the Annenberg School for Communication and Journalism at the University of Southern California, she went right to work as an experiential marketer and event manager. She swiftly rose to become global production manager for the Creators Project, a partnership of VICE Media and Intel. In that role, she produced grand-scale events globally focused on the intersection of technology, music, and art in places such as Brazil, France, Korea, China, and the United States. Then, a couple of years ago, feeling burned out from the event-producer lifestyle and seeking to strengthen her intellectual fire-power, she applied to and was accepted into the esteemed global media master's degree program at the London School of Economics, where she wrote a thesis entitled "The Deconstruction of Truth in a Post Truth Era."

Since returning from London and securing a great job as head of business development for LA-based marketing firm Wondros, working alongside visionary founder Jesse Dylan (Bob's son), she likes to lecture me about what's wrong with Western medicine. Although I applaud her curiosity, her enthusiasm sometimes causes me to roll my eyes and sigh. She tells me, "You don't get it, Dad." Recently, Casey was home visiting, and she asked me why I was so resistant to the new ways of thinking about the body and mind. The following discussion ensued.

Casey: Dad, I know you know a lot about the body and mind, but I want to know why you are so unwilling to consider new approaches to health. Can we discuss, and can I record this?

Ken: Sure, and thanks for asking. Let me start by giving you some background. Until I was five, we lived on Lehigh Avenue in Newark, New

Jersey, in the same house as my mom's parents—my grandparents Max and Clara Siderman. Up the block, in a pleasant duplex, was the medical office of Dr. Victor Tepper, our family physician. If there was ever anything wrong, you went to see Dr. Tepper. If we were unable to leave the house for some reason, Dr. Tepper would show up at our front door with his medical bag to do an exam in our home. He usually checked what were then believed to be the key vital signs, so he used his stethoscope to hear how your heart was beating and how your lungs sounded. And he took your temperature and looked at your tongue. That was pretty well it.

Casey: Was that okay? Did you and your family feel that you were getting great medical care?

Ken: We didn't know better, so we thought it was fine. Dr. Tepper sure seemed like a kind and wise physician. Besides, back then, anyone who went to medical school was usually thought to be a stand-out individual. Before entrepreneurs, corporate executives, and hedge fund billionaires became glamorized, doctors were professional royalty.

Although we eventually moved into our own home a few miles away, Dr. Tepper remained our family doctor until I went off to college. Back then, you didn't really question what the doctor said, you just did what he told you to do. If the doctor said you should do this or that, you did it. You may think this is unimaginable, but when I was growing up, doctors wrote prescriptions in Latin. The idea was that you, the patient, were not supposed to understand what was in a prescription: that was not your business. Instead, you'd take the prescription to the local pharmacist, who was trained to read these Latin requests—and then you took your medicine as prescribed. And in time, you got better or you didn't. Of course, there was no Internet, there were no articles or research on health and wellness available to the general public. Medicine was a mysterious science, and doctors, with their healing and helping powers, were seen as almost God-like.

Then, in the late 1960s, as mass media and mind-expanding education began to open the world up to us, we boomers were being taught to question authority. As you know, what emerged was a rebellious, antiauthoritarian mood: it was rebellion against militarism, materialism, gas-guzzling cars, the sexual mores of our parents and grandparents' generations, and even medicine. That movement opened up a can of worms, for sure.

Women—lead by the Boston Women's Health Book Collective—and then men—began to believe that people should have knowledge about and control of their own bodies.

Around that time, as you know, I dropped out of college in order to fully immerse myself in the human potential movement at Esalen. As I upped my daily yoga practice to four hours each day (two hours each morning, an hour in the late afternoon, and an hour before going to sleep), I found that the Hindus don't see the body as Dr. Victor Tepper did. They believe that the body is a vibrating, pulsing energy field organized around seven vortices, called chakras. It wasn't some New Age idea—this yogic approach to health had been around for more than a thousand years. Maybe I was very open-minded or maybe I was foolishly gullible (or some combination of both), but I began to wonder if our whole notion of medicine in terms of blood pressure and heartbeat and lungs, and treatment with pharmaceuticals and surgery, was all bullshit. I wasn't alone. This kind of questioning was popping up in progressive—or impressionable—cities such as New York, LA, Chicago, and San Francisco. When cultural influencers such as the Beatles started having Indian gurus, lots of folks began to wonder if we should all become yogis.

But there was a catch. In our immediate-gratification-oriented lives, the Hindu approach to personal development was very slow moving. Far swifter approaches to mind-body health were swirling—primarily in New York and California. One of Sigmund Freud's medical students, Dr. Wilhelm Reich, believed that if you wanted to be mentally or physically healthy, you needed to free up your blocked emotions, fears, trauma, or sexual frigidity through intense psychotherapy and by practicing a variety of energetic and expressive movements. Reich believed that the body and mind were united and that at their core they were energy, which he called "orgone." Long before there were Samadhi isolation tanks and cryotherapy chambers at the local malls, Reich invented a wooden chamber that you could sit in to rebalance and recharge your energy. The FDA didn't agree. In 1956 they sent Reich to jail, proclaiming that he was selling quackery, not medicine. While imprisoned, Reich died the following year of a heart attack.

Just when everyone was trying to blend the Hindu and Reichian—Eastern and Western—approaches, elderly Bronx-born biochemist Dr. Ida Rolf showed up with an entirely different approach that promised optimal physical and mental health through ten structured deep-massage sessions.

A smart, old-fashioned scientist, Ida Rolf believed that since your body existed in a gravitational field, how you stand and move and how your myofascial tissue is either fluid or tight could create disruptions in your overall physical makeup and, in turn, your mind. If you could free up the myofascial tissue that was holding the body in imbalanced and misaligned ways, you could allow the body to return to a beautiful, balanced, upright, graceful, healthy, happy version of itself. People flocked from far and wide to get Rolfed by either Ida or one of her trained practitioners. During those years, I was Rolfed more than 150 times and also became friends with Ida.

Casey: Okay, Dad. Since you were in the middle of all this, wasn't it getting confusing? Were people doing crazy things? How did you know what was solid and what was nuts?

Ken: You can't even begin to imagine the range of things people were willing to try to find a shortcut to the fountain of health—even enlightenment. Suddenly you had a marketplace for anything and everything that promised to make you feel better. And the boundaries between mental and physical health were getting very fuzzy, which I guess I had contributed to a little.

Casey: Didn't people's common sense guide their openness to try these new things?

Ken: It was all really confusing. I remember wondering if I should practice yoga, be acupunctured, get Rolfed, or attempt a primal scream. For the record, I tried them all!

Then, swirling up from all this, when I moved to Berkeley from Big Sur, a diverse and high-minded group of doctors, psychologists, tai chi teachers, acupuncturists, psychics, biofeedback scientists, bodyworkers, and nutritionists got together and formed a study group to try to imagine a new model of medicine in which the mind and body weren't separated and all therapeutic possibilities could be examined. No one was motivated by money—instead everyone was driven by curiosity. Everyone was interested in sharing what they knew and learning from one another. For example, one week we were visited by Drs. Carl cancer Simonton and Stephanie Matthews-Simonton from Texas, who believed that cancer could be cured through meditation and visualization of healthy cells battling with and beating cancer cells. Another week we had a lengthy multidisciplinary discussion about healthy bowels, constipation, and diarrhea. One of the participants introduced the idea of "floaters" and "sinkers." What was her proposition? That if when you pooped you had floaters, you had the right amount of fiber in your diet. If you produced sinkers, you didn't.

As you know, from these meetings, Gay Luce, Eugenia Gerrard, and I started the Holistic Health Council and then the SAGE Project. At the same time, Eugenia Gerrard's husband, Don, came up with a bold idea. Because he had been a book distributor for years, Don thought that there were all these way-out and possibly revolutionary things going on in the Bay Area that the rest of the world was not aware of. So he went to New York and met with Random House with a proposal: "Let's create a joint book imprint, and I'll find cutting-edge authors and you give me some operating money and we'll distribute these books through your sales network and split the profits." They agreed to try it out. The very first book published by Bookworks/Random House was called *The Well Body Book* written by Mike Samuels and Hal Bennett. Nothing like it had ever existed before. It was an oversized book filled with drawings of human anatomy that clearly explained how your body worked—and how to get it to work better. It took the things that only doctors and nurses had known and made them understandable to laypeople so they could take charge of their own health.

Casey: Wait a minute. I know that the Internet wasn't invented yet, so there was no Google or YouTube, but there had to be wellness guidebooks. Weren't there?

Ken: No. As hard as it may be for you to consider, there weren't any. You may have taken a class on personal hygiene in high school, or there were a few pages about how to deal with accidents, cuts, or bruises in the *Boy Scouts Manual*. Now it seems inconceivable, but making this kind of mind/body/health information accessible to everyone was considered revolutionary. And you know what else? Don Gerrard was a publishing genius. *The Well Body Book* swiftly sold over a million copies.

Then a young Bay Area physician named John Travis, trained at Tufts and Johns Hopkins, found himself taken by Abraham Maslow's radical suggestion that you didn't have to be mentally ill to focus on being more mentally well. Travis applied that notion to the practice of medicine. He was the man who popularized the word "wellness." At the time the medical establishment thought Travis had totally gone off the rails!

Casey: Did you write *Bodymind* during this period?

Ken: Yes, it came out in 1977.

Casey: Nice work, Dad. So I guess that you were one of the pioneers of all this.

Ken: Thanks, Casey.

Casey: Looking back, what do you think was the major point of the book?

Ken: It's all right there in the title: *Bodymind*—one word. My publisher initially wanted to hyphenate it "Body-Mind." I insisted that we needed to shake up the way we thought about human beingness and all of the systems designed to improve us as well. After the book came out, I became curious about nutrition, which I hadn't known much about. I tracked down a world-renowned nutritionist, Paavo Airola, ND, from Finland. His book *How to Get Well* was a best seller. I tried to learn everything I could from him and many other popular experts. He told me, "Mental and physical health will not be achieved by being Rolfed, doing yoga, or being psychoanalyzed. Good nutrition is what causes mental and physical health; bad nutrition is what causes mental and physical disease. If we all knew what and how to eat, we'd all be super-healthy and super-happy."

Casey: Wait a minute. "Food as medicine" is a new idea—my generation is popularizing it.

Ken: Wrong. Sorry, Casey. After Airola, and Frances Moore Lappe's *Diet for a Small Planet*, Nathan Pritikin captured a lot of attention for a while starting in the late 1970s. Pritikin had taken note that during the Second World War in England, when there was limited access to meat and butter, the Brits' health got better—specifically, incidences of heart disease and diabetes declined dramatically. So, he said, if you replace high-fat-content foods with a multitude of grains, fruits, and vegetables, you can rid the body of heart disease and diabetes. Although the Pritikin diet wasn't fun—it was quite austere—it worked, and it became the rage. That got my attention: I haven't eaten meat since.

What does this all sound like to you, Casey?

Casey: Honestly, it all sounds so interesting but confusing too.

Ken: Exactly... and that's what I was thinking then. Some people tried to connect a number of dots in their pursuit of a new health paradigm. My friend Dr. Dean Ornish followed up on Pritikin's diet with a more comprehensive program of nutrition, yoga, meditation, and supportive group co-counseling sessions. His book *Dr. Dean Ornish's Program for Reversing Heart Disease* became a best seller, and even President Clinton became a vocal fan of Dean's approach. Here's an interesting tidbit. Years ago, Mom and I were invited to Dean's second wedding. It was a beautiful affair, presided over by both a rabbi and Swami Satchidananda. When we arrived at the venue, we were dazzled by the gorgeous flowers that covered the entire hall. As we were ushered to our seat, I turned to Mom and said, "Did you notice who our usher was?" She took another look at the handsome young man who had just seated us, and we laughed as we realized it was Steve Jobs. Mom was seated next to a manly older guy, whom I immediately recognized as Clint Eastwood, and I was sitting next to Arianna Huffington. Right in front of me was Quincy Jones. In fact, the whole room was filled with Hollywood and Silicon Valley royalty. Mom and I realized that many of these folks, if not all, were Dean's patients. Think about it. If you were rich and famous, you'd probably pair your world-class traditional doctor with your world-class alternative doctor to hedge your bets. I learned a key lesson about the pursuit of health at that gathering: rich people are very willing to be early adapters when they think something can make them either healthier or more youthful.

Over the decades, alternative approaches to health have multiplied like bunnies. One "holistic" approach tries to upstage another. One "alternative" nutritional campaign does battle with another. Similarly, the relatively straightforward world of yoga practice has morphed into hot yoga, vipassana yoga, hip-hop yoga, yin yoga, yang yoga, kundalini yoga, earth and sea yoga, indigo yoga, et cetera. Now in this far more entrepreneurial, capitalistic era, we're being sold skin preparations, hormone therapies, vitamins, prepared meals, pillows, mantras, brain wave supplements, self-help apps, and exercise technology along with books and seminars.

Casey: Are you saying that these people are frauds? This takes me back to my opening question: Are you a skeptic regarding the very holistic health movement you helped create?

Ken: Some are frauds and some aren't—and it's not always easy to figure out who is, who isn't, and who's just full of shit. Also, just because someone has an interesting insight doesn't mean they have the knowledge or skills to properly fix the problem. Over the past fifty years, I have heard and seen a thousand different "experts" make the case that they've got the secret sauce or treatment that can cure almost everything. Usually they make their case by first proclaiming, "You've got some things wrong with you that your Western trained doctor doesn't properly understand." Then they usually layer in how "Big Pharma doesn't want you to get better because they make more money when you're sick." I've heard that from nutritionists, supplement sellers, energy medicine practitioners, anti-aging doctors, psychologists, chiropractors, life coaches, and biohackers.

Casey: Don't you believe in people taking responsibility for their own health?

Ken: Yes. I'm a big believer in self-empowerment. But because there's so much information out there and so many choices, it can be utterly confusing and overwhelming. Sometimes it's even just plain wrong, since much of what's now posted on the Internet is not vetted for truthfulness.

Do I think that everyone should become their own doctor? No, I don't. Do I think we should have another era of Dr. Victor Teppers using their stethoscopes and thermometers to check a few vital signs? No. Do I think healthcare should include a wide range of alternative therapies? I do. Ultimately, I believe that in this modern age each of us should be an activist consumer trying to find healthcare providers who either individually or collectively can take a far more holistic approach to helping us manage our health and well-being at every stage in our lives. I think it's about a partnership. For example, my doctor is at University of California San Francisco, and she follows a practical, high-tech, and traditionally allopathic approach to medicine. In addition, I regularly see an acupuncturist, have been counseled by nutritionists, get several kinds of bodywork and chiropractic regularly, and try to practice yoga and work out every day. And I'll see a psychotherapist from time to time to sort my way through challenges or life issues. Because I have both high cholesterol and high blood pressure, I also take medications. For me, it's more of a concert of care than anything, but I do not think I know more than my doctor. If I did, I'd get a better doctor.

Casey: Okay, Dad. So you've been there, done that for a lot of what I'm now just learning about. What's in your crystal ball now? What do you see as the future of medicine?

Ken: A big part of the challenge is that while there are many similarities among us humans, there are lots of differences, too. And since now there might be literally thousands of things to measure and thousands of ways to improve one's health, how can any one person know for sure which approach or which combination of approaches—with which practitioners—will get the best results? I can't imagine that any one practitioner can mastermind or curate the right approach to a more holistic medicine for each and every individual.

However, I think that within a few years, due to advances in artificial intelligence and machine learning, we're going to transition relatively swiftly from this somewhat chaotic period of health diagnosis and treatment to an era of "precision medicine." We're soon going to see scientific breakthroughs that will allow us to arrive at a far deeper and richer understanding of the interactions between our genes, nutrients, molecular activity, and brain-body interactions so that we'll be able to "holistically" track thousands of biomarkers. And if the AI is informed by a wide range of potential solution paths—allopathic, naturopathic, homeopathic, Ayurvedic, and others (always evolving based on outcomes research)—it could be far more effective at precisely diagnosing what's not working right and then proposing the ideal constellation of solutions for each individual. This will create an entirely new science and practice of medicine, geared to optimizing physical and mental health, enhancing well-being and happiness, and maybe even forestalling aging.

Casey: Will this new health platform be available to everyone?

Ken: Eventually, but I worry that probably not at first. A few years ago I was giving a keynote address for the esteemed Business Council, which is composed of the chairs of the Fortune 100. I was feeling a bit playful and asked the group, "Imagine that you're a bit older than you are now and you're beginning to get worried about physical and mental aging. If I had a pill or a therapy of some sort that could cause you to look and feel like you were forty again, what percentage of your total net worth would you give me for that?"

Assuming that the average net worth in the room was around $100 million, I was curious about their reactions. I asked, "How many of you would give me five percent of your total net worth for that?" Every hand in the room went up. I pressed further: "Ten percent? Fifteen percent? Twenty percent? Fifty percent?" Every hand in the room remained up until I eventually hit 90 percent. The room grew silent as everyone realized that something highly revealing and provocative had just surfaced. That evening at dinner, this theme became the topic of conversation. These powerful folks said that it wasn't so much about wanting to be a young person again. They liked who there were. Rather, it was their growing awareness that if their bodies were beginning to fall apart, they would wish they could have youthful vitality and health once more.

And here we'll have an ethical issue. If optimal health is available to everyone, that would be grand, but if it's only available to corporate billionaires, that doesn't seem fair. If you think that income inequality is a big deal, how do you think folks will feel about longevity inequality, which already exists but could multiply?

Casey: Thanks, Dad, for this gift. Hearing your views on all of this was fun and has given me a lot to think about.

Ken: Of course, Casey. And thank *you* for your curiosity and willingness to listen to me. I sure love you.

ATTEMPTING THOUGHT LEADERSHIP
LEARNING FROM TRIALS AND ERRORS

"Do not go where the path may lead; go instead where there is no path and leave a trail." —Ralph Waldo Emerson

Like many people, I have always been drawn to and curious about modern thought-leaders. For example, what made John F. Kennedy so compelling? How did Martin Luther King capture our imagination so profoundly with his "I Have a Dream" speech? How did Bob Dylan shift cultural consciousness? How did Steve Jobs repeatedly reinvent himself? While I've never attended leadership school, in my own way I have been attempting to be a thought leader in the modern field of gerontology for decades. Through lots of trials and lots of errors, through some successes and many failures, I've come to believe there are five key ingredients for getting out in front and becoming and remaining a leader.

First, you must have—and effectively communicate—a forward-facing vision and mission. You've got to imagine how you'd like things to be, the path to getting there, and what roles others will need to play to realize that vision. Your ideas must be compelling enough for people to want to take that trip with you. Backward-facing vision may be fascinating and make for an insightful historical perspective, but forward-facing vision is a requirement of leadership.

And you must do your best to cultivate excellent communication skills. In a less media-engaged era, you might have been able to carry on by teaching a college course or publishing a timely study. That's not enough anymore. Today you must be a persuasive multimedia communicator. Some people think effective communication is a natural talent. I disagree: whatever natural skills you may or may not have, you can learn how to get better, you can improve with hard work and practice, and you can use classes, workshops, and coaching to leapfrog forward.

When I began trying to spread the word about a new image of aging, I started taking courses in selling. I doubt there's ever been a course at a gerontological meeting on how to be a persuasive salesperson, but in the field of life insurance and home realty, they know how to sell. So I enrolled in many programs in those sectors to hone my skills as a persuasive communicator in my own field. And as the years have unfolded, there has not been any point in my professional life when I didn't have a speaking coach of one sort or another to help me improve my game.

Third, your content must be airtight. When you are vetted by the White House or asked to speak in front of world leaders, CEOs, or experts in any field, and your facts are wrong, it's over. The subjects that have interested me the most—human potential, wellness, aging, and longevity—are often misunderstood, and people may have a biased or uninformed point of view about them. I've also learned that you must be even more expert in what others think than in what you think. Do your homework and know what you're talking about and what they're thinking about. Which includes admitting what you're not sure of.

For example, years ago I didn't think I understood the history of aging well enough, so I reached out to Dr. Andy Achenbaum—the country's leading expert on this subject and the author of *Old Age in the New Land*—and asked him to tutor me. He graciously agreed. I flew across the country to his doorstep, paid him for his time and wisdom, and he took me swiftly up the learning curve. He offered up a vast panorama of big ideas—and I've been grateful and better informed ever since. Similarly, when I found myself getting increasingly involved with the economic implications of the age wave, I sought out numerous financial experts, such as Sir John Bond (HSBC), Andy Sieg and Rich Wald (Merrill Lynch), and Ric Edelman (Edelman Financial Engines) to school me on the fundamentals of finance.

Fourth, be prepared to course correct. No matter who you are or what path you're on, you'd probably benefit from good editing. This requires a willingness to learn new things and adjust your orientation. For example, in my early thirties I was straddling three different fields—human-potential-oriented psychology, body-mind-oriented holistic health, and gerontology. One night over dinner with our good friends Marilyn and Bob Kriegel (authors of *The C Zone: Peak Performance Under Pressure*), they argued that if my attention remained so diffuse, I'd run the risk of not getting much done in any of these fields. They challenged me to pick one field and allow the other interests to fall in line. That discussion directly led to the creation of Age Wave, Inc.

A few years later, Monsignor Chuck Fahey and I were sitting on a panel together at a conference; Chuck turned to me and initiated a serious discussion about the importance of the civil rights movement and the kind of caring values and morals that were needed to form the foundation of the field of aging. He made some important points that I hadn't fully considered. At that moment I was just completing seven years of work on my eighth book, *Age Wave*. After the talk with Fahey, my views shifted, and I decided to rewrite the whole book. It took me another year and a half, but I'm so glad I did it.

Which leads me to my fifth point: have mentors. I don't know how anybody can become a leader in any field without mentors—and I don't mean cheerleaders. And don't be afraid to reach high. The most influential gerontology-related mentors to me were Maggie Kuhn and Bob Butler. However, many of my mentors were from the worlds of communications, business, and politics. When I was asked to give a speech at Georgia Southwestern State University, I wound up with President Carter as a friend and mentor. Our exchanges had a profound impact on my life. You don't always get a former US president to be your mentor. But a coworker could make an equally lasting impact. It could be one of your students or clients. It could be your grandchild. It could be all of the above. Throughout this book, I have been attempting to share some of the insights I have gained from both short- and long-term mentors. My good friend Chip Conley, successful entrepreneur, philanthropist, and author of numerous *New York Times* best-selling books, including most recently the prescient *Wisdom@ Work: The Making of a Modern Elder*, has conjured up the idea of a "mentern," a cross between a mentor and an intern. A director of Burning Man and the hospitality guru behind the meteoric success of Airbnb, Chip believes that great leaders are both wise and continually curious.

In addition to these skills and resources, you'll also need courage, a strong will, a resilient heart, and a supportive team. Being a leader can sometimes be tough—very tough. While there will be moments of affirmation, even acclaim, you will also be disagreed with and disappointed. You may also be pigeonholed. Some things that you're dreaming about and hoping for won't happen. Some days you'll say things that you think are brilliant and people won't care. Being a leader on a complicated topic and one where you must fight for the rights of other people is particularly challenging.

Finally, I strongly recommend you surround yourself with people who will support you—because you will get wounded again and again. Whether it's your faith, your community, your team, or your family. In my case, it's all of the above but my sturdiest base of support has come from my wife, my children, my brother, my work partners, and earlier, my parents.

At the same time, if you're wonderfully successful and you experience any fame, for a moment or a while, you may very well start drinking too much of your own Kool-Aid. If that occurs, you'll need people who will make sure you don't go off to Elvisville (my affectionate term for the state of unreality that some famous people relocate to). Either way, be sure there are people who love you, who will be honest with you, and who will give you the support you need to go out and change the world.

Note: The most extraordinary leader I have ever personally encountered was Nelson Mandela. When he keynoted the World Economic Forum in Davos, Switzerland, in 1999, I arrived at the main auditorium three hours early to insure a seat in the front row. The theme of his speech was democracy, but what I remember most was his exceptional humanity. He stepped out onto the stage, tall, lean, and handsome, with a welcoming smile. At eighty-one years of age, he seemed frail, yet he exuded the strength of a bull. His presence was kind and gentle, but everyone in the room was engulfed by his superhuman intensity. He didn't brag or posture. Instead, he was such a magnificent human being that you simply wanted to learn from anything and everything he shared.

THE APPRENTICE MEETS
THE SORCERER

Life isn't about finding yourself. Life is about creating yourself.
—George Bernard Shaw

One of the advantages of asking for help to get to where you're trying to go is that sometimes the person who's helping you will show you a route you never would have considered. I was so captivated by the thought-provoking session with psychotherapist Jim Bramson regarding The Sorcerer's Apprentice that when I met with Jay Golden, my deep-thinking storytelling coach, a few days later, I couldn't wait to tell him all about it.

As I told Jay about my new insights on the Mickey Mouse character in "The Sorcerer's Apprentice," he stopped me and gently reminded me that there were *two* protagonists in that story.

Jay said, "Here's something to think about, Ken. Maybe what you're in the middle of now in your life, triggered by the death of your dad, but maybe also by your children leaving home to pursue their own dreams, is that you're searching for a comfortable way to think about your own aging, not as a decline or diminishment but rather as a new and maybe even more powerful stage of your life. Aren't you Mr. Age Wave? Didn't you write a book called *The Power Years* a few years ago? Maybe you're shifting from being the apprentice to becoming the teacher—the sorcerer. And isn't that what you've always wanted? And isn't that what a sorcerer's apprentice is supposed to do one day anyhow? He's not supposed to remain an apprentice forever."

He was right.

Jay added, "It's not lost on me that this subject, elderhood as an important and powerful stage of life, is what you're supposed to be an expert on."

"Easier said than done," I responded.

As a mischievous smile appeared on his face, Jay jumped right in and made a suggestion. "I know all about when you got kicked out of your house in Big Sur in 1973, which both disrupted the path you were on and also led to all sorts of new challenges and opportunities. I want you to close your eyes and imagine that you somehow are able to travel back in time and go to the house where twenty-three-year-old Ken Dychtwald was living in the redwood forest next to the Big Sur River. Go there to a time when nothing of what was coming was known to you. Go find the young, yoga-practicing, New Age Esalen hippie guy."

"Okay," I said. "I'm closing my eyes, and I'm imagining that. What should I do now?"

"Walk around the house, look in the windows, and see what's going on inside. If you feel inclined and when you're ready, knock on the front door and meet yourself."

So that's exactly what I did. My little house was just a worn-out old cabin, surrounded by redwood trees and sitting right next to a burbling river. A rectangular box with a front door painted mustard yellow by the previous resident—a stoned hippie, no doubt. There was a tiny kitchen, one small bedroom with a mattress on the floor, and a bathroom across the hall with a shower stall. While living there, I had spent most of my time in the funky living room, heated by a potbellied wood-burning stove and furnished with a beat-up old couch and a desk that I had constructed out of a big sheet of plywood, stained brown. Per Jay's suggestion, the sixty-nine-year-old me walked around the cabin and peeked into the living room. And there, sitting in front of the plywood desk, was the twenty-three-year-old, long-haired, bell-bottomed me hammering away on a Smith Corona typewriter, a trusty little jar of Wite-Out nearby to fix the many typos I'd make. Van Morrison's *Moondance* was playing on my record player. Of course, there was no TV, no computer, no video games, no cell phone.

I stood outside there for quite a while watching my younger self working on what the current me knew would ultimately become my first book, *Bodymind*. However, while imagining all of this, I remembered that back then I had never published anything and had no clue that my rambling notes and stories would one day become a book that would be translated into a dozen languages. As the sixty-nine-year-old me was watching all this through the living room windows, the twenty-three-year-old me sighed, stood up and stretched, threw some more logs into the wood stove, and then went to the bedroom to change into yoga pants. I then watched my younger self roll out a mat in front of the fire (as I remembered doing nearly every night during the cold and wet winter to take a break from the writing) and slowly worked his way through a set of flowing yoga postures.

At that point in my visualization, I got up my nerve to go to the front door and knock. After a few moments the young me opened the door and took a good long look at the current me, as though he thought he might remember me from somewhere. He said, "Hi. Do I know you?"

I responded, "I'm you, forty-six years from now."

"What???" he responded. "What are you talking about?"

"It's true," I said. "Can I come in?" Understandably confused by all of this but having been a fan of time-travel science fiction for some time already (which I, of course, knew), he said, "Sure. Why don't we sit in the living room? It's this way."

I told him I knew where the living room was.

We sat facing each other on the old couch, and the twenty-three-year-old me, trying to break the ice, asked, "If you're me, how did you let yourself get so fat?" While it's true that I now weigh fifty pounds more than I did then, I sidestepped his question and said, "I don't quite know how to tell you this, but I've come from the future and you might forget this visit, or you might think it happened in a dream, but you're about to set out on a grand adventure. You'll be leaving Big Sur soon, and you'll get involved with people and projects that you can't even imagine right now. You'll be tested, jostled, torn, and stretched in ways you can't conceive of."

To his credit, the twenty-three-year-old me got right to the point. He asked, "If you're me four-plus decades from now, who are you and what have you made of yourself? What becomes of my life?"

I held his hands—my hands—looked into his eyes—my eyes—and said, "I'm not here to tell you what stocks to buy or what horses to bet on like in Bradbury's "A Sound of Thunder," a sci-fi story I knew that he liked—and I still liked. "Instead I want you to know that I have lived a wonderful life and although I'm nearly three times your age, I think I've got plenty of roadway still in front of me. Most important, I found love. When I was thirty-three, I married Maddy Kent, a caring, smart, playful, talented, and radiantly beautiful woman. By the way, even though we got together here in California, she grew up not far from me—from you. She's a Jersey girl. You've already met her—at a party, but that's all I'm going to say about that now. In fact, I love her so much I have remarried her every year, each time in a different location with a different religion. And we have two extraordinary kids, Casey, who is thirty-two, and Zak, who is twenty-nine. They are both healthy, vibrant, athletic, curious, adventurous young people who want to see, feel, and taste the world. I love them like crazy. I imagine that you'd be interested in knowing that I had an honorable and loving relationship with my parents—your parents—who have passed away after very long lives—and with my (your) brother Alan, who is healthy and active. I've made many friends, and I work with terrific people. I have written books—an early draft of the first one is on your desk right there. I have produced several documentaries and given lectures to more than two million people around the world.

As I looked at the twenty-three-year-old me, I felt his youthful energy and his drive. I also saw his inexperience, confusion, and yearning. As he studied me, he saw a gray-haired, elderly man (remember this was 1973, and for him someone at sixty-nine was surely elderly!), still healthy but a bit stiff and paunchy. I was admittedly nervous about how he would respond.

And then the twenty-three-year-old me looked into my eyes, which were surrounded by wrinkles, and to my surprise he said, "Wow. I have never imagined that I would have a life that has turned out as loving, productive, and influential as what you just described." Then the young me asked, perhaps more out of curiosity than anything, "Did you figure out how to make money anytime along the way? Because I'm struggling to afford the hundred-fifty-dollar-a-month rent for this cabin."

"I did," I told him. "But you'll have to learn about that for yourself."

The twenty-three-year-old me closed his eyes and thought about all this for a while, and then he looked up and I was gone. I was back in Berkeley facing my storytelling coach. Jay knew something unexpected and important had just transpired, and he asked me, "How are you doing?"

With a big sigh and then a smile, I told Jay I felt wonderful. I felt good knowing that the young me, when confronted with an older, seasoned me, was pleased with where his life was heading.

In that imaginary exchange, the twenty-three-year-old version of me was the judge of the sixty-nine-year-old version of me, and the reaction was thumbs-up. In the days that followed, as I reflected on this moment, something shifted in me. I realized that notwithstanding my craving to remain forever youthful, I was no longer only the Mickey Mouse character with whom I had so identified. I was also the old gray-bearded master with some chops for stirring up cosmic magic. I think that's at the heart of the transition I've been struggling with: evolving from a young man to an elder man. From the student to the mentor. From the apprentice, through the trials and lessons, to the sorcerer.

But this sorcerer still asks for directions and guidance when he's lost, which, one way or another, is much of the time.

AND THEN, THE MOST PECULIAR THING HAPPENED

You can't connect the dots looking forward; you can only connect them looking backward. S, you have to trust that the dots will somehow connect in your future. You have to trust in something—your gut, destiny, life, karma, whatever.
—Steve Jobs

Just when I least expected it, as I approached my seventieth birthday, a door seemed to be opening to another chapter in my life—an experience I'd had several times before. In early March there was news about some sort of novel coronavirus that had taken root in Wuhan, China, and might be spreading. Hmmmm... I wonder what that's all about? What? No NBA?

The day before my birthday in late March, I was supposed to keynote the general session at the American Society on Aging conference in Atlanta. I had thought it would be a great way to highlight the transition from my seventh to my eighth decade of life. From there, Maddy and I planned to fly to meet our kids in the Caribbean to spend the week bonding, playing, and partying. Instead, for my birthday, we had a group Zoom call at home.

I asked something different of Maddy, Casey, Zak, and my brother, Alan. "Rather than trying to find a gift," I said, "I'd just like each of you to tell me three things from your heart. First, what do you feel was the best experience we ever had together? Second, what quality of mine do you love the most? And third, what has been the best day of your life so far?"

As it turned out, what they said in that Zoom call were the most wonderful gifts I could ever receive.

I had felt sad going into my birthday. I couldn't travel, I couldn't be with all the people I love most (except Maddy), but that call helped me feel so much gratitude for this life I'm living. That night Maddy cooked me a fantastic, healthy dinner of salmon and veggies, after which we cuddled up all by ourselves watching a movie on Netflix. It was the most tender birthday I have ever had.

During the past months we have all been told that we must shelter in place. I've chosen not to think about this as "sheltering." When I was a kid, we had a bomb shelter in our house in Newark. That was clearly protection from fear. I prefer to think about what we're doing right now as "cocooning."

Just as a caterpillar takes time to cocoon in order to reconstitute itself before reemerging as a butterfly (Gideon-style), I believe we're in the middle of a COVID-19-driven pause, a collective chrysalis. The whole world is going through a near-death experience—perhaps the life you were living just died, or you're worried about someone you love dying or you're thinking about your own mortality. I'm hoping we can all come through this together and find a way to make a better world. Maybe I'm a dreamer, but I'm hopeful that we're at a critical turning point in American history, a moment of real change for the better. The main questions are: During this profound moment of collective pause, what have we learned? How will each of us emerge as better humans as a result of this rough experience. And what will we teach?

OUR OAK TREE

This oak tree and me, we're made of the same stuff. — Carl Sagan

When Maddy and I moved into our home in Orinda, California, in 1989, it was already thirty-four years old. Built in 1955, it was a beautiful, spacious, comfortable home set on the side of a hill, with a gorgeous expanse of land and an unobstructed view of two symmetrical mountains off in the distance. Right between those mountains is where the sun rises each morning. Since Casey was two and Maddy was pregnant with Zak, we were looking for a place where we could raise our kids with good public schools and maybe other kids in the neighborhood for them to play with. We were also hoping for a little land, as our last home in Berkeley was built on the side of a cliff, with no backyard at all. As a kid who grew up in the neighborhoods of Newark, I'd never imagined that I'd live in a home as dreamy and wonderful as ours. Before that, I lived in a little house behind a Chinese restaurant, before that I lived in a small cabin in the woods of Big Sur, and before that I lived in my van. As the real estate agent walked us through the house and around the backyard, one of the things that took our breath away was a massive, multi-limbed oak tree that had been growing majestically on the side of the hill for several hundred years. The tree was gorgeous and dominated the backyard, with long, sturdy limbs and lush branches that reached for the sky.

Over the decades, as Casey and Zak grew up and enjoyed the backyard with their buddies (and my buddies too)—like Justin, Liza, Tristen, and Trevor—that beautiful oak tree was always there to protect us all and provide some shade in the hot days of summer. After our kids left home for college, and as our wheel of life continued to turn, this oak tree seemed immortal to us. Maddy and I always thought of the tree as a combination anchor and beacon. We loved it and what it stood for.

Last year we were told that the tree had a rare disease—ominously called sudden oak death—and was struggling to survive. We reached out to numerous oak tree specialists to see if the tree might be treated and cured. However, all attempts failed, and we were told that the entire tree would have to be taken down—and we'd have to do it soon so that other trees in the area wouldn't be infected.

This deeply rattled us, and we couldn't avoid thinking of the death of this beautiful tree as an omen—a bad omen. Maybe it represented our own aging process? Maybe it was signaling the end of an era in our lives? Maybe it portended bad things?

Last week, on the exact day that I was finishing this sort-of-memoir, a five-man crew arrived in our yard, and within three days the entire tree was removed. First it was dismantled, the limbs and branches sawed apart and hauled away. Then the stump, which was quite deep and more than six feet in diameter, was ground down. When I came home on the third afternoon, there was no sign that the tree had ever been there. It was completely gone.

But to our surprise, what was in its place? Spaciousness. A glorious swath of sun, sky, and beautiful distant hills were now beaming to us in places that had previously been totally blocked. Our next-door neighbor, an older woman whose husband had passed away, rejoiced that she now had more light and scenery than she had had for fifty years, since her children were small. We agreed that we were all grateful for the light.

Maddy and I are now thinking of the removal of this once towering tree as a different kind of omen—a good omen, representing our own reinvention process and portending good things. With this grand view that was always there (even if we didn't know it), we have been given a wonderful gift: the beginning of a new, more spacious era in our lives.

ACKNOWLEDGEMENTS

I am deeply grateful to the following very special people for their contribution to this book—and even more important, to my life:

Maddy Dychtwald, for your unboundaried love, respect, support, encouragement, humor, patience, positivity, beauty, playfulness, and adventuresome spirit.

Pearl and Seymour Dychtwald, for giving me the gift of life and for your unrelenting presence— past, present, and future.

Alan Dychtwald, for being my best buddy and my soul-mate brother.

Stan Kent and Sally and Ray Fusco, for adopting and loving me as your son (in-law).

Richard, Linda, David, Michelle, Annie, Jonah, Jacob, Joel, Patty, and Lucas Kent, my wonderful second family.

Elyse Pellman, for being my favorite co-warrior and extraordinary friend.

Robyn Reynolds, for guiding, managing, nurturing, and improving my dreams at every turn.

Master storytelling coach Jay Golden and ingenious psychotherapist Jim Bramson, for midwifing my legacy stories.

All of the colorful and helpful teachers who have shared their lessons and encouraged me to "breathe, learn, teach, and repeat," including Will Schutz, Michael Murphy, Jean Houston, Gay Luce, Eugenia Gerrard, Joel Kramer, Bob Butler, Joseph Campbell, Dick Price, Dean Ornish, Maggie Kuhn, Jimmy Carter, Ronald Reagan, Jesper Juul, Bill Clinton, Charlie Lynch, Eugene Kleiner, Huston Smith, John McCain, Bucky Fuller, Arnold Schwarzenegger, Anna Halprin, Bob Reich, Fernando Torres-Gil, Father Charles Fahey, and Gregory Bateson.

My wonderful friends and coconspirators: Jayme and Gayle Canton, Danny, Nancy, Justin, and Liza Katz, Joe Max Floyd, Stuart Pellman, Neil Steinberg, Bob Morison, Luke Van Meter, Dan Veto, Stacy Cranston, Katy Flick, Ruth Bercovich, Thi Truong, Celine Santos, Jason Welshonse, Michael and Dulce Murphy, Nancy Lunney and Gordon Wheeler, Chungliang "Al" Huang, Matthew and Jessica Upchurch, George Vradenburg, Meryl Comer, Mary Furlong, Terry and Kim Gilbey, Michael and Leslie Krasny, Kenny and Sandie Dorman, Dave, Robin, and Grace Zaboski, Bob and Judy Huret,

Jay, Ahri, Izzy and Sofie Golden, Lisa Genova, Peter Diamandis, Rich Wald, Sam Stern, Candis Isphoring and Roxy, Jim Bernstein, Bruce Clark, Mark Goldstein, Marc Freedman, Chip Conley, Fernando Torres-Gil, Ric and Jean Edelman, Deborah Medow, Danny Bianchetta, Peggy Horan, Ellen Watson, Brita Ostrom, Nora Matten, Sabina Loetscher, Bill Newman, Don and Katherine Mankin, Chip Baird, Jeff Tolvin, Paul Felsen, Jeff Rubin, Larry Fischer, Herman Rosenfeld, Bob Spindel, Ken Teitelbaum, Dan Kadlec, Deborah Szekely, Becca Derrough, Carrie MacFadden, Lucia Horan, and Douglas Drummond, Colin and Julie Milner.

The Esalen community for repeatedly reminding me that I can get color out of my black-and-white set.

My brilliant agent, Will Lippincott, who believed that my personal stories and life lessons could be of interest and value to others.

Unnamed's Olivia Smith, who saw to the heart of my journey.

My absolutely extraordinary editor, Chris Heiser, who used his heartful magic to turn straw into gold.

My wonderful copy editors, Amy Garcia and Margaret Wimberger, for cleaning up my occasional writing messes.

ABOUT THE AUTHOR

Dr. Ken Dychtwald is a psychologist, gerontologist, visionary thinker, author of 18 books including *Bodymind, Age Wave* and *What retirees Want: A Holistic View of Life's Third Age,* celebrated public speaker and teacher, successful entrepreneur, documentary film-maker, and CEO of Age Wave. He has been helping people look ahead for decades, both at their own—and their clients, consumers, patients and voters'—futures as well as the culture at large. Dychtwald has given presentations to over two million people worldwide and his ideas and research have garnered nearly fifteen billion media impressions. His client list has included over half the Fortune 500. He has served as a Fellow of the World Economic Forum, has keynoted two White House Conferences on Aging, and is the recipient of the McKinsey Prize from the *Harvard Business Review.* Ken has twice received the distinguished American Society on Aging Award for outstanding national leadership and although he's not an economist, he was honored by *Investment Advisor* as one of the 35 most influential financial thought leaders over the past 35 years. Ken and his wife, Maddy are the recipients of the Esalen Prize for their outstanding contributions to advancing the human potential of aging men and women worldwide. Ken was recently awarded the Inspire Award from in the International Council on Active Aging for his efforts to make a difference in the lives of older adults worldwide. He is a Trustee of the XPrize Foundation.

@unnamedpress

facebook.com/theunnamedpress

unnamedpress.tumblr.com

www.unnamedpress.com

@unnamedpress